Spelling
Workout

Phillip K. Trocki

Modern Curriculum Press
is an imprint of

SAVVAS
LEARNING COMPANY

COVER DESIGN: Pronk & Associates

ILLUSTRATIONS: Jim Steck

PHOTOGRAPHS: Cover: *t.r.* AHMAD FAIZAL YAHYA/Fotolia, *b.l.* Artbase Inc.
5: © Photos.com. 8: © David Woolfenden/Fotolia.com. 9: © Clarence Alford/Fotolia.com. 16: © Thye Aun Ngo/Fotolia.com.
17: © Mickael IRLES/Fotolia.com. 21: © Michelle Chrin/Fotolia.com. 26: © Yi Liu/Fotolia.com. 29: © objectsforall/Fotolia.com.
32: © Jimmy/Fotolia.com. 33: © ilumus photography/Fotolia.com. 36: © Carolyn Mitchell/Fotolia.com. 37: © valdezrl/Fotolia.com.
41: © Josep Pena/Fotolia.com. 44: © Mike Price/Fotolia.com. 45: © AlienCat/Fotolia.com. 48: © Charles Kaye/Fotolia.com.
53: NASA Images. 57: © Graça Victoria/Fotolia.com. 61: © Comstock/Thinkstock. 64: Library of Congress. 65: © Photos.com/
Thinkstock. 69: © Lee Barnwell/Fotolia.com. 72: © Judy Tejero Photography/Fotolia.com. 77: © Natalia Bratslavsky/Fotolia.com.
80: © zora/Fotolia.com. 81: © Mark Atkins/Fotolia.com. 84: © Comstock/Thinkstock. 85: © Marina Krasnovid/Fotolia.com.
88: © Andi Taranczuk/Fotolia.com. 89: © philipus/Fotolia.com. 91: © Edsweb/Fotolia.com. 92: © Comstock/Thinkstock.
93: © Katherine Haluska/Fotolia.com. 96: © James Lewis/Fotolia.com. 97: © Lida Salatian/ Fotolia.com. 101: © Lifesize/Thinkstock.
104: © Comstock/Thinkstock. 105: © Mist/Fotolia.com. 109: © Davidpstephens/Fotolia.com. 112: © dlrz4114/Fotolia.com.
113: © Jgz/Fotolia.com. 116: © dtedesco/Fotolia.com. 117: © Comstock/Thinkstock. 120: © Michael Cornelius/Fotolia.com.
122: © Olga Barbakadze/Fotolia.com. 125: © Shariff Che'Lah/Fotolia.com. 128: © Brand X Pictures. 129: © Rob/Fotolia.com.
132: © E.T/Fotolia.com. 133: © Irina B/Fotolia.com. 137: © Photos.com/Thinkstock. 141: © Dorling Kindersley.

Acknowledgments

ZB Font Method Copyright © 1996 Zaner-Bloser.

Some content in this product is based upon WEBSTER'S NEW WORLD DICTIONARY, 4/E. Copyright ©2013 by
Houghton Mifflin Harcourt Publishing Company. Reprinted by permission of Houghton Mifflin Harcourt Publishing
Company. All rights reserved.

ISBN-13: 978-0-7652-2483-5
ISBN-10: 0-7652-2483-6
37 21

Table of Contents

Learning to Spell a Word

1. Say the word.
   Look at the word and say the letters.

2. Print the word with your finger.

3. Close your eyes and think of the word.

4. Cover the word and print it on paper.

5. Check your spelling.

Keeping a Spelling Notebook

A spelling notebook will help you when you write. Write the words you're having trouble with on a separate sheet of paper or in the **Spelling Notebook** at the back of the book.

What stunt was performed by a woman nearly a century ago?

Every year, thousands of people brave the **traffic** to travel to Niagara Falls. The famous waterfall lies between New York and Canada and is about 170 feet high, or more than **twelve** stories tall. Most people just watch the falls. On October 24, 1901, one person did more than just look. She was the first person to go over the falls in a wooden **barrel**!

Her name was Anna Taylor. This, her first real adventure, could have been her last. She was sure that if she survived the fall, she would find **fame** and fortune.

Several **hundred** people stood along the banks of the Niagara River. They cheered as the barrel was released in the water. The barrel floated with the **swift** current. Then, it tumbled over and down the falls. For a while, there was no sign of Anna Taylor. The crowd was **silent until** finally the oak barrel bobbed into view.

The barrel was brought ashore. As Anna was released from the barrel, the crowd went **wild** with cheers.

Taylor was famous for a little while. **Later** on, she earned money posing for photographs.

Look back at the boldfaced words. Say each word. What consonant sounds do you hear in each word?

LIST WORDS

1. banner
2. hundred
3. fame
4. later
5. seven
6. hammer
7. twelve
8. barrel
9. dollar
10. letters
11. silent
12. wild
13. until
14. swift
15. bottles
16. pineapple
17. film
18. gallon
19. traffic
20. eleven

Listening for Consonant Sounds

Write one consonant or two different consonants to complete each **list word**.

1. f a ___ e
2. t w e ___ ___ e
3. w i ___ ___
4. e ___ e ___ e n
5. l a ___ e r
6. s w i ___ ___
7. s e ___ e n
8. h u n ___ ___ e d
9. f i ___ m
10. ___ i ___ e n t
11. u n ___ i ___

Write a double consonant to complete each of these **list words**.

12. b a ___ ___ e l
13. b a ___ ___ e r
14. l e ___ ___ e r s
15. h a ___ ___ e r
16. g a ___ ___ o n
17. b o ___ ___ l e s
18. d o ___ ___ a r
19. t r a ___ ___ i c

Write four consonants to complete the **list word**.

20. p i ___ e a ___ ___ ___ e

Read each definition clue. Write **list words** in the spaces. Then use the numbered letters to solve the riddle.

1. cars ___ ___ ___ ___ ___ ___
           11   4

2. 12 − 1 = ___ ___ ___ ___ ___ ___
                9

3. a flag ___ ___ ___ ___ ___
                7

4. quiet ___ ___ ___ ___ ___ ___
      2   6

5. not tame ___ ___ ___ ___
          8

6. fast ___ ___ ___ ___ ___
      3

7. popularity ___ ___ ___ ___
         1

8. writing marks ___ ___ ___ ___ ___ ___ ___
                10

9. a movie ___ ___ ___ ___
      5

Riddle: What runs and falls but never walks?

Answer: ___ ___ ___ ___ ___ ___ ___ ___ ___ ___ ___
     1   2   3   4   5   6   7   8   9   10   11

Write **list words** under the correct headings. The first one has been done for you.

numbers

1. eleven

2. ___

3. ___

4. ___

fruit

5. ___

money

6. ___

tool

7. ___

measurement

8. ___

containers

9. ___

10. ___

time words

11. ___

12. ___

Spelling and Writing

- ⬭ spelling mistake
- ≡ capital letter

Proofreading

This travel article has ten mistakes. Use the proofreading marks to fix each mistake. Then, write the misspelled **list words** correctly on the lines.

When traveling to niagara Falls during the summer, be ready for some delays. The traffik can be heavy. When you finally get to the falls, spend some time watching the wyild, swiff water. Don't worry. it's unlikely that a barral will come crashing down. Latar, after you leave, your ears will still hear the roar of the water. take plenty of filmm, and send leterz and postcards home to friends. There are many scenic places you'll want to share.

1. _____   2. _____

3. _____   4. _____

5. _____   6. _____   7. _____

Writing a News Story

Imagine that you had watched Anna Taylor go over Niagara Falls. Write a brief news story telling what you saw, heard, and felt. Include what happened when it was all over. Use as many **list words** as you can. Proofread your news story and fix any mistakes.

_____

_____

_____

_____

_____

BONUS WORDS

vessel

slipper

splendid

enemy

instant

Spelling Words in Action

What type of sculpture disappears with the tide?

DIG IT

It all starts when the tide goes out. The artists come to the beach with their pails and shovels. They lift, sift, and **stamp** to make **bumps** in the sand. This is the annual sand castle **contest** in Carmel, California. In this contest, artists make not only castles, but also animals, cars, buildings, and anything else they can think of.

Carmel is not the only place with a sand sculpture contest. From Jesolo, Italy, to Galveston, Texas, people of all ages get together to **practice** their sand-building skills.

The contestants mold and carve the wet sand into **solid** works of art. They use pails, shovels, **sticks**, and other small tools. Mostly, they use their **hands**. By the end of the day, sand sculptures **stand** all over the beach. The results are sometimes wacky. They are always creative and fun to see. It's difficult to **judge** a winner.

When the contest is over, the sculptors don't have to put the sand back. In time, their creations are **lifted** and washed away by the tide.

Look back at the boldfaced words. Say each word. Listen for the short-vowel sounds. What short-vowel sound do you hear in each word?

TIP

The letters **a**, **e**, **i**, **o**, and **u** are vowels. If a word or syllable has one vowel and it comes at the beginning or between two consonants, it usually stands for the short-vowel sound. Study these examples.

a in <u>stand</u>   **e** in <u>spent</u>
i in <u>sticks</u>   **o** in <u>locked</u>
u in <u>judge</u>

LIST WORDS

1. hands
2. dentist
3. lifted
4. crack
5. bumps
6. practice
7. solid
8. clasp
9. sticks
10. spent
11. locked
12. adopt
13. judge
14. contest
15. stand
16. shrimp
17. stamp
18. trust
19. fender
20. pencil

Short-Vowel Sounds

Write each **list word** under the correct short-vowel sound. If a word has two short-vowel sounds, use the stressed syllable.

a as in <u>band</u>

1. _____   2. _____
3. _____   4. _____
5. _____   6. _____

i as in <u>fit</u>

7. _____   8. _____
9. _____

u as in <u>pup</u>

10. _____   11. _____
12. _____

e as in <u>set</u>

13. _____   14. _____
15. _____   16. _____

o as in <u>pot</u>

17. _____   18. _____
19. _____   20. _____

Replace the Words

Write the **list word** that goes with the underlined word or phrase in each sentence.

1. They asked him to be the <u>person to decide the winner.</u> _____

2. The door was <u>bolted shut</u> from the inside. _____

3. Someone always <u>knocks against</u> me while I am in line. _____

4. The father <u>raised</u> the box onto the counter. _____

5. I <u>paid out</u> a lot of money for skiing lessons. _____

6. My brother won first prize in the spelling <u>match.</u> _____

7. The diamond bracelet has a gold <u>fastener.</u> _____

8. They made a bonfire from <u>small branches and twigs.</u> _____

9. The team must <u>choose</u> a new method of training. _____

10. I can <u>rely on</u> my friend Karen to help me. _____

11. He used his feet to <u>press</u> down the sand. _____

Hidden Words

Each word given is hidden in a **list word**. Write the **list word** on the line. Circle the letters that spell the hidden word.

1. rust _____

2. lid _____

3. hand _____

4. rim _____

5. den _____

6. tick _____

7. pen _____

8. end _____

9. tan _____

10. rack _____

11. act _____

12. test _____

Spelling and Writing

Proofreading

The following how-to instructions have nine mistakes. Use the proofreading marks to fix each mistake. Then, write the misspelled **list words** correctly on the lines.

Proofreading Marks

⬭ spelling mistake

⊙ add period

Here's how to create a solud sand sculpture that won't disappear with the tide First, mix together two cups of sand, one cup of cornstarch, and one cup of water. Next, heat the mixture over low heat until thick. Then, let the mixture cool After it cools, use your handz to mold your sculpture and smooth out the bomps. Use the tip of a pensil to create designs. Finally, let your sculpture dry and harden Invite your friends to create sculptures, too. Hold a contess, and ask a parent or teacher to be the judj.

1. _____   2. _____

3. _____   4. _____

5. _____   6. _____

Writing an Advertisement

Use the **list words** to create a poster to advertise a sand sculpture contest. Don't forget to include important information, such as when and where the contest will take place. Remember to proofread your poster and fix any mistakes.

_____

_____

_____

_____

BONUS WORDS

timid

mascot

extend

public

fond

Spelling Words in Action

What are some rules for playing the tuba?

Tuba Tips

You might have the **idea** that tubas only go with oom-pah bands. The **tuba**, however, has a warm, rich **musical** sound. It is an important part of marching bands and orchestras.

Tubas are the largest of the brass instruments. They have the lowest sound. A musician plays the tuba by blowing into the mouthpiece and vibrating the lips. Special valves help the musician change notes.

If you want to learn how to play the tuba, **these** are some **rules** to think about:

- **Locate** a good teacher.
- Practice every day even if you have a **tight** schedule.
- Listen to recordings of professional tuba players to remind you of your goals.
- Oil the valves on your tuba every day.
- Grease the sliding parts once a month.
- Bathe your tuba once a year. You can **safely** bathe your tuba with a garden hose, a soft cloth, and a mild soap. Dry the tuba with soft cloths, then oil and grease it.

Whether practicing a solo or a simple **scale**, always take **pride** in playing your tuba.

Look back at the boldfaced words. Say each word. Listen for the vowel sounds. What long-vowel sound do you hear in each word?

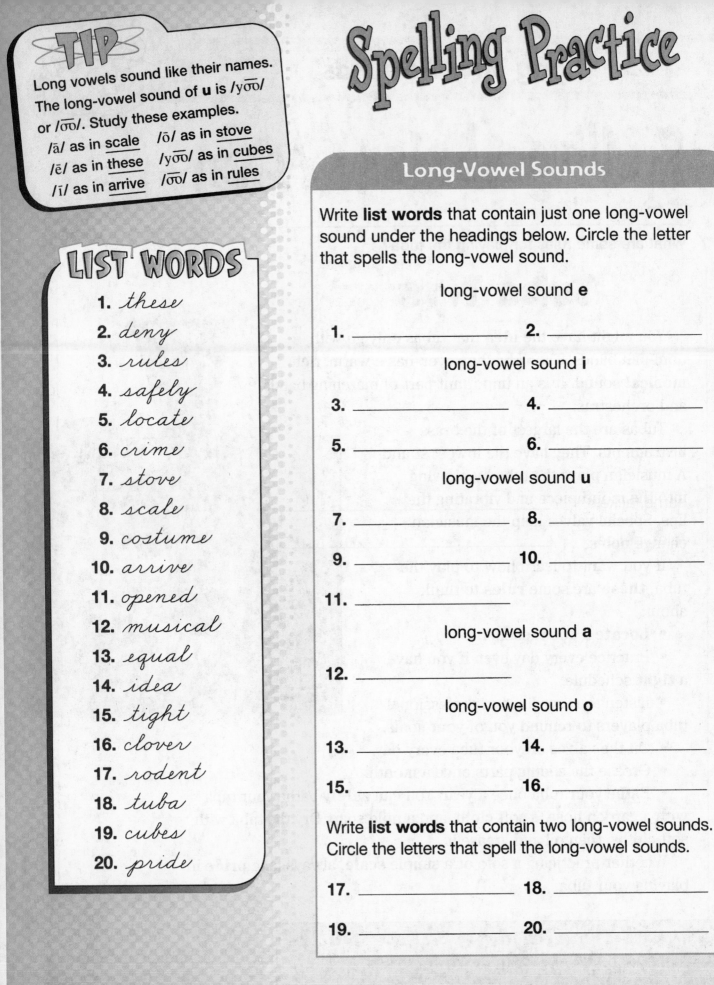

Classification

Write the **list word** that belongs in each group.

1. sink, refrigerator, _____
2. piano, flute, _____
3. find, place, _____
4. this, those, _____
5. play, show, _____
6. mask, makeup, _____
7. laws, orders, _____
8. squares, boxes, _____
9. thought, plan, _____
10. rat, mouse, _____
11. same, alike, _____
12. thief, police, _____

Word Building

Add and subtract letters to form **list words**.

1. right – r + t = _____
2. rival – riv + equ = _____
3. arrow – ow + ive = _____
4. rover – r + cl = _____
5. pale – p + sc = _____
6. any – a + de = _____
7. timely – tim + saf = _____
8. price – ce + de = _____
9. loaned – loa + ope = _____
10. time – t + cr = _____
11. drive – dri + sto = _____
12. moose – moo + the = _____
13. gate – g + loc = _____
14. turtle – rtle + ba = _____

Spelling and Writing

Proofreading

Proofreading Marks

spelling mistake

add something

The following story has nine mistakes. Use the proofreading marks to fix each mistake. Then, write the misspelled **list words** correctly on the lines.

Yesterday, Bo and I went to our first community orchestra concert. As we walked in, the musicians were playing a scail to warm up. The usher helped us logate our seats. Then, everything went silent as the conductor walked on stage. He turned to the orchestra and oapened the score on the music stand.

"Look There are two tubah players in the orchestra," Bo said.

"Doesn't the first one look familiar" I asked.

"That's our music teacher! Bo said with praide.

"That gives me an idea. Let's go see him after the concert. I bet he'll be surprised," I said.

Just then, the conductor raised his baton and beautiful musicle sounds began to fill the auditorium.

1. _____

2. _____

3. _____

4. _____

5. _____

6. _____

Writing a Narrative Paragraph

What is your favorite kind of music? Write a paragraph that tells about the music you like best and why. Try to use as many **list words** as you can. Remember to proofread your paragraph and fix any mistakes.

_____

_____

_____

_____

BONUS WORDS

remove

spice

rude

cone

tomato

Spelling Words in Action

What kind of sculpture never gets into a museum?

Cool as Ice

If someone wore ski pants, heavy kneepads, a warm jacket, a baseball cap, and warm gloves, who could that person be? A skier? A **strange**-looking baseball player? Possibly, but that person could also be an ice sculptor. An ice sculptor carves works of art out of giant blocks of ice. Not a very **common** job, is it?

It can take an ice sculptor hours of cutting, chipping, and smoothing to complete a single carving. A good sculptor can **decide** to turn a block of ice into almost anything. The result might be an animal full of **energy**, a **gentle** mermaid, a horse-drawn chariot, or even a frozen **cactus**.

Unlike most works of art, ice sculptures are not meant to last. Once they're displayed, they melt. These **graceful** figures are often used as party decorations. They are usually placed in the **center** of a food table, in a **corner**, or on a **stage**. Talking about the sculptures puts guests at ease. They can easily "break the ice" by talking about the frozen art.

Say each boldfaced word. Listen for the sounds that c and g make. What do you notice about the sounds for c and g?

Spelling Practice

TIP

The letter **c** makes a hard sound as in <u>cactus</u> and a soft sound as in <u>force</u>. Hear the hard and soft sound of **c** in <u>circle</u>.

The letter **g** makes a hard sound as in <u>gifts</u> and a soft sound as in <u>edge</u>. Hear the hard and soft sound of **g** in <u>baggage</u>.

Often **c** and **g** are soft when followed by **e**, **i**, or **y**.

LIST WORDS

1. edge
2. common
3. circle
4. cactus
5. gifts
6. gentle
7. stage
8. strange
9. corner
10. graceful
11. center
12. baggage
13. category
14. gerbil
15. cement
16. prices
17. force
18. celery
19. decide
20. energy

Hard and Soft c and g

Write each **list word** under the correct heading. Four words will be written more than once.

hard c as in <u>carton</u>

1. _____
2. _____
3. _____
4. _____
5. _____

hard g as in <u>grade</u>

14. _____
15. _____
16. _____
17. _____

soft c as in <u>cent</u>

6. _____
7. _____
8. _____
9. _____
10. _____
11. _____
12. _____
13. _____

soft g as in <u>germ</u>

18. _____
19. _____
20. _____
21. _____
22. _____
23. _____
24. _____

Missing Words

Write a **list word** to complete each sentence.

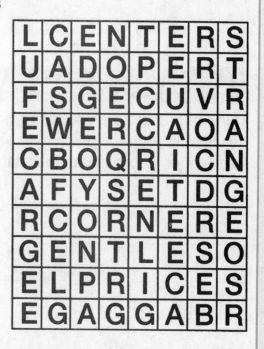

1. A _____ makes a cuddly, little pet.

2. Sidewalks are usually made from _____.

3. One kind of desert plant is a _____.

4. A play is usually performed on a _____.

5. The opposite of <u>uncommon</u> is _____.

6. The sun produces solar _____.

7. A ring is in the shape of a _____.

8. The dolphin sculpture was in a _____ all by itself.

9. _____ are often given at a birthday party.

10. Lettuce, cucumbers, and _____ are used in salads.

Word Search

Ten **list words** are hidden in the puzzle. Some words go across, some go down, some go diagonally, and some go backward. Circle each word. Then, write the words in alphabetical order.

1. _____   2. _____

3. _____   4. _____

5. _____   6. _____

7. _____   8. _____

9. _____   10. _____

L	C	E	N	T	E	R	S
U	A	D	O	P	E	R	T
F	S	G	E	C	U	V	R
E	W	E	R	C	A	O	A
C	B	O	Q	R	I	C	N
A	F	Y	S	E	T	D	G
R	C	O	R	N	E	R	E
G	E	N	T	L	E	S	O
E	L	P	R	I	C	E	S
E	G	A	G	G	A	B	R

Spelling and Writing

Proofreading

The following review has nine mistakes. Use the proofreading marks to fix each mistake. Then, write the misspelled **list words** correctly on the lines.

Proofreading Marks

⬭ spelling mistake

⌃ add something

Paul Matisse's sculpture, "The Musical Fence," is generating a great amount of energee at the Sculpture Park! The graseful, wave-like outline of the sculpture makes it interesting to look at and to hear. People can use wooden sticks to make gentel strikes on the aluminum bars. This creates a pleasant sound. The sculpture certainly is not kommon, but it also doesn't take senter staje at the park. Many people, though, deside to go see it. Who knows Perhaps "The Musical Fence" will encourage other artists to work in this particular categorry of sculpture art.

1. _____

2. _____

3. _____

4. _____

5. _____

6. _____

7. _____

8. _____

Writing a Descriptive Paragraph

Think of a sculpture you might like to create. Write a paragraph describing your sculpture. Use as many **list words** as you can. Remember to proofread your paragraph and fix any mistakes.

_____

_____

_____

_____

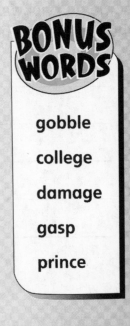

BONUS WORDS

gobble

college

damage

gasp

prince

What sport was once called "baggataway" or "tekwaarathon"?

Lacrosse

Historians can **trace** the game of lacrosse back to Indians living in Canada. These North American Indians called it "baggataway" or "tekwaarathon." The game was played with as many as a thousand warriors. There were very few **strict** rules. Later, French settlers adopted the game and gave it the name *lacrosse*. They added a few rules to make it safer to play.

In 1867, lacrosse was made the national game of Canada. It was first played in the Olympic Games in 1904. Today, it is a popular sport in such faraway places as Australia.

A **proper** game of lacrosse requires both **speed** and **skill** as well as **brains**. Today, lacrosse is played by two teams on a grassy area a little larger than a football field. Each team usually has ten players. They wear heavy **gloves**, helmets, and shoulder pads to **protect** themselves. Each player carries a **straight** stick called a *crosse*. It is usually made of wood and has a small pocket at one end. The pockets are made with **screens** of loose net. A player uses the crosse to catch and throw the ball. Only the goalkeepers can touch the ball with their hands. The object of the game is to score goals. The team scoring the most goals wins.

Say each of the boldfaced words. How many consonant sounds do you hear at the beginning of each word?

TIP

A **consonant blend** is two or more consonants that come together in a word. Their sounds blend together, but each sound is heard. Listen to the sounds of these consonant blends:

gl as in <u>gl</u>oves
dr as in <u>dr</u>eam
str as in <u>str</u>aight
scr as in <u>scr</u>eens

LIST WORDS

1. gloves
2. speed
3. skill
4. screens
5. protect
6. front
7. craft
8. brains
9. scared
10. proper
11. trace
12. dream
13. straight
14. splinter
15. screech
16. spaces
17. stuff
18. greedy
19. sprinkle
20. strict

Beginning Consonant Blends

Add the **sc**, **sk**, **sp**, or **st** consonant blend to each group of letters to form a **list word**.

1. _____uff_____   2. _____ill_____

3. _____ared_____   4. _____eed_____

5. _____aces_____

Add the **br**, **cr**, **dr**, **fr**, **gl**, **gr**, **pr**, or **tr** consonant blend to each group of letters to form a **list word**.

6. _____oper_____   7. _____otect_____

8. _____eam_____   9. _____ains_____

10. _____eedy_____   11. _____ace_____

12. _____aft_____   13. _____ont_____

14. _____oves_____

Add the **scr**, **spl**, **spr**, or **str** consonant blend to each group of letters to form a **list word**.

15. _____ict_____   16. _____inter_____

17. _____eens_____   18. _____eech_____

19. _____inkle_____   20. _____aight_____

Rhyming Words

Use the clues to write **list words**. Each **list word** must rhyme with the underlined word.

1. As I chopped wood last <u>winter</u>, I got a _____.

2. My sister <u>loves</u> to wear red _____.

3. Stand up _____ and perform a <u>stunt</u>.

4. Studying <u>trains</u> takes _____.

5. Sandpaper is <u>rough</u> _____.

6. I heard a _____ at the <u>beach</u>.

7. _____ the <u>wrinkle</u> to make it smooth.

8. To win the race, you will <u>need</u> _____.

9. Tiny _____ make fancy <u>laces</u>.

10. Hiking up mountains takes a lot of <u>hill</u> _____.

Puzzle

Fill in the crossword puzzle by writing a **list word** to answer each clue.

ACROSS

2. wire window coverings
3. to watch over or keep safe
5. afraid
7. not willing to share
8. harsh or stiff

DOWN

1. to copy a picture
2. not crooked or bent
3. correct or suitable
4. work that takes special skill
6. a sleeping person's mind picture

Spelling and Writing

Proofreading

The article below has ten mistakes. Use the proofreading marks to fix each mistake. Then, write the misspelled **list words** correctly on the lines.

Proofreading Marks

◯ spelling mistake

≡ capital letter

Kickball races are popular among many native peoples in mexico, especially the Tarahumara. in a race, two teams of players kick a ball made of wood for many miles. The race can last for several hours or even days. Some tarahumara players race barefoot with nothing to protekt their feet. They move the ball in frunt of them with great skil and spead. they have to keep the ball going as strayht as possible in order to win. Sometimes, they kick the ball across flat spases to gain more ground and move ahead.

1. _____

2. _____

3. _____

4. _____

5. _____

6. _____

Writing a Comparison

What is your most favorite sport? What is your least favorite sport? Write a paragraph that compares and contrasts the two sports. Use as many **list words** as you can. Remember to proofread your comparison and fix any mistakes.

_____

_____

_____

_____

BONUS WORDS

glow

crazy

program

scramble

strength

24   Lesson 5 • Beginning Consonant Blends

In lessons 1–5, you learned about consonant sounds, short- and long-vowel sounds, the hard and soft sounds of c and g, and beginning consonant blends.

Check Your Spelling Notebook

Look at the words in your spelling notebook. Which words for lessons 1 through 5 did you have the most trouble with? Write them here.

_____

_____

Practice writing your troublesome words with a partner. Try writing the letters of each word in the air. Your partner can spell the word aloud as you write.

Lesson 1

 TIP In most words, you can hear the sound of each consonant, as in <u>later</u>. Some words have double consonants that stand for one sound, as in <u>letters</u>.

Write a **list word** that belongs in each group. Not all of the **list words** will be used.

List Words
banner
hammer
twelve
dollar
silent
wild
swift
bottles
pineapple
film
traffic

1. nickel, quarter, _____

2. quiet, hushed, _____

3. wrench, pliers, _____

4. apple, peach, _____

5. quick, fast, _____

6. jars, packages, _____

7. free, untamed, _____

8. camera, movie, _____

9. four, eight, _____

10. flag, shield, _____

TIP Vowels can stand for short sounds, as in <u>contest</u> and <u>judge</u>.

List Words

dentist
lifted
practice
solid
clasp
adopt
judge
shrimp
trust
pencil

Write two **list words** next to each short-vowel sound. If a word has two short-vowel sounds, use the stressed syllable.

1. a as in <u>hat</u>   _____ _____

2. e as in <u>egg</u>   _____ _____

3. o as in <u>hop</u>   _____ _____

4. i as in <u>hit</u>   _____ _____

5. u as in <u>up</u>   _____ _____

TIP Vowels can also stand for long sounds, as in <u>these</u> and <u>stove</u>.

List Words

deny
safely
locate
costume
equal
idea
clover
rodent
tuba
pride

Write a **list word** to complete each sentence.

1. A _____ is a musical instrument.

2. Ramon was filled with _____ when he won.

3. Anna wore a chicken _____ to the party.

4. Please help me _____ my lost book.

5. I can't _____ I'm happy it's summer.

6. We split the melon into _____ halves.

7. People say a four-leaf _____ is lucky.

8. Juan has a clever _____ for a story.

9. A field mouse is a _____ .

10. Drive _____ to avoid accidents.

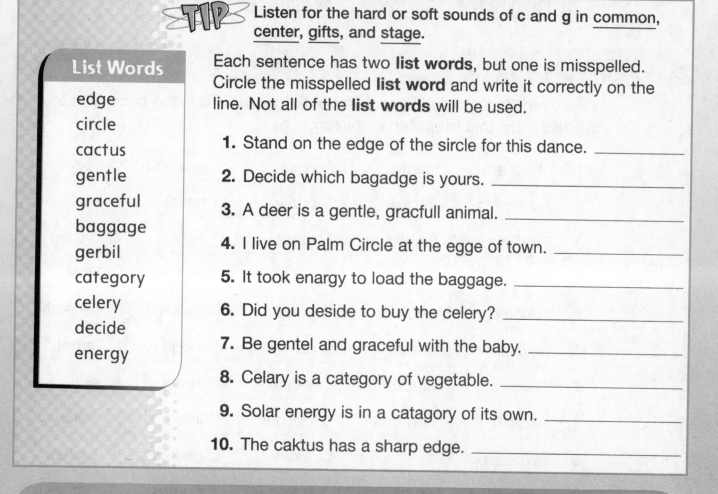

TIP Listen for the hard or soft sounds of **c** and **g** in <u>common</u>, <u>center</u>, <u>gifts</u>, and <u>stage</u>.

List Words

edge
circle
cactus
gentle
graceful
baggage
gerbil
category
celery
decide
energy

Each sentence has two **list words**, but one is misspelled. Circle the misspelled **list word** and write it correctly on the line. Not all of the **list words** will be used.

1. Stand on the edge of the sircle for this dance. _____

2. Decide which bagadge is yours. _____

3. A deer is a gentle, gracfull animal. _____

4. I live on Palm Circle at the egge of town. _____

5. It took enargy to load the baggage. _____

6. Did you deside to buy the celery? _____

7. Be gentel and graceful with the baby. _____

8. Celary is a category of vegetable. _____

9. Solar energy is in a catagory of its own. _____

10. The caktus has a sharp edge. _____

TIP In a consonant blend, you can hear the sound of each consonant in a word, as in <u>sprinkle</u> and <u>protect</u>.

List Words

gloves
protect
scared
proper
trace
straight
splinter
screech
greedy
strict

Write each group of **list words** in alphabetical order.

greedy scared straight proper gloves	trace screech strict protect splinter

1. _____   6. _____

2. _____   7. _____

3. _____   8. _____

4. _____   9. _____

5. _____   10. _____

Show What You Know

One word is misspelled in each set of **list words**. Fill in the circle next to the **list word** that is spelled incorrectly.

1. ○ banner   ○ stamp   ○ equal   ○ graceful   ○ spead
2. ○ strikt   ○ decide   ○ crime   ○ hands   ○ swift
3. ○ traffic   ○ locked   ○ these   ○ edge   ○ branes
4. ○ sprinkle   ○ cement   ○ tight   ○ dentiss   ○ later
5. ○ hunred   ○ bumps   ○ scale   ○ gentle   ○ screech
6. ○ gloves   ○ circle   ○ safely   ○ judge   ○ barral
7. ○ hammer   ○ stycks   ○ locate   ○ strange   ○ skill
8. ○ gready   ○ common   ○ opened   ○ lifted   ○ seven
9. ○ pineapple   ○ trust   ○ stove   ○ cactuss   ○ protect
10. ○ straght   ○ stage   ○ rules   ○ contest   ○ bottles
11. ○ fame   ○ praktice   ○ deny   ○ prices   ○ spaces
12. ○ dreem   ○ center   ○ cubes   ○ crack   ○ until
13. ○ letters   ○ solid   ○ costume   ○ cornuh   ○ stuff
14. ○ front   ○ bagage   ○ pride   ○ pencil   ○ film
15. ○ wild   ○ stand   ○ tubah   ○ gifts   ○ screens
16. ○ splintter   ○ force   ○ arrive   ○ spent   ○ silent
17. ○ eleven   ○ clasp   ○ musicle   ○ energy   ○ trace
18. ○ craft   ○ catagory   ○ clover   ○ shrimp   ○ dollar
19. ○ gallon   ○ fender   ○ idea   ○ cellery   ○ scared
20. ○ proper   ○ gerbil   ○ rodent   ○ adopt   ○ twelf

Lesson 7

Spelling Words in Action

What problems might a two-headed snake have?

Double Header

A snake **crept** along the forest floor at **dusk**, but there was something very unusual about it. It had two heads! There is a saying that "two heads are better than one." This is definitely not true when it comes to snakes. **Different** kinds of animals have been born with two heads, but no one knows for sure why a large number of them have been snakes.

One might think that there are advantages in being a two-headed snake. For instance, a snake with two heads might perhaps have better hearing. This, though, doesn't apply, because a snake can't hear **sounds** since it has no ears. As a result, a snake cannot hear the **crunch** of a footstep. A snake can, however, feel the vibrations of a footstep. Two heads would not help the snake to make sounds either. A snake has no vocal cords and therefore can only make hissing noises.

There is also a **risk** that comes with having two heads. Each head might decide to be **independent** of the other. What would happen if one head wanted to **stretch** out and the other head wanted to coil up? Everything would grind to a **halt**. The heads would fritter away all their time **protesting**, and the snake wouldn't move at all.

Say each boldfaced word in the selection. Listen for the consonant blends. What do you notice about where the blends are in the words?

Spelling Practice

LIST WORDS

1. crept
2. crunch
3. sounds
4. dusk
5. refund
6. colder
7. skunk
8. unfold
9. risk
10. milk
11. halt
12. different
13. protesting
14. twister
15. independent
16. absent
17. stretch
18. printing
19. blended
20. product

Writing Consonant Blends

Add one or two consonant blends to each group of letters to form a **list word**.

1. differe ___ ___
2. ___ ___ ___ etch
3. refu ___ ___
4. twi ___ ___ er
5. du ___ ___
6. prote ___ ___ ing
7. unfo ___ ___
8. ___ ___ oduct
9. sou ___ ___ ___
10. indepe ___ ___ ent
11. ___ ___ unk
12. abse ___ ___
13. ___ ___ unch
14. ha ___ ___
15. ble ___ ___ ed
16. mi ___ ___
17. ___ ___ inting
18. co ___ ___ er
19. ___ ___ ept
20. ri ___ ___

Word Meaning

Write the **list word** that relates to the word or phrase given.

1. chance or gamble _____
2. extend _____
3. white drink _____
4. stop _____
5. return of money paid _____
6. unusual _____
7. mixed _____
8. tornado _____
9. complaining _____
10. writing _____
11. self-governed _____
12. chillier _____
13. open up _____
14. missing _____
15. tones or noises _____
16. nightfall _____
17. crush or chew _____
18. crawled _____
19. something made _____

Word Building

Add and subtract letters to form **list words**.

1. grounds – gr + s = _____
2. duty – ty + sk = _____
3. bunch – b + cr = _____
4. about - ou + sen = _____
5. hunk – h + sk = _____
6. mind – nd + l k = _____
7. deduct – de + pro = _____
8. cooler – ol + ld = _____
9. sound – so + ref = _____
10. retold – ret + unf = _____

Spelling and Writing

Proofreading

Proofreading Marks

- ⬭ spelling mistake
- ⊙ add period
- ⌄ add apostrophe

The following paragraph has ten mistakes. Use the proofreading marks to fix each mistake. Then, write the misspelled **list words** correctly on the lines.

When dusc falls, the spotted scunk looks for food. Its an indepedant animal that might take over another animal's home If a dog krept up on a spotted skunk, it would be taking a risc. Youd hear some prootesting howls when the skunk sprayed the dog with a terrible smelling liquid

1. _____
2. _____
3. _____
4. _____
5. _____
6. _____

Writing Dialogue

Write a conversation between a skunk and a dog that have accidentally met. Use as many **list words** as you can. Remember to proofread your dialogue and fix any mistakes.

_____

_____

_____

_____

_____

_____

BONUS WORDS

harvest

slender

stumble

branch

bask

How can you turn garbage into art?

Recycling for Art

Before you toss out that milk **carton** or pair of **dirty** old shoes, take **heart**. Think about keeping them. Why? You'd keep them for art, of course!

Believe it or not, **garbage** can change you into an **artist**. With a little imagination, you can turn discarded materials into artistic treasures. The best part is that you are also recycling! So, don't make the **error** of setting that trash by the **curb**. Use it creatively.

Recycling for art is not a new idea. Sculptors have used everything from broken teacups to **spare** tires. Painters have created masterpieces on everything from old **boards** to discarded clothing. Some very famous paintings have been painted on top of other paintings. Very often, artists could not afford the price of a new canvas, so they simply painted over an old one.

The challenge for you is to find objects that no one wants, then make them into something someone would love to have. If the idea of turning junk into art bothers you, don't think of it as art. **Cheerfully** think of it as just another way to clean up!

Look back at the boldfaced words. Say each word. What do you notice about the way the vowels sound in each word?

33

TIP

When the letter **r** comes after a vowel or vowels, it sometimes changes the vowel sound. Say each pair of words. Notice how the **r** changes the sound that the vowel or vowels make.

heat—heart (ar sound)
spot—sports (or sound)
cub—curb (ur sound)

LIST WORDS

1. carton
2. heart
3. sports
4. artist
5. spare
6. dirty
7. shore
8. curb
9. fair
10. sherbet
11. boards
12. fearless
13. journal
14. cheerfully
15. garbage
16. organ
17. error
18. sparks
19. harbor
20. perfume

Listening for Vowels with <u>r</u>

Say each word below. Then, write each **list word** under the word with the same vowel sound. If a **list word** has two syllables, use the vowel sound in the stressed syllable. Remember that some words use different letters to spell the same sound.

<u>part</u>   <u>short</u>

1. _____   12. _____

2. _____   13. _____

3. _____   14. _____

4. _____   15. _____

5. _____   <u>care</u>

6. _____   16. _____

<u>fur</u>   17. _____

7. _____   18. _____

8. _____   <u>year</u>

9. _____   19. _____

10. _____   20. _____

11. _____

Definitions

Write the **list word** that matches each definition.

1. something extra

_____

2. edge of the street

_____

3. festival

_____

4. not afraid

_____

5. trash

_____

6. a dessert like ice cream

_____

7. a musical instrument

_____

8. mistake

_____

9. not clean

_____

10. land at the edge of the sea

_____

11. a person who draws or paints

_____

12. diary

_____

Hidden Words

Each word below is hidden in a **list word**. Write the **list word** on the line. Circle the letters that spell the hidden word.

1. ports _____

2. cart _____

3. fume _____

4. park _____

5. air _____

6. full _____

7. hear _____

8. oar _____

9. less _____

10. arbor _____

11. ore _____

12. our _____

Spelling and Writing

Proofreading

The editorial below has nine mistakes. Use the proofreading marks to fix each mistake. Then, write the misspelled **list words** correctly on the lines.

Proofreading Marks

⬭ spelling mistake

⌃ add something

What is the problem with garbaje There is just too much of it. Who likes to look at dirtee beaches or smell a polluted harber Who wants to see a milk cartone lying on the kerb It is time for people to stop this mess and be fare to our planet.

1. _____ 2. _____

3. _____ 4. _____

5. _____ 6. _____

Writing an Advertisement

Imagine you are exhibiting "garbage art" that you created. Write an advertisement to tell about your show. Make it sound like something everyone would want to see. Use as many **list words** as you can. Remember to proofread your ad and fix any mistakes.

_____

_____

_____

_____

_____

_____

_____

_____

BONUS WORDS

starve

nurse

nervous

forth

hearth

What should you do if lightning strikes?

Flash! The lightning **reaches** swiftly across the sky. Then, **thunder** roars **sharply** as the softball team scatters. Your family's car is parked **farther** away than you'd like, but you reach it as rain starts to fall.

Air is always filled with static electricity. When a major storm develops, the electricity separates into positive and negative charges. Because opposites attract, the positive and negative charges meet. The path of electricity between them is lightning.

What should you do if you're stuck outside when a lightning storm strikes? Don't **bother** to **gather** your belongings. Don't be **foolish** either and attempt to hide under a tree. Lightning usually strikes the highest point nearby, such as a tree or **chimney,** so stay close to the ground if you can't find a building to wait in. Get down on your hands and knees to remain low if you have to. One of the safest places to seek refuge is in a car or truck with the doors and windows closed tight.

The lightning has stopped, but now it's pouring rain. You wait **awhile**, but it doesn't let up. Nobody wants to play "water" sports, so the game is called off until **Thursday.**

Look back at the boldfaced words. Say each word. Can you find two consonants together in each word that make only one sound?

Spelling Practice

LIST WORDS

1. thunder
2. farther
3. reaches
4. chicken
5. wheat
6. Thursday
7. foolish
8. gather
9. brother
10. awhile
11. chimney
12. sharply
13. leash
14. bother
15. shipment
16. feathers
17. charge
18. shovel
19. whiskers
20. crush

Listening for Consonant Digraphs

Write each **list word** under the correct heading.

wh as in whale

1. _____   2. _____

3. _____

th as in thimble

4. _____   5. _____

sh as in dish

6. _____   7. _____

8. _____   9. _____

10. _____   11. _____

ch as in peach

12. _____   13. _____

14. _____   15. _____

th as in mother

16. _____   17. _____

18. _____   19. _____

20. _____

Missing Words

Write a **list word** to complete each sentence.

1. The driver turned _____ to avoid the dog.

2. Smoke goes up the _____ of the fireplace.

3. The _____ lays several eggs each day.

4. Jason felt a little _____ for wearing such a silly costume.

5. The spelling books will arrive in next month's _____.

6. Hand Greta a _____ so she can dig, too.

7. The oil on a duck's _____ helps it keep dry.

8. My cat has long, white _____.

9. Kim used a hammer to _____ the stone.

10. Keep your dog on a _____ at all times.

What **list words** can you make from the letters in these words? Use each letter once. The first one has been done for you.

1. rend, hut __thunder__

2. aces, her _____

3. we, hat _____

4. has, Trudy _____

5. her, tag _____

6. both, err _____

7. hail, we _____

8. the, rob _____

9. he, crag _____

10. her, raft _____

Spelling and Writing

Proofreading

The news report below has ten mistakes. Use the proofreading marks to fix each mistake. Then, write the misspelled **list words** correctly on the lines.

Strange weather hit our our area last Thurzday. The day was was warm until noon, when dark clouds began to gathur. heavy rain fell awile until there was a loud crash of thundur. Suddenly, the rain turned to hail! this was the first hail storm our area has seen since 1963. The the hail came down so hard that one woman said it knocked the fithers off her prize chikin!

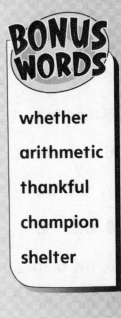

1. _____   2. _____

3. _____   4. _____

5. _____   6. _____

Writing a Descriptive Paragraph

A thunder and lightning storm can be exciting and scary. Write a description of a storm you have experienced. Use as many **list words** as you can. Remember to proofread your description and fix any mistakes.

_____

_____

_____

_____

_____

_____

BONUS WORDS

whether

arithmetic

thankful

champion

shelter

Spelling Words in Action

What do you do on a photo safari?

Photo Opportunities

Once a safari meant hunting animals with guns. Today, a safari is more likely to involve cameras. The **trophy** is not an animal head hanging on a wall or sitting on a **shelf**. Instead, it is a picture of a living animal in its natural environment.

Every year, people travel to Africa to go on **photo** safaris. Africa's wildlife and **geography** provide **enough** opportunities for almost any photographer. There's nothing **phony** here. **Elephants** can be seen in their natural environment. A camera may capture a **giraffe** lumbering across the plains. The safari van may have to stop as a pride of lions crosses the road. An untimely **cough** may set a herd of zebras stampeding. Such photo opportunities are priceless.

After visiting Africa, people could go on safari to India or Australia. Both countries possess many wildlife sites.

If a destination close to home is desired, a photo safari to the countryside nearby, a local park or zoo, or a wildlife rehabilitation center might be possible.

Look back at the boldfaced words. Listen for the sound of f in each word. How many different spellings for the sound of f do you find?

Spelling Practice

TIP

The sound of **f** is usually spelled with **f**, as in <u>after</u>. It can also be spelled with **ff**, as in <u>stiff</u>. Sometimes the **f** sound is spelled with **ph**, as in <u>photo</u> and <u>graphs</u>. The **f** sound can also be spelled with **gh**, as in <u>cough</u> and <u>laughs</u>.

LIST WORDS

1. photo
2. graphs
3. laughs
4. cough
5. trophy
6. roughly
7. enough
8. alphabet
9. shelf
10. after
11. stiff
12. elephants
13. giraffe
14. geography
15. nephew
16. phase
17. orphan
18. dolphin
19. phony
20. autograph

Writing Words with the f Sound

Write each **list word** under the correct heading.

f sound spelled ph

1. _____
2. _____
3. _____
4. _____
5. _____
6. _____
7. _____
8. _____
9. _____
10. _____
11. _____
12. _____

f sound spelled gh

13. _____
14. _____
15. _____
16. _____

f sound spelled f

17. _____
18. _____

f sound spelled ff

19. _____
20. _____

Comparing Words

The first two underlined words or word pairs in each sentence are related. Write the **list word** that relates to the third underlined word or word pair.

1. Music is to CD as _____ is to camera.

2. Charts is to chart as _____ is to graph.

3. Sufficient is to lacking as _____ is to skimpy.

4. Bricks are to wall as letters are to _____.

5. Chair is to table as _____ is to bookcase.

6. Hard is to soft as _____ is to relaxed.

7. Living things are to biology as the Earth is to _____.

8. Niece is to aunt as _____ is to uncle.

9. Season is to year as _____ is to moon.

10. Honest is to true as fake is to _____.

11. Title is to book as _____ is to person.

Puzzle

This is a crossword puzzle without word clues. Study the length and the letters already done for nine **list words**. Then, complete the puzzle.

Spelling and Writing

Proofreading

This article has eleven mistakes. Use the proofreading marks to fix each mistake. Then, write the misspelled **list words** correctly on the lines.

how many wild animals are in trouble today There are enouph that we should be concerned. Elefant herds have been greatly reduced, and a young elephant can be made an orfan because of ivory hunting. some animals, like the jirafe, are forced out of their homes by people looking for places to build and farm. Afffter a large fishing net is hauled in, a dolfin is sometimes found tangled up in the net along with the fish. when will people learn to share the Earth with animals

1. _____

2. _____

3. _____

4. _____

5. _____

6. _____

Writing Captions

Draw pictures of elephants, giraffes, dolphins, or other wild animals. Write captions to go with the pictures. Use as many **list words** as you can. Remember to proofread your captions and fix any mistakes.

_____

_____

_____

_____

BONUS WORDS

affection

phrase

earmuffs

perfect

tough

What is the "ghost galleon"?

Ghost Ship

Through the years, **folks** have loved to **listen** to stories of **ghost** ships. **Often**, these stories are more myth than fact. The story of the *Santa Margarita*, however, is true.

Savage winds ripped her sails. Fierce waves spilled over her decks. A thundering crack was heard. Suddenly, the towering mainmast collapsed into the sea. The *Santa Margarita* was at the mercy of the wind and sea. In a short while, the mighty ship was gone, and over 120 people had drowned trying to take **flight**. In one of the most mysterious **wrecks** of all time, the *Santa Margarita* disappeared in 1622. Since then, she has been **known** as the "ghost galleon."

In 1980, the *Santa Margarita* was located. Pieces of the ship's cargo were found under the sand and water near an **island** in the Florida Keys. When the treasure-hunting divers saw the cargo, they quickly changed the nickname to the "gold-chain wreck" due to the great amount of gold found scattered on the ocean floor. As divers untangled a mass of gold chains, they counted 43 glittering chains that reached a total length of 180 feet! Each link was as thick as the **knuckle** of a **thumb**. In the 1600s, people often carried gold in the form of chains. Links could be unhooked and used like coins.

Say each of the boldfaced words in the selection. Which letters in the words do not make a sound?

LIST WORDS

1. ghost
2. thumb
3. known
4. often
5. folks
6. wrist
7. halfway
8. listen
9. knuckle
10. comb
11. wrecks
12. flight
13. honest
14. island
15. Wednesday
16. numb
17. wrench
18. crumb
19. soften
20. answer

Identifying Silent Letters

Write each **list word** under the correct heading.

silent b

1. _____
2. _____
3. _____
4. _____

silent w

11. _____
12. _____
13. _____
14. _____

silent h

5. _____
6. _____

silent l

15. _____
16. _____

silent gh

7. _____

silent d

17. _____

silent k

8. _____
9. _____

silent t

18. _____
19. _____
20. _____

silent s

10. _____

Fill in the crossword puzzle by writing a **list word** to answer each clue.

ACROSS

2. day of the week
4. people
6. part of the way
10. a spirit
11. land surrounded by water
13. understood or realized
15. tool used on the hair
16. tiny bit
17. to make soft

DOWN

1. destroys
3. response to a question
5. many times
6. truthful
7. trip on a plane
8. one of the fingers
9. part of each finger
12. to try to hear
14. without feeling

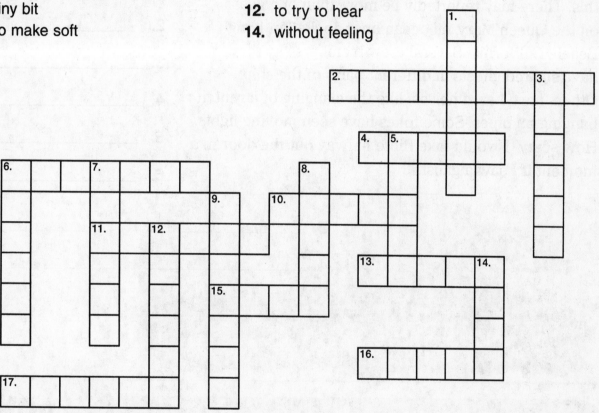

Rhyming Words

Write the **list word** that rhymes with each word below.

1. bench _____
2. right _____
3. decks _____
4. fist _____
5. own _____
6. most _____

Spelling and Writing

Proofreading

This story has eight mistakes. Use the proofreading marks to fix each mistake. Then, write the misspelled **list words** correctly on the lines.

Imagine being on a haunted ship Well, lissen to this. There may reportedly be more than one goast on the Queen Mary, an ocean liner docked in Long Beach, California. Several crew members say they have sighted ghosts in different parts of the ship. Others have heard noises, like the clanging of a rentch banging on pipes. Some fokes have seen moving lights. How scary I would take flihte hafway out the door in a moment if I saw a ghost.

1. _____

2. _____

3. _____

4. _____

5. _____

6. _____

Writing a News Story

Imagine what it would be like to find a shipwreck full of treasure. Write a news story that reports the discovery. Use as many **list words** as you can. Remember to proofread your story and fix any mistakes.

_____

_____

_____

BONUS WORDS

daughter

bomb

knowledge

whistle

wrinkle

In lessons 7–11, you learned how to spell words with consonant blends and digraphs, vowels with **r**, silent letters, and the sound of **f**.

Check Your Spelling Notebook

Look at the words in your spelling notebook. Which words in lessons 7 through 11 did you have the most trouble with? Write them here.

_____

_____

Practice writing your troublesome words with a partner. Try writing the letters for each word in a tray of sand, salt, or sugar. Your partner can check your spelling as you write.

Lesson 7

TIP In a consonant blend, you can hear the sound of each letter. A blend may be found anywhere in a word, such as **tw** in twister, **ld** in colder, and **nds** in sounds.

Write a **list word** to complete each sentence. Not all of the **list words** will be used.

List Words

crept
crunch
dusk
refund
skunk
unfold
milk
halt
twister
stretch
blended
product

1. Bob _____ the ingredients.

2. A _____ is black and white.

3. The sky begins to darken at _____.

4. The store would not _____ my money.

5. Thin the batter with a cup of _____.

6. Bike riders must _____ at stop signs.

7. The rabbit _____ into my garden.

8. Try to _____ the hat to fit.

9. My report was the _____ of hard work.

10. I heard the _____ of snow under my boots.

TIP When the letter **r** comes after a vowel, it often changes the sound the vowel stands for.

cub—curb (**ur** sound)   spots—sports (**or** sound)

Write the **list word** that belongs in each group. Not all the **list words** will be used.

List Words

heart
artist
spare
dirty
sherbet
fearless
journal
garbage
organ
error
harbor
perfume

1. diary, autobiography, _____

2. ice cream, pudding, _____

3. musician, dancer, _____

4. soiled, messy, _____

5. ocean, river, _____

6. valentine, love, _____

7. piano, violin, _____

8. trash, wastepaper, _____

9. mistake, blunder, _____

10. lipstick, powder, _____

TIP Two consonants together can form a consonant digraph, making a new sound, such as **wh** in awhile, **sh** in foolish, **th** in gather, and **ch** in charge.

List Words

thunder
chicken
wheat
brother
chimney
leash
shipment
feathers
shovel
whiskers

Add a consonant digraph to each group of letters to form a **list word**.

1. ___ ___ imney

2. fea ___ ___ ers

3. ___ ___ under

4. ___ ___ icken

5. bro ___ ___ er

6. ___ ___ iskers

7. ___ ___ ipment

8. lea ___ ___

9. ___ ___ eat

10. ___ ___ ovel

TIP The sound **f** can be spelled with **f**, **ff**, **ph**, or **gh**.
Find it in <u>after</u>, <u>stiff</u>, <u>phony</u>, and <u>laughs</u>.

List Words

cough
trophy
roughly
enough
shelf
after
stiff
giraffe
nephew
phase
orphan
dolphin

Build **list words** by adding or subtracting letters. Not all of the **list words** will be used.

1. knew – kn + neph _____

2. tough – t + c _____

3. stick – ck + ff _____

4. though – th + en _____

5. than – t + orp _____

6. girl – l + affe _____

7. thin – th + dolph _____

8. shed – d + lf _____

9. tropical – pical + phy _____

10. route – te + ghly _____

TIP Some words contain silent letters, such as **h**, **b**, and **d**. Look for the silent letters in <u>ghost</u>, <u>numb</u>, and <u>Wednesday</u>.

List Words

known
folks
wrist
knuckle
comb
flight
wrench
crumb
soften
answer

Write each group of **list words** in alphabetical order.

wrist flight soften wrench folks	known crumb comb knuckle answer

1. _____

2. _____

3. _____

4. _____

5. _____

6. _____

7. _____

8. _____

9. _____

10. _____

Show What You Know

One word is misspelled in each set of **list words**. Fill in the circle next to the **list word** that is spelled incorrectly.

1. ○ crunch   ○ durty   ○ bother   ○ listen   ○ laughs

2. ○ gerafe   ○ folks   ○ leash   ○ error   ○ absent

3. ○ refund   ○ organ   ○ awhile   ○ nuckle   ○ after

4. ○ foto   ○ ghost   ○ thunder   ○ carton   ○ crept

5. ○ printing   ○ journal   ○ chimney   ○ honest   ○ elefants

6. ○ nephew   ○ comb   ○ gather   ○ kurb   ○ milk

7. ○ halt   ○ sherbert   ○ feathers   ○ wrecks   ○ stiff

8. ○ geografy   ○ thumb   ○ reaches   ○ sports   ○ twister

9. ○ sounds   ○ heart   ○ wheat   ○ flight   ○ enuf

10. ○ alphabet   ○ Wenesday   ○ farther   ○ artist   ○ dusk

11. ○ unfold   ○ fair   ○ foolish   ○ wriss   ○ phony

12. ○ dolphin   ○ rench   ○ crush   ○ sparks   ○ risk

13. ○ colder   ○ boards   ○ sharpley   ○ island   ○ graphs

14. ○ trofhy   ○ numb   ○ charge   ○ fearless   ○ stretch

15. ○ diffrent   ○ shore   ○ shovel   ○ crumb   ○ phase

16. ○ cough   ○ sofen   ○ chicken   ○ spare   ○ product

17. ○ independant   ○ garbage   ○ shipment   ○ halfway   ○ shelf

18. ○ autograph   ○ answer   ○ whiskers   ○ cheerfuly   ○ protesting

19. ○ blended   ○ parfume   ○ brother   ○ known   ○ roughly

20. ○ orphan   ○ ofen   ○ Thursday   ○ harbor   ○ skunk

Spelling Words in Action

What happened on the Apollo 13 mission?

MISSION: CUT SHORT

Fra Mauro Hill seemed the ideal place for the next lunar **landing**. The crew of the Apollo 13 mission were ready and well trained, but something would go terribly wrong before they ever got to the moon. They would be lucky to get back to Earth at all.

Apollo 13 was launched on April 11, 1970. For the first two and a half days, the mission went smoothly. Then, on the 13th, the astronauts **remembered** hearing a big bang. They quickly set about **checking** what had happened. **Following** the bang, they discovered that a faulty switch had caught fire, **leading** to the explosion of two oxygen tanks. Without oxygen, there would be no power, water, or air to breathe. The astronauts **guessed** they would never make it back to Earth. The mission was **turning** into a nightmare.

Back on Earth, the mission control people were **watching** the drama unfold. They anxiously tried to figure out what to do. They knew the Lunar Module aboard the spacecraft had extra power supplies. It also had stores of water and oxygen. **Bending** all the rules, scientists worked hastily to design a way of connecting the two systems. Finally, they had a solution, **finishing** just in time.

The astronauts returned to Earth, tired, hungry, cold, and thirsty. In one way, though, they were fortunate. If the accident had happened after landing on the moon, supplies in the Lunar Module would have been used up. The ending would have been very different.

Look back at the boldfaced words. Did the base words change when <u>ing</u> or <u>ed</u> was added?

TIP

You can add **ed**, **er**, or **ing** to some words without changing the spelling of the base word. Study these examples:

clean + **ed** = cleaned
wish + **ing** = wishing
learn + **er** = learner
sing + **er** = singer

Find the unchanged base word in each **list word**.

LIST WORDS

1. watching
2. checking
3. finishing
4. learner
5. bending
6. cleaned
7. sorted
8. missed
9. singer
10. guessed
11. teacher
12. walker
13. remembered
14. following
15. tossed
16. turning
17. wishing
18. landing
19. leading
20. catcher

Writing Words with er, ed, or ing

Write each **list word** under the correct heading.

Base word + **er**

1. _____
2. _____
3. _____
4. _____
5. _____

Base word + **ed**

6. _____
7. _____
8. _____
9. _____
10. _____
11. _____

Base word + **ing**

12. _____ 13. _____
14. _____ 15. _____
16. _____ 17. _____
18. _____ 19. _____
20. _____

Classification

Write the **list word** that belongs in each group.

1. pitcher, batter, _____

2. hoping, wanting, _____

3. supposed, imagined, _____

4. runner, jogger, _____

5. seeing, looking, _____

6. dancer, actor, _____

7. threw, pitched, _____

8. divided, grouped, _____

9. thought of, recalled, _____

10. curving, stooping, _____

11. pupil, student, _____

12. avoided, escaped, _____

Riddles

Use **list words** to answer these riddles.

1. I'm not beginning. I'm just ending. What am I doing? _____

2. You can usually find me in the classroom. What am I? _____

3. I'm looking. I'm just making sure. What am I doing? _____

4. I rhyme with <u>leaned</u> and <u>screened</u>. What am I? _____

5. I'm not leading. I'm behind. What am I doing? _____

6. I do this when I'm going around a corner. What am I doing? _____

7. After descending, airplanes do this on a runway. What are they doing? _____

8. I'm the first. I'm not following. What am I doing? _____

Spelling and Writing

Proofreading

The paragraph below has ten mistakes. Use the proofreading marks to fix each mistake. Then, write the misspelled **list words** correctly on the lines.

Proofreading Marks

⬭ spelling mistake

≡ capital letter

℮ take out something

Yesterday, I went to an air show with my friend david and his mother, who is a teachr. We were waching six jets jets streak across the sky, one folowing the other. Suddenly, the plane that was leeding began to turn. The others followed. we stared in amazement as the jets did loops and dips. When the pilots came in for the landng, the crowd cheered! We wouldn't have mised that that show for anything!

1. _____   2. _____

3. _____   4. _____

5. _____   6. _____

Writing a Journal Entry

Imagine that you are the first astronaut to land on an unknown planet. Write a journal entry to describe what you see and hear. Use as many **list words** as you can. Remember to proofread your writing and fix any mistakes.

_____

_____

_____

_____

_____

_____

_____

Bonus Words

gulped

performer

mending

sinking

soared

Spelling Words in Action

What snack food has been popular for hundreds of years?

Pop Quiz

What food explodes as it cooks, **giving** about 20 to 40 times the original amount? It's popcorn, of course.

Long before the Pilgrims landed in the New World, American Indians were **sharing** this explosive treat among themselves. A kernel of popcorn found in Utah **proved** to be over 1,000 years old! For hundreds of years, people **loved** eating it plain and hot. In the early 1900s, movie houses began selling popcorn. Moviegoers loved munching it during the **coming** attractions. Theater owners **served** it topped with butter and salt. That made the popcorn eaters so thirsty that they bought something to drink, too.

It's not **surprising** that popcorn is one of America's best-loved treats. It is happily eaten by nearly everyone, from the ballet **dancer** to the furniture **mover**. Every year, people eat millions of pounds of the fluffy stuff! Today, popcorn is sold in all kinds of shops and in all kinds of flavors.

Comparing popcorn to other snack foods results in a pleasant surprise. Popcorn is high in fiber and very low in calories. It's good for you—so long as you skip the butter, that is.

Look at the base words in the boldfaced words. What do you notice about their spelling?

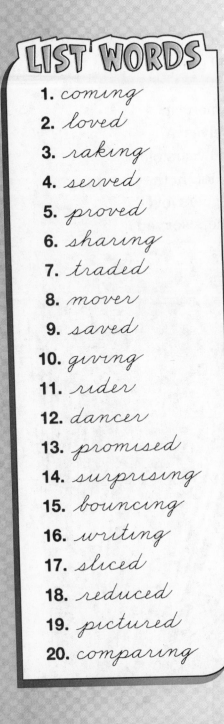

TIP

When a word ends in silent **e**, the **e** is usually dropped before adding an ending or suffix that begins with a vowel.

trade + **ed** = traded

move + **er** = mover

surprise + **ing** = surprising

LIST WORDS

1. coming
2. loved
3. raking
4. served
5. proved
6. sharing
7. traded
8. mover
9. saved
10. giving
11. rider
12. dancer
13. promised
14. surprising
15. bouncing
16. writing
17. sliced
18. reduced
19. pictured
20. comparing

Identifying Endings and Suffixes

Write the **list words** that tell about actions that are happening in the present. Circle the ending in each word.

1. _____ 2. _____

3. _____ 4. _____

5. _____ 6. _____

7. _____ 8. _____

Write the **list words** that tell about actions that happened in the past. Circle the ending in each word.

9. _____ 10. _____

11. _____ 12. _____

13. _____ 14. _____

15. _____ 16. _____

17. _____

Write the **list words** that name people and what they do. Circle the suffix in each word.

18. _____ 19. _____

20. _____

Missing Words

Write the **list word** that best completes each sentence.

1. Tom is _____ the leaves in the yard.

2. Leah _____ twenty dollars to buy a new purse.

3. The magician was _____ everyone with magic tricks.

4. The runner _____ his weight by fifteen pounds.

5. My grandparents are _____ to visit us in July.

6. Mom _____ in her old car for a brand new one.

7. The ballet _____ leaped gracefully.

8. I am _____ the two shirts to see which one I like better.

9. Anna _____ the cheese into several pieces.

Riddle

Read each definition clue. Write **list words** in the spaces. Then, use the numbered letters to solve the riddle.

1. adored ___ ___ ___ ___ ___
    12 3

2. waited on ___ ___ ___ ___ ___ ___
    8

3. showed to be correct ___ ___ ___ ___
    14 13

4. giving away ___ ___ ___ ___ ___ ___
    2 9 5

5. someone who rides ___ ___ ___ ___ ___
    10

6. moving up and down ___ ___ ___ ___ ___ ___ ___
    11 4 7

7. using paper and pencil ___ ___ ___ ___ ___ ___ ___
    1 6

Riddle: When is a piece of wood like a king?

Answer: ___ ___ ___ ___ ___ ___ ___ ___ ___ ___ ___ ___ ___ ___
 1 2 3 4 5 6 7 8 9 10 11 12 13 14

Spelling and Writing

Proofreading

The advertisement below has twelve mistakes. Use the proofreading marks to fix each mistake. Then, write the misspelled **list words** correctly on the lines.

A snack that's beyond compareing,
One youll surely enjoy shairing.
Its a moveer in the store!
You're sure to shout, "Lets have more"
So if youve promisde yourself a treat,
Or pichtured something great to eat,
Go right ahead and munch some Yummy—
What a thrill youll be giveing your tummy!

1. _____   2. _____

3. _____   4. _____

5. _____   6. _____

Writing a Descriptive Paragraph

Some people love popcorn. What is your favorite snack? Write a description of it. Use as many **list words** as you can. Remember to proofread your writing and fix any mistakes.

_____

_____

_____

_____

_____

_____

BONUS WORDS

driving

stared

shaking

rising

skater

Spelling Words in Action

What kind of race uses giant canoes?

Culture and Canoes

The sky is bright and sunny. Light winds ripple the water. Six anxious competitors are **sitting** inside a giant canoe. Each one is **grabbing** onto a paddle, waiting for the signal. Other canoes are **bobbing** in the water. They are also waiting. Suddenly, the sound of an airhorn pierces the silence.

The sound marks the **beginning** of a 41-mile race from the Hawaiian island of Molokai to the island of Oahu. In moments, the canoes are **skimming** across the water. Onlookers are yelling and **chatting** as they watch the canoes **slipping** off into the distance.

The Molokai Outrigger Canoe Race is not just a race. It has historical importance as well. Many years ago, giant canoes were the only way to travel among the Hawaiian Islands. Each boat was usually carved from a single tree—mainly the Koa tree. The canoes were **outfitted** to be used as fishing boats, warships, and even ferries. Over time, these giant boats were replaced by more efficient means of transportation.

The tradition of the outrigger canoe hasn't been **dropped**, though. It continues today with the annual Molokai Race. The competitors who win the race aren't the only **winners**. Everyone wins, because the race preserves an important part of Hawaiian culture.

Look back at the boldfaced words. What do you notice about the spelling of the base words?

TIP

When a short-vowel word ends in a single consonant, the consonant is usually doubled before adding an ending that begins with a vowel:

hum + **ing** = humming

In words with two or more syllables, the final consonant is usually doubled if the last syllable has a short vowel followed by a single consonant:

outfit + **ed** = outfitted

LIST WORDS

1. beginning
2. humming
3. dropped
4. sitting
5. slipping
6. joggers
7. grabbing
8. bobbing
9. tripped
10. padded
11. skimming
12. scrubbing
13. winners
14. outfitted
15. wrapped
16. clapping
17. dragging
18. chatting
19. quitter
20. trimmer

Doubling Consonants

Write each **list word** under the correct heading. Then, circle the base word in each **list word**.

ing

1. _____
2. _____
3. _____
4. _____
5. _____
6. _____
7. _____
8. _____
9. _____
10. _____
11. _____

ed

12. _____
13. _____
14. _____
15. _____
16. _____

er or ers

17. _____
18. _____
19. _____
20. _____

Word Meaning

Write the **list word** that relates to the word or phrase given.

1. dressed _____
2. washing _____
3. covered _____
4. starting _____
5. let go of _____
6. being seated _____
7. runners _____
8. not losers _____
9. cushioned _____
10. reaching for _____
11. reading quickly _____
12. floating _____
13. singing _____
14. applauding _____
15. hair cutter _____
16. stumbled _____

Rhyming

Write the **list words** whose base words rhyme with the words given.

that

1. _____

stop

2. _____

hit

3. _____
4. _____
5. _____

dim

6. _____
7. _____

strap

8. _____
9. _____

wag

10. _____

sum

11. _____

hip

12. _____
13. _____

Spelling and Writing

Proofreading

The paragraphs below have ten mistakes.
Use the proofreading marks to fix each mistake.
Then, write the misspelled **list words** correctly
on the lines.

Proofreading Marks

⬭ spelling mistake

⊙ add period

¶ indent paragraph

The Inuit people built the first kayaks thousands of
years ago In the begining, kayaks were made of animal
skins stretched over wooden frames. Siting inside the
kayak, the kayaker wraped the skin around his waist to
make the boat watertight The Inuit used their kayaks
for fishing and hunting in the cold Arctic waters.

   The modern kayak looks something like a canoe, but
it is trimer and sleeker A kayaker is outfited with a
double-ended paddle to move the boat. The narrow
shape and light weight of a kayak make it easy to
control in the water

1. _____   2. _____

3. _____   4. _____

5. _____

Writing a Narrative Paragraph

Write a paragraph about a kayak race. Describe the action and
what is happening. Use as many **list words** as you can.
Remember to proofread your paragraph and fix any mistakes.

_____

_____

_____

_____

BONUS WORDS

snapping

stepped

patrolling

dimmed

mugger

Why would a scientist want to fly a kite during a lightning storm?

A Man of Many Talents

Benjamin Franklin **applied** his talents in many ways. He was a printer, writer, civic leader, and scientist. **Relying** on his famous **replies** and clever sayings, he often convinced people of his ideas. Today, no one **denies** Franklin's genius.

Almost 250 years ago, Benjamin Franklin conducted his most famous experiment. He proved that lightning is electricity. The exact details of his experiment are not known. Some people think Franklin may have flown a kite at the beginning of an electrical storm. Lightning may have struck a wire **carried** by the kite. It then might have traveled down the hairs of the kite string to a key. There, it created a spark. The experiment **supplied** information Franklin needed to invent the lightning rod.

Franklin also invented the Franklin stove. It produced twice as much heat as a fireplace and used much less fuel. He invented bifocal glasses, which had both reading and distance lenses. Franklin discovered that disease **multiplied** in stuffy rooms. He was the first to show that a rough sea could be calmed by pouring oil on it. He also thought up daylight-saving time, **buying** people more daylight in the summer.

Many people **copied** Franklin's ideas. Franklin, though, refused to make a profit from any of his inventions. He was **satisfied** if his inventions gave people a better life.

Look back at each boldfaced word. Identify the base word. Did it change when an ending was added?

65

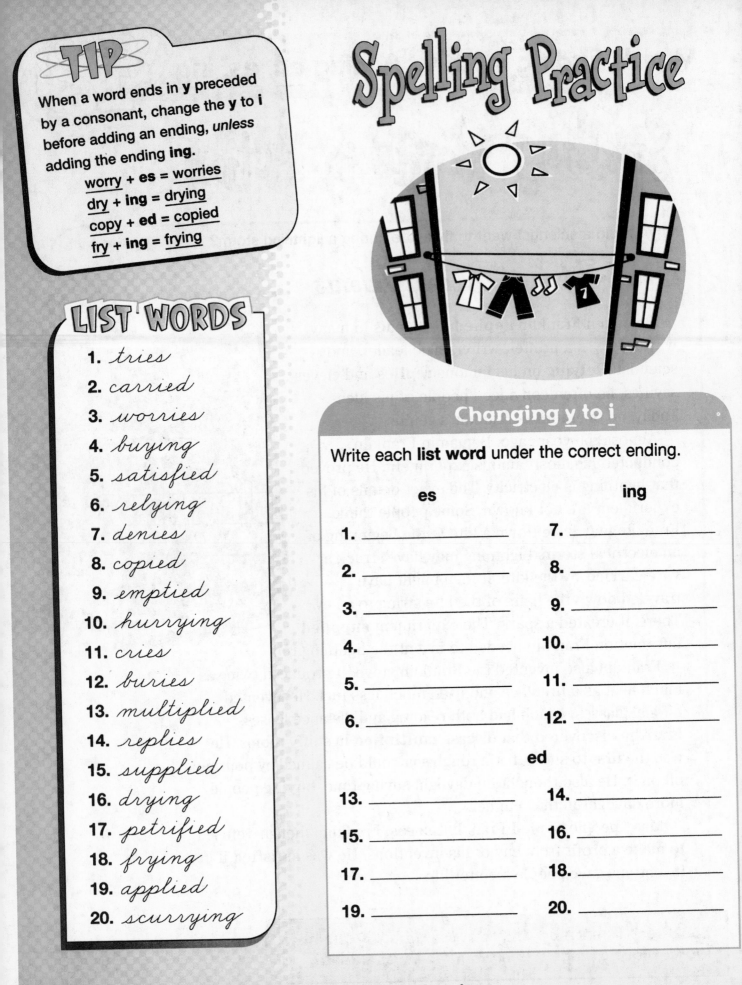

TIP

When a word ends in **y** preceded by a consonant, change the **y** to **i** before adding an ending, *unless* adding the ending **ing**.

worry + **es** = worries
dry + **ing** = drying
copy + **ed** = copied
fry + **ing** = frying

Spelling Practice

LIST WORDS

1. tries
2. carried
3. worries
4. buying
5. satisfied
6. relying
7. denies
8. copied
9. emptied
10. hurrying
11. cries
12. buries
13. multiplied
14. replies
15. supplied
16. drying
17. petrified
18. frying
19. applied
20. scurrying

Changing y to i

Write each **list word** under the correct ending.

es

1. _____
2. _____
3. _____
4. _____
5. _____
6. _____

ing

7. _____
8. _____
9. _____
10. _____
11. _____
12. _____

ed

13. _____
15. _____
17. _____
19. _____

14. _____
16. _____
18. _____
20. _____

Write the **list word** that matches each clue. Then, read down the shaded boxes to solve the riddle.

1. puts underground or hides

2. imitated

3. sobs

K

4. transported

5. rushing

6. says something is not true

7. depending

8. feels anxious

9. answers

10. increased

Riddle: What kind of music do stone workers and bakers like?

Answer: _____ _____ _____

Write the **list word** formed from each base word below.

1. apply _____

2. petrify _____

3. scurry _____

4. satisfy _____

5. dry _____

6. supply _____

7. buy _____

8. empty _____

9. try _____

10. fry _____

Spelling and Writing

Proofreading

The article below has twelve mistakes. Use the proofreading marks to fix each mistake. Then, write the misspelled **list words** correctly on the lines.

Proofreading Marks

⬯ spelling mistake

∧ add something

℮ take out something

What is a popular activity in Japan. It's kite-flying! At different times of the year, children are hurreing and scurying about, biyng supplies to to make kites. As the glue is driing, the children might be thinking about the colorful paints that will be applyied to their kites.

What happens after the children are satisfyed with their creations The kites are carryed to an open area area and flown. Sometimes, one team of kite-flyers tryes to knock another team's kites out of the sky!

1. _____

2. _____

3. _____

4. _____

5. _____

6. _____

7. _____

8. _____

Writing Instructions

Do you know how to fly a kite? Have you ever made one? Write instructions to a friend to tell how to make a kite or another kind of toy. Use as many **list words** as you can. Remember to proofread your instructions and fix any mistakes.

_____

_____

_____

BONUS WORDS

dairies

horrified

pitying

magnifying

mysteries

Spelling Words in Action

Which fruit is more than just a delicious food?

An Apple a Day

What do McIntosh, Granny Smith, and Cortland have in common? They're all apples. Some fruits may be **fancier** and others **prettier**, but few can be enjoyed in more ways than the apple. Apples can be made into apple pie, applesauce, and apple butter. The **juiciest** ones can be squeezed into apple juice or apple cider. Of course, the **easiest** way to enjoy an apple is to eat it raw.

Apples are more than just a delicious food. They're part of our language. Someone special can be described as "the apple of my eye." New York City is called "The Big Apple." The lump in a person's throat is called the "Adam's apple."

There are some interesting facts about apples. The **heaviest** apple weighed three pounds, two ounces. That's **heavier** than a bunch of eight or nine bananas! In **earlier** times, George Washington and Thomas Jefferson both grew apples. The **earliest** mention of apples in ancient writing was about 6,000 years ago. Today, about 300 different kinds of apples are grown in the United States. Some of the **funnier** names include Winter Banana, Summer Rambo, and Kidd's Orange Red.

About 200 years ago, a man named John Chapman traveled across the United States planting apple seeds. A **happier** or friendlier person would have been hard to find. People called him Johnny Appleseed. Thanks to John, apple growing is one of America's largest farm industries.

Look back at the base word in each boldfaced word. How did each base word change?

Spelling Practice

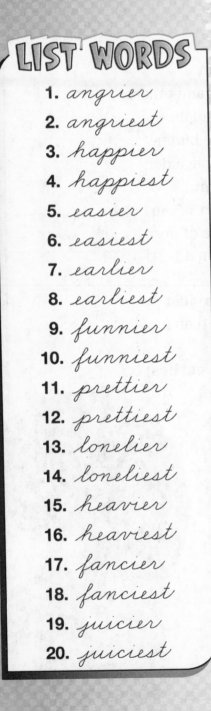

TIP

Adjectives ending in **er** compare two things. Adjectives ending in **est** compare three or more things. To add **er** or **est** to an adjective that ends in **y**, change the **y** to **i** first.

happy + er = happier
happy + est = happiest

LIST WORDS

1. angrier
2. angriest
3. happier
4. happiest
5. easier
6. easiest
7. earlier
8. earliest
9. funnier
10. funniest
11. prettier
12. prettiest
13. lonelier
14. loneliest
15. heavier
16. heaviest
17. fancier
18. fanciest
19. juicier
20. juiciest

Changing y to i

Write the **list words** that compare two things. Circle the ending on each word.

1. _____ 2. _____

3. _____ 4. _____

5. _____ 6. _____

7. _____ 8. _____

9. _____ 10. _____

Write the **list words** that compare three or more things. Circle the ending on each word.

11. _____ 12. _____

13. _____ 14. _____

15. _____ 16. _____

17. _____ 18. _____

19. _____ 20. _____

Replace the Words

Write the **list word** that best replaces the underlined word or phrase.

1. Joe was the <u>first</u> person to arrive at the party. _____

2. That was the <u>most humorous</u> joke I ever heard. _____

3. I think roses are <u>more beautiful</u> than tulips. _____

4. Mary was <u>madder</u> at the insult than I was. _____

5. The test was <u>simpler</u> than I thought it would be. _____

6. I felt <u>more alone</u> than ever before. _____

7. The costumes were <u>showier</u> than before. _____

8. Marge was the <u>most pleased</u> I had ever seen her. _____

9. The peaches were <u>more filled with juice</u> this year than last year. _____

10. This suitcase is <u>of greater weight</u> than that one. _____

11. Lisa was <u>the maddest</u> of all about the accident. _____

12. This is <u>the simplest</u> way to make a book. _____

Scrambled Words

What **list words** can you make from the letters in these words? Use each letter once.

1. its, juice _____   **2.** tease, is _____

3. rare, lie _____   **4.** fine, run _____

5. tin, faces _____   **6.** pear, hip _____

7. pretest, it _____   **8.** eel, in, slot _____

9. have, site _____   **10.** are, sting _____

11. shape, tip _____   **12.** reel, lion _____

13. let, raise _____   **14.** ten, if, sun _____

Spelling and Writing

Proofreading

The paragraph below has nine mistakes. Use the proofreading marks to fix each mistake. Then, write the misspelled **list words** correctly on the lines.

The best apple pies are made with the firmest apples, not with watery or mushy ones. making an apple pie will be easer if the Crust is prepared ahead of time. A top crust can be made fansier and prettyer with cutouts. Remember though—the more flour in a crust or the longer you work with the crust, the heaver and tougher it will be. tough crusts make cooks the angryest. Flaky crusts make cooks—and pie-eaters—happyer.

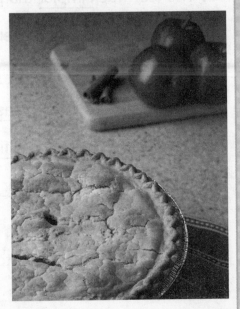

1. _____   2. _____

3. _____   4. _____

5. _____   6. _____

Writing a Poem

Some people like apples. Write a short poem to describe your favorite fruit. Is it the juiciest fruit you've ever eaten? Is it heavier than another fruit? Use as many **list words** in your poem as you can. Remember to proofread your poem and fix any mistakes.

_____

_____

_____

_____

_____

_____

BONUS WORDS

tastier

loveliest

clumsier

luckiest

curlier

Lessons 13–17 · Review

In lessons 13–17, you learned how to add **ed**, **er**, **es**, **est**, and **ing** to the ends of words, including words that end with **y** or silent **e**.

Check Your Spelling Notebook

Look at the words in your spelling notebook. Which words for lessons 13 through 17 did you have the most trouble with? Write them here.

_____

_____

Practice spelling your troublesome words with a partner. Take turns writing a word equation for each word.

apply **- y + i + ed =** applied

Lesson 13

TIP You can add **ed**, **er**, or **ing** to some words without changing the spelling of the base word, as in sorted, learner, and checking.

Write a **list word** that means the same or almost the same as each word or phrase. Not all of the **list words** will be used.

List Words

watching
finishing
cleaned
singer
guessed
teacher
walker
remembered
tossed
wishing
landing
catcher

1. vocalist _____

2. threw _____

3. touch down _____

4. recalled _____

5. viewing _____

6. ending _____

7. figured out _____

8. hoping _____

9. instructor _____

10. jogger _____

TIP When a word ends in silent **e**, the **e** is usually dropped before adding an ending that begins with a vowel, as in sharing and served.

Write each **list word** under the correct category.

List Words

loved
proved
saved
dancer
promised
surprising
bouncing
sliced
pictured
comparing

One Syllable

1. _____
2. _____
3. _____
4. _____

Two Syllables

5. _____
6. _____
7. _____
8. _____

Three Syllables

9. _____
10. _____

TIP When a short-vowel word or final syllable ends in a single consonant, the consonant is usually doubled when an ending that begins with a vowel is added, as in slipping and quitter.

Write the **list word** that belongs in each group.

List Words

beginning
humming
joggers
tripped
scrubbing
outfitted
wrapped
clapping
dragging
chatting

1. talking, speaking, _____
2. stumbled, fell, _____
3. runners, racers, _____
4. opening, starting, _____
5. covered, sealed, _____
6. pulling, towing, _____
7. dressed, equipped, _____
8. cheering, applauding, _____
9. singing, whistling, _____
10. washing, cleaning, _____

TIP When a word ends in a consonant and **y**, the **y** is changed to **i** before an ending other than **ing** is added, as in supplied and denies.

Write a **list word** to complete each sentence. Not all of the **list words** will be used.

List Words

worries
buying
satisfied
copied
emptied
cries
multiplied
replies
petrified
frying
scurrying

1. Four _____ by two is eight.

2. I saw Jo _____ a new baseball.

3. I expect the _____ to my letters to come soon.

4. The truck _____ a load of sand.

5. The delicious meal _____ my hunger.

6. Al _____ his story.

7. The baby _____ when she's tired.

8. Aunt Jan _____ if I'm late.

9. I watched a cat _____ up a tree.

10. _____ wood is as hard as rock.

TIP When **er** or **est** are added to an adjective ending in **y**, the **y** changes to **i**, as in prettier and earliest.

Write the **list word** that contains the base word given.

List Words

angriest
happier
easiest
earlier
funnier
prettiest
lonelier
heaviest
fancier
juiciest

1. early _____   2. angry _____

3. happy _____   4. funny _____

5. heavy _____   6. pretty _____

7. fancy _____   8. juicy _____

9. easy _____   10. lonely _____

Show What You Know

One word is misspelled in each set of **list words**. Fill in the circle next to the **list word** that is spelled incorrectly.

1. ○ tossed ○ padded ○ rakeing ○ drying ○ earlier
2. ○ angier ○ frying ○ proved ○ joggers ○ watching
3. ○ checking ○ humming ○ ridder ○ replies ○ lonelier
4. ○ happiest ○ buying ○ giving ○ chating ○ teacher
5. ○ bending ○ winners ○ bounceing ○ hurrying ○ funnier
6. ○ juicyest ○ scurrying ○ promised ○ dropped ○ catcher
7. ○ singer ○ sitting ○ reduced ○ petrifyed ○ prettier
8. ○ heavyest ○ tries ○ sharing ○ slipping ○ turning
9. ○ landing ○ triped ○ saved ○ buries ○ fancier
10. ○ denies ○ happyer ○ traded ○ outfitted ○ missed
11. ○ sorted ○ begining ○ coming ○ carried ○ juicier
12. ○ quitter ○ following ○ earlyest ○ cries ○ dancer
13. ○ walker ○ claping ○ mover ○ heavier ○ emptied
14. ○ funnyest ○ worries ○ loved ○ skimming ○ wishing
15. ○ leading ○ scrubing ○ sliced ○ copied ○ easier
16. ○ relying ○ easiest ○ surpriseing ○ wrapped ○ guessed
17. ○ grabbing ○ learner ○ writting ○ fanciest ○ satisfied
18. ○ multiplyed ○ loneliest ○ pictured ○ cleaned ○ trimmer
19. ○ bobbing ○ compareing ○ applied ○ prettiest ○ finishing
20. ○ dragging ○ remembered ○ supplyed ○ angriest ○ served

Spelling Words in Action

What is the "Great Outdoors" like?

Camping Anyone?

Millions of people go camping every year. They enjoy the sense of **freedom** that comes from living in the great outdoors. To some, nothing can **approach** the feeling of sleeping under the stars or watching an **eagle** flying across the sky.

Camping can cost a little or a lot depending on campers' preferences. For example, there are different kinds of sleeping bags to choose from in all price ranges. Where campers stay can also affect how much money they spend. **Instead** of renting an expensive cabin, some people rough it with a tent. Setting up a tent **between** trees or large rocks can provide shelter from a cool **breeze** or a fierce wind. In the end, though, it really doesn't matter how much or how little money is spent. The most important **reason** to go camping is to have fun!

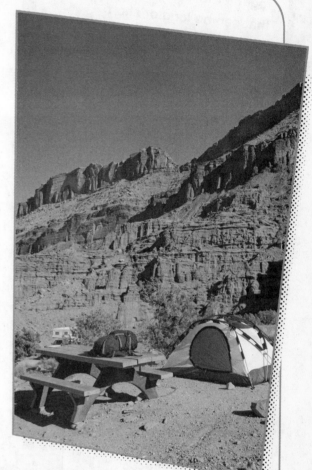

It has been said that people haven't lived until they've **roasted** a marshmallow over a crackling fire or smelled a fresh **meadow** in the early morning hours. It's all part of the camping experience. So, why not join the millions of people who've been **treating** themselves to something special—camping! After all, there's nothing better than the "Great Outdoors."

Say the boldfaced words in the selection. What sounds do the two vowels that are together make in these words?

TIP

In vowel pairs, two vowels come together to make one long vowel sound. The second vowel is silent.
- **ee** and **ea** as in <u>fleet</u> and <u>reason</u>
- **oa** and **oe** as in <u>loaned</u> and <u>hoed</u>
- **ue** as in <u>clues</u>

In vowel digraphs, two vowels come together to make a vowel sound that can be long or short.
- **ea** as in <u>measure</u>

Spelling Practice

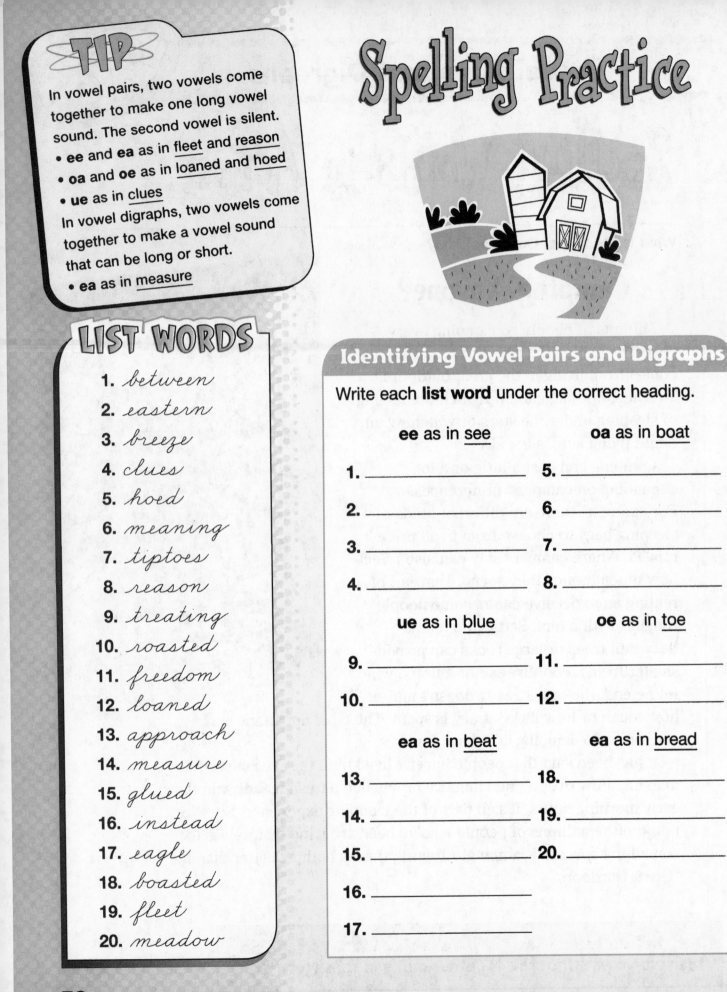

LIST WORDS

1. between
2. eastern
3. breeze
4. clues
5. hoed
6. meaning
7. tiptoes
8. reason
9. treating
10. roasted
11. freedom
12. loaned
13. approach
14. measure
15. glued
16. instead
17. eagle
18. boasted
19. fleet
20. meadow

Identifying Vowel Pairs and Digraphs

Write each **list word** under the correct heading.

ee as in <u>see</u>

1. _____
2. _____
3. _____
4. _____

oa as in <u>boat</u>

5. _____
6. _____
7. _____
8. _____

ue as in <u>blue</u>

9. _____
10. _____

oe as in <u>toe</u>

11. _____
12. _____

ea as in <u>beat</u>

13. _____
14. _____
15. _____
16. _____
17. _____

ea as in <u>bread</u>

18. _____
19. _____
20. _____

Missing Words

Write the **list word** that best completes each sentence.

1. At the school play, I sat _____ Sue and Miguel.

2. I _____ my science book to Carter on Friday.

3. Use a ruler to _____ the size of the photograph.

4. Mel owns a farm with a beautiful, grassy _____.

5. Keep to your left as you _____ the school.

6. Jen _____ the pictures into her new scrapbook.

7. Mr. Hall _____ that he was the smartest man in town.

8. The _____ to the crossword puzzle were not too hard.

9. A beautiful _____ soared through the trees across the sky.

10. Walk on _____ so no one will hear you when you enter.

Word Search

Ten **list words** are hidden in the puzzle below. The words go across, down, diagonally, backward, or upside down. Circle each word. Then, write the words in alphabetical order on the lines.

1. _____   2. _____

3. _____   4. _____

5. _____   6. _____

7. _____   8. _____

9. _____   10. _____

S	E	A	S	T	E	R	N
A	O	B	E	E	T	Q	R
I	M	R	O	E	C	D	O
H	O	E	D	L	B	A	A
R	D	E	A	F	X	E	S
O	E	Z	D	N	M	T	T
A	E	E	E	E	I	S	E
P	R	E	A	S	O	N	D
L	F	S	C	L	P	I	G
G	N	I	T	A	E	R	T

Spelling and Writing

Proofreading

There are ten mistakes in the paragraphs below. Use the proofreading marks to fix each mistake. Then, write the misspelled **list words** correctly on the lines.

Animal tracks are cluez. If you know what to look for, you can uncover their meening. You can tell what kind of animal left them. Sometimes, you can figure out what the animal was doing. You can meashur a track to get an idea of the animal's size. With some experience, learning to read animal tracks is a breaze.

The tracks of some animals are similar toeach other. For example, dogs foxes, and wolves belong to the same family. Their tracks show the pads that cover the bottoms of their feet. If you look carefully, though, you can tell the differences betwean them. Deer elk, and moose leave the imprint of their hooves. The tracks of most birds show three narrow toes in front and one inthe rear. Insted of footprints, snakes leave trails that show their gliding movement through sand and mud.

1. _____ 2. _____ 3. _____

4. _____ 5. _____ 6. _____

Writing a Persuasive Paragraph

Do you like to hike or camp? Write a persuasive paragraph that will convince people of the joys of the "Great Outdoors." Use as many **list words** as you can. Remember to proofread your paragraph and fix any mistakes.

_____

_____

_____

_____

BONUS WORDS

cheat

forehead

sneeze

groan

dues

Spelling Words in Action

What should runners do to take care of their feet?

Tenderfeet

It seems that everywhere you look, people are running. You see them on smooth streets, rough roads, sandy beaches, and grassy **fields**. Running can be good for your health. Doctors **believe** it can strengthen your heart. However, whether **brief** or long, running **amplifies** the wear and tear on your feet.

As your feet hit the ground, they each **receive** an impact equal to three times what you **weigh**. This means that when a 90-pound person runs, each foot hits the ground with 270 pounds of pressure. That's quite a jolt for those bones and muscles! That's **chiefly** why your feet may need **relief**. Here are some tips for tending your toes:

- Check your feet every day for any signs of injury or calluses. If you **perceive** any foot problems, see a doctor.
- After washing your feet, dry them well.
- Wear light-colored socks that breathe and keep your feet dry.
- Be sure your running shoes fit well and give good support.
- Tie your shoes snugly, but not tightly.

Pass these tips on to friends and **neighbors**. Their feet will be glad you did.

Look back at the boldfaced words. Notice that each word contains <u>ie</u> or <u>ei</u>. Say each word. How many different vowel sounds do you hear?

TIP

The letters **ie** and **ei** can be vowel pairs or digraphs. They are vowel pairs in <u>pies</u> and <u>seize</u>. They are vowel digraphs in <u>brief</u> and <u>sleigh</u>. Use this rhyme to spell words with **ie** and **ei**:

I before E
except after C
or when sounded as A
as in <u>neighbors</u> and <u>weigh</u>!

LIST WORDS

1. died
2. fields
3. brief
4. relief
5. shriek
6. weigh
7. believe
8. sleigh
9. receive
10. eighteen
11. seize
12. neighbors
13. receipt
14. amplifies
15. chiefly
16. freighter
17. deceive
18. perceive
19. pies
20. diet

Spelling with ei and ie

Write each **list word** under the correct heading.

long a sound spelled ei

1. _____
2. _____
3. _____
4. _____
5. _____

long e sound spelled ei

6. _____
7. _____
8. _____
9. _____
10. _____

long e sound spelled ie

11. _____   12. _____
13. _____   14. _____
15. _____   16. _____

long i sound spelled ie

17. _____   18. _____
19. _____

Write the **list word** in which the letters **ie** have two separate sounds.

20. _____

Puzzle

Fill in the puzzle by writing a **list word** to answer each clue. Then, read down the shaded boxes to solve the riddle.

1. record of purchases
2. people who live close by
3. easing of pain
4. a vehicle to ride in snow
5. stopped living
6. stretches of open land
7. a ship for carrying freight
8. to measure with a scale
9. makes stronger or louder
10. to accept as true and real
11. scream

Riddle: What wears shoes but has no feet?

Answer: ___ ___ ___   ___ ___ ___ ___ ___ ___ ___ ___

Missing Vowels

Add **ie** or **ei** to each group of letters to form a **list word**. Then, write the whole word on the line.

1. p ___ ___ s _____
2. dec ___ ___ ve _____
3. ch ___ ___ fly _____
4. ___ ___ ghteen _____
5. br ___ ___ f _____
6. d ___ ___ t _____
7. rec ___ ___ ve _____
8. perc ___ ___ ve _____
9. s ___ ___ ze _____
10. rec ___ ___ pt _____

Spelling and Writing

Proofreading

The following article has nine mistakes. Use the proofreading marks to fix each mistake. Then, write the misspelled **list words** correctly on the lines.

Proofreading Marks

⬭ spelling mistake

∧ add something

If you perceev that you need more exercise, you probably do. Many people beleive there are more choices in exercise programs today. Those who want to recieve the best in fitness can do walking running aerobics and step classes. When you combine exercise with dyeit, you can be sure you will look and feel better. Some people feel better after a breif time, while others need a little longer because they want to lose weight, as well as feel fit. So sieze the moment. Get in shape!

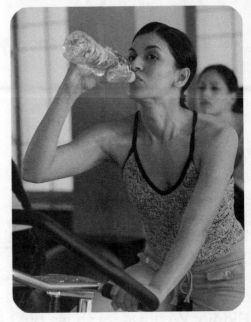

1. _____   2. _____

3. _____   4. _____

5. _____   6. _____

Writing a Description

Have you ever seen or heard about a bed race or a soap box derby? Use as many **list words** as you can to describe an unusual or funny race that you may have seen or heard about. Remember to proofread your description and fix any mistakes.

_____

_____

_____

_____

_____

BONUS WORDS

ceiling

hygiene

veil

achieve

allies

How can a little animal build a dam?

Little Lumberjacks

If you've ever seen **drawings** of beavers, you may think they look a little strange. Beavers have stout little bodies, small heads, tiny **claws**, and tails that look like ping-pong paddles. A beaver may look **awkward**, but in the water it is a fast, graceful, and strong swimmer.

Beavers are nature's best builders of dams. In the spring and summer, they begin their work at the break of **dawn**. They **gnaw** on trees and branches. A beaver has long teeth and a strong **jaw** that can cut through a thick tree in minutes. Once the trees and branches are cut, the beavers **launch** them into a stream. Then, they push the logs and branches into place to make a dam. The dam is packed with mud and **straw** to hold back the water.

Beavers usually make their homes in the ponds that form behind their dams. A beaver lodge has many underwater entrances. Inside, it is a warm and dry place for the beavers to live and store food.

Beavers must chew on wood even during the winter months. If they don't, their teeth keep growing and become too long, **causing** them harm. They will live in the same area for many years. Humans are usually at **fault** when beavers leave their homes.

Each boldfaced word in the selection is spelled with <u>au</u> or <u>aw</u>. Say each word. What do you notice about the sound each makes?

Spelling Practice

LIST WORDS

1. claws
2. fault
3. causing
4. dawn
5. straw
6. drawings
7. launch
8. sauce
9. jaw
10. haunt
11. yawn
12. fawns
13. awkward
14. gnaw
15. audience
16. scrawl
17. fraud
18. gaunt
19. restaurant
20. shawl

Writing Consonant Blends

Write each **list word** under the correct heading.

/ô/ spelled **aw**

1. _____
2. _____
3. _____
4. _____
5. _____
6. _____
7. _____
8. _____
9. _____
10. _____
11. _____

/ô/ spelled **au**

12. _____
13. _____
14. _____
15. _____
16. _____
17. _____
18. _____
19. _____
20. _____

Rhyming

Use the clues to write **list words**. Each **list word** must rhyme with the underlined word.

1. The cat's _____ had no <u>flaws</u>.

2. I began to _____ at the break of <u>dawn</u>.

3. The horse chewed the <u>straw</u> with the motion of its _____.

4. What's _____ all the <u>pausing</u>?

5. It isn't my _____ you ate the <u>salt</u>.

6. A worm writes with a <u>crawl</u> _____.

7. The creamy _____ lost its <u>gloss</u>.

8. The captain gave the boat a <u>staunch</u> _____.

9. A beaver's <u>jaw</u> helps it _____ wood to keep its teeth short.

10. The lady's _____ was rolled up into a <u>ball</u>.

Word Meaning

Write the **list word** that relates to the word or phrase given.

1. sunrise _____

2. thin _____

3. pictures _____

4. eating place _____

5. baby deer _____

6. fake _____

7. listeners _____

8. scarf _____

9. dried grass _____

10. chew _____

11. clumsy _____

12. frighten _____

13. throw _____

14. sharp nails _____

15. scribble _____

16. gravy _____

Lesson 21 • Vowel Digraphs **au** and **aw**   87

Spelling and Writing

Proofreading

This description has twelve mistakes. Use the proofreading marks to fix each mistake. Then, write the misspelled **list words** correctly on the lines.

Do you know what is fun to do Watch the otters at the High desert museum. The museum is not far from bend, Oregon. These otters love an awdience. They are up at daun, playing and swimming. They lawnch themselves down hills and slide into the water, making people laugh. can you guess what happens then They do it all over again. it's also fun to watch an otter eat. It floats, holding food in its claus. It's like a show at a restawrant.

1. _____   2. _____

3. _____   4. _____

5. _____

Proofreading Marks

⬯ spelling mistake

≡ capital letter

⌃ add something

Writing a Description

Have you ever watched a wild animal at work or at play? Write a description of what you saw. Use as many **list words** as you can. Remember to proofread your paragraph and fix any mistakes.

_____

_____

_____

_____

_____

_____

BONUS WORDS

drawn

saucer

automatic

author

lawyer

Spelling Words in Action

How can a town be turned into a museum?

End of the Trail

The front door of Butch Cassidy's cabin stands open, **swaying** on its hinges. A stagecoach is parked outside the general store, but no horses are restlessly pawing the gray dust. No **voices** can be heard from the well-traveled trail. In fact, the only **noises** that can be heard are whispering breezes and chirping insects.

You may think this is a ghost town, but it's really a museum called Old Trail Town. It stands outside Cody, Wyoming, and was established by Bob Edgar and his wife, Terry, in 1967. Among the **displays** are 26 buildings, 100 horse-drawn vehicles, and hundreds of treasures from the old Wild West.

Years ago, Bob noticed old cabins standing empty in the **broiling** sun of the open range. Some were falling in, and others were being **destroyed** by grazing cattle. Bob felt it was **disloyal** to let these historical relics disappear. So, the Edgars **appointed** themselves to save this part of America's history.

After working hard and sacrificing much time and money, the Edgars' dream came to life. Now, they are **praised** for preserving a long-ago way of life. Many people are interested in seeing how cowhands and pioneers really lived. A visit to Old Trail Town will not **disappoint** them.

Say each boldfaced word in the selection. How are the words with the /ā/ sound spelled? How are the words with the /oi/ sound spelled?

89

TIP

The vowel pairs **ai** and **ay** make the /ā/ sound you hear in <u>waist</u> and <u>fray</u>. Diphthongs are different from vowel pairs in that the two vowels blend together to make one sound. The diphthongs **oi** and **oy** make the /oi/ sound you hear in <u>voices</u> and <u>employ</u>.

LIST WORDS

1. voices
2. sprain
3. noises
4. disloyal
5. employ
6. waist
7. destroyed
8. fray
9. broiling
10. swaying
11. displays
12. praised
13. disappoint
14. railroad
15. royalty
16. appointed
17. crayon
18. boiling
19. soybean
20. spoiled

Spelling with ai, ay, oi, and oy

Write each **list word** under the correct heading.

/ā/ spelled **ai**

1. _____
2. _____
3. _____
4. _____

/ā/ spelled **ay**

5. _____
6. _____
7. _____
8. _____

/oi/ spelled **oi**   ### /oi/ spelled **oy**

9. _____   16. _____

10. _____   17. _____

11. _____   18. _____

12. _____   19. _____

13. _____   20. _____

14. _____

15. _____

Classification

Write the **list word** that belongs in each group.

1. pen, pencil, _____

2. baking, boiling, _____

3. bang, crash, _____

4. soprano, alto, _____

5. dissatisfy, fail, _____

6. rice, potato, _____

7. queens, kings, _____

8. untrue, unfaithful, _____

9. moving, rocking, _____

10. chosen, assigned, _____

Move the Words

Each underlined **list word** must be moved to a different sentence to make sense.
Write the correct **list word** for each sentence in the blank at the end.

1. The water in the kettle is <u>spoiled</u>. _____

2. My sleeves are beginning to <u>railroad</u>. _____

3. Don't <u>employ</u> your back lifting that box. _____

4. The two dogs are <u>waist</u> rotten. _____

5. The <u>displays</u> station was a landmark. _____

6. The belt wouldn't go around my <u>praised</u>. _____

7. The store wants to <u>destroyed</u> more people. _____

8. The team was <u>boiling</u> for winning. _____

9. The waves <u>sprain</u> the sand castle. _____

10. The newly built museum <u>fray</u> art. _____

Spelling and Writing

Proofreading

The paragraph below has eleven mistakes. Use the proofreading marks to fix each mistake. Then, write the misspelled **list words** correctly on the lines.

Proofreading Marks

⬭   spelling mistake

⊙   add period

ℓ   take out something

The pioneers who came west in covered wagons are to be praysed Even with an appoynted leader, they had to use all their skills just to survive. Long days were spent riding in in the swaiying wagons in boyling hot or icy cold weather. Accidents could and did happen! A wagon wheel could be destroied by by the rough terrain, or someone could have a sprained ankle with with no one to treat it When the rallroad came, traveling west became easier, but it was still an adventure.

1. _____

2. _____

3. _____

4. _____

5. _____

6. _____

Writing a Narrative Paragraph

Cowhands worked hard at herding cattle. Yet, they had fun, too. Write a paragraph telling what you think it was like to be an Old West cowhand. Use as many **list words** as you can. Remember to proofread your paragraph and fix any mistakes.

_____

_____

_____

BONUS WORDS

entertain

delay

embroider

loyal

raisin

What bird can be as small as a sparrow or as big as a dog?

Night Prowlers

Owls aren't seen as often as other birds, but that's because they prefer the **hours** of darkness. Even if we don't see them, owls are there. In fact, owls are found throughout the world in places like **mountain** forests and dry deserts. There are more than 130 different kinds of owls. Some are as small as **sparrows**, like the elf or pygmy owls. Others are very large, such as the great horned owl. It's as big as some dogs!

Owls often live in nests left behind by other birds. Sometimes, they use **hollow** trees or logs for their homes. When they live near **towns**, owls may move into deserted buildings or barns.

Most owls sleep during the day. When dusk comes, they glide through the air **without** making a sound, looking for food. Owls can see even with a small **amount** of light and can spot food in the darkest places. Their keen eyes can't move, but an owl's long, thin neck **allows** it to turn its head in almost a complete circle so that it can easily spot prey. An owl's hearing is as **powerful** as its sight, **although** some people may not believe this. After all, if owls can hear so well, why do they always say "whoo"?

Look back at the boldfaced words. Say each word. Listen for the /ō/ and /ou/ sounds. What do you notice about the way these sounds are spelled?

TIP

The diphthongs **ou** and **ow** can make the /ou/ sound, as in <u>without</u> and <u>towns</u>.

The letters **ow** can also be a vowel pair making the /ō/ sound, as in <u>hollow</u>.

The letters **ou** can make the /ō/ sound in <u>although</u>, the /ô/ sound in <u>thought</u>, or the /u/ sound, as in <u>southern</u>.

LIST WORDS

1. *hours*
2. *sparrows*
3. *towns*
4. *powerful*
5. *amount*
6. *without*
7. *allows*
8. *shower*
9. *brought*
10. *sought*
11. *hollow*
12. *swallowed*
13. *southern*
14. *thousand*
15. *thought*
16. *trouble*
17. *bouquet*
18. *although*
19. *mountain*
20. *chowder*

Spelling with <u>ou</u> and <u>ow</u>

Write each **list word** under the correct heading.

/ou/ spelled ou

1. _____
2. _____
3. _____
4. _____
5. _____

/ou/ spelled ow

6. _____
7. _____
8. _____
9. _____
10. _____

/ô/ spelled ou

11. _____
12. _____
13. _____

/ō/ spelled ow

14. _____
15. _____
16. _____

/ō/ spelled ou

17. _____
18. _____

/u/ spelled ou

19. _____
20. _____

Puzzle

Read each clue. Write the **list word** that means the same or almost the same as each word given. Then, read down the shaded boxes to solve the riddle.

1. minus
2. problem

3. rain
4. permits
5. 1,000

6. sum

7. idea
8. empty
9. soup
10. hill

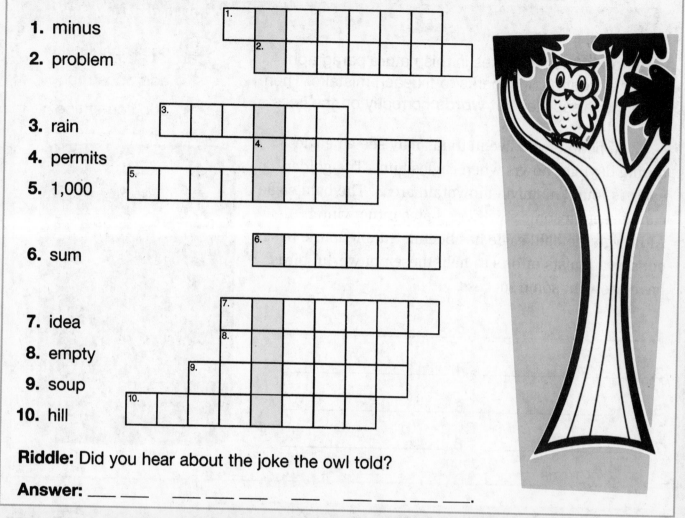

Riddle: Did you hear about the joke the owl told?

Answer: ___ ___ ___ ___ ___ ___ ___ ___ ___ ___ ___ ___ .

Dictionary Guide Words

For each set of dictionary guide words, write the **list words** that could be found on that page. Write the words in alphabetical order.

alter/cat

1. _____
2. _____
3. _____
4. _____

skip/thorn

5. _____
6. _____
7. _____
8. _____

In a dictionary, guide words at the top of a page show the first and last entries on that page.

maybe/mountain

Spelling and Writing

Proofreading

Look for thirteen mistakes in this nature paragraph. Use the proofreading marks to fix each mistake. Then, write the misspelled **list words** correctly on the lines.

Even people who live in touns may see an eagle during daylight howrs when eagles hunt. The golden eagle is found mainlyin mowntain areas. The bald eagle canbe seen in some sowthern states inthe winter. Althowgh the bald eagle has beenin trauble in the past, conservationists efforts to help these pouwerful birds have browght some success.

1. _____   2. _____

3. _____   4. _____

5. _____   6. _____

7. _____   8. _____

Writing a Journal Entry

Write a journal entry about an interesting bird you have seen recently. Don't forget to include the date you saw the bird. Use as many **list words** as you can. Remember to proofread your entry and fix any mistakes.

_____

_____

_____

_____

_____

BONUS WORDS

scouts

drowned

marshmallow

couple

fought

In lessons 19–23, you have learned how to spell words with vowel pairs, vowel digraphs, and diphthongs.

Check Your Spelling Notebook

Look at the words in your spelling notebook. Which words for lessons 19 through 23 did you have the most trouble with? Write them here.

_____

_____

Practice writing your troublesome words with a partner. Form the letters of each word with clay, pipe cleaners, or string while your partner spells the words aloud.

Lesson 19

TIP The vowel pairs **ee** and **ea** can spell /ē/, as in fleet and reason; **oa** and **oe** spell /ō/, as in boasted and tiptoes; and **ue** spells /o͞o/, as in clues; the vowel digraph **ea** can spell /e/, as in instead.

Add and subtract letters to form **list words**.

List Words
breeze
hoed
meaning
roasted
freedom
approach
measure
glued
eagle
meadow

1. cued – c + gl = _____

2. tasted – ta + roa = _____

3. each – ch + gle = _____

4. house – use + ed = _____

5. approve – ve + ach = _____

6. freeze – f + b = _____

7. lining – li + mea = _____

8. meant – nt + dow = _____

9. random – ran + free = _____

10. treasure – tr + m = _____

TIP The letters **ie** can spell /ī/, as in <u>died</u>, or /ē/, as in <u>fields</u>.
The letters **ei** can spell /ē/, as in <u>seize</u>, or /ā/, as in <u>weigh</u>.

Write the **list word** that belongs in each group.

List Words

brief
shriek
believe
sleigh
receive
neighbors
receipt
amplifies
chiefly
freighter

1. canoe, sailboat, _____
2. scream, yell, _____
3. sled, ski, _____
4. friends, partners, _____
5. mainly, mostly, _____
6. short, small, _____
7. feel, think, _____
8. increases, boosts, _____
9. get, obtain, _____
10. check, ticket, _____

TIP The vowel digraphs **au** and **aw** both spell /ô/, as in <u>haunt</u> and <u>claws</u>.

Write each **list word** in the correct category.

List Words

fault
drawings
launch
sauce
awkward
gnaw
audience
scrawl
gaunt
restaurant

one syllable

1. _____
2. _____
3. _____
4. _____
5. _____
6. _____

two syllables

7. _____
8. _____

three syllables

9. _____
10. _____

TIP Vowel pairs **ai** and **ay** spell /ā/, as in <u>waist</u> and <u>fray</u>.
Diphthongs **oi** and **oy** spell /oi/, as in <u>voices</u> and <u>employ</u>.

Write each group of **list words** in alphabetical order.

List Words

sprain
disloyal
employ
destroyed
displays
disappoint
railroad
royalty
soybean
spoiled

sprain royalty railroad soybean spoiled	disloyal employ destroyed displays disappoint

1. _____   6. _____

2. _____   7. _____

3. _____   8. _____

4. _____   9. _____

5. _____   10. _____

TIP The letters **ou** and **ow** can be diphthongs that make the sound /ou/, as in <u>amount</u> and <u>towns</u>. The letters can also be vowel pairs with the /ō/ sound, as in <u>hollow</u> and <u>although</u>, and vowel digraphs with the /u/ sound, as in <u>trouble</u>, or the /ô/ sound, as in <u>thought</u>.

List Words

hours
sparrows
powerful
shower
brought
hollow
swallowed
bouquet
mountain
chowder

Write a **list word** to match each definition.

1. a very high hill _____

2. units of 60 minutes _____

3. strong or forceful _____

4. a light rainfall _____

5. carried or delivered _____

6. having empty space inside _____

7. a thick soup _____

8. gray and brown songbirds _____

9. a bunch of flowers _____

10. passed down the throat _____

Show What You Know

One word is misspelled in each set of **list words**. Fill in the circle next to the **list word** that is spelled incorrectly.

1. ○ launch ○ royalty ○ meaning ○ powerful ○ cheifly
2. ○ hours ○ sleigh ○ praysed ○ reason ○ sauce
3. ○ hoed ○ towns ○ soybean ○ claws ○ wiegh
4. ○ crayon ○ deceive ○ betwean ○ sparrows ○ fault
5. ○ deid ○ eagle ○ shower ○ employ ○ dawn
6. ○ boiling ○ bouquay ○ meadow ○ believe ○ causing
7. ○ rooasted ○ allows ○ waist ○ straw ○ eighteen
8. ○ southern ○ sieze ○ jaw ○ fray ○ freedom
9. ○ glewed ○ diet ○ awkward ○ sprain ○ swallowed
10. ○ amount ○ pies ○ treeting ○ haunt ○ railroad
11. ○ recieve ○ spoiled ○ loaned ○ hollow ○ yawn
12. ○ chowder ○ displays ○ frawd ○ fields ○ clues
13. ○ broiling ○ measure ○ drawings ○ sawght ○ relief
14. ○ mountain ○ nieghbors ○ fawns ○ noises ○ eastern
15. ○ gnaw ○ voices ○ brieze ○ without ○ brief
16. ○ tiptoes ○ shreek ○ brought ○ audience ○ disloyal
17. ○ thousand ○ shawl ○ receipt ○ destroyed ○ approoch
18. ○ amplifyes ○ scrawl ○ swaying ○ instead ○ thought
19. ○ trouble ○ boasted ○ freighter ○ disappoint ○ gawnt
20. ○ restaurant ○ appointed ○ fleat ○ although ○ perceive

Spelling Words in Action

How do you keep a bike in tip-top shape?

Clean Machine

You have to work hard to keep a bike in tip-top shape. The best time to care for a bike is before anything goes wrong. Clean off **splashes** of dirt with soap and water, then dry your bike with soft, clean towels. Pay attention to the reflectors that give off **flashes** of light. The cleaner they are, the easier it is for the driver of a car to see you. To protect the shine, apply a coat of car or bicycle wax. Most **waxes** can be applied using a soft, clean cloth, then removed using another cloth.

To keep your bike safe, keep its chain in good condition. Old **toothbrushes** are great for removing grime. Oil the chain with bike chain oil. Don't use too much! Oily **chains** become gummy and collect dirt. If your bike has hand brakes, check the brake **shoes**. These are the rubber pads that grip the tires. Replace them if they are worn. You want the brakes to work well, so you can avoid **crashes** or riding into **ditches**.

Once your bike is in good working order, take it out for a test run and put it through its **paces**. Then, pack some **sandwiches**, bike to your favorite spot, and have a picnic.

Look back at the boldfaced words. What letter or letters are added to each word to make it plural?

101

TIP

You make most singular words plural by adding just **s** to the singular form.

<u>shoe</u> + **s** = <u>shoes</u>

If a singular word ends in **x**, **ss**, **sh**, or **ch**, you usually add **es** to make it mean more than one.

<u>fox</u> + **es** = <u>foxes</u>

LIST WORDS

1. axes
2. chains
3. bosses
4. shoes
5. kisses
6. waxes
7. foxes
8. splashes
9. ashes
10. crashes
11. matches
12. sandwiches
13. toothbrushes
14. eyelashes
15. sashes
16. ditches
17. flashes
18. churches
19. paces
20. clashes

Forming Plurals

Finish spelling each **list word**.

1. ki _____
2. sh _____
3. as _____
4. cr _____
5. wa _____
6. bo _____
7. ax _____
8. fl _____
9. di _____
10. cla _____
11. cha _____
12. fo _____
13. ma _____
14. pa _____
15. sas _____
16. chu _____
17. sand _____
18. spla _____
19. eye _____
20. tooth _____

Rhyming Words

Use the clues to write **list words** that could make sense in each sentence. Each **list word** must rhyme with the underlined word.

1. The snake <u>hisses</u> when it _____.

2. If it <u>rains</u> on my _____, they'll rust.

3. Playing in the _____ might give you <u>rashes</u>.

4. He _____ with loose <u>laces</u>.

5. Put the <u>batches</u> of _____ in a safe place.

6. Wily _____ don't like <u>boxes</u>.

7. He <u>pitches</u> rocks in the _____.

8. The reflectors makes <u>slashes</u> of _____.

9. The tourist <u>searches</u> elaborate _____.

10. She <u>lashes</u> _____ around her waist.

Word Building

Add and subtract letters to form **list words**.

1. flashes – f + eye = _____

2. nailbrushes – nail + tooth = _____

3. apes – p + x = _____

4. hisses – hi + bo = _____

5. shirts – irt + oe = _____

6. sandworm – orm + iches = _____

7. watch – tch + xes = _____

8. classic – sic + hes = _____

Spelling and Writing

Proofreading

This poem has twelve mistakes. Use the proofreading marks to fix each mistake. Then, write the misspelled **list words** correctly on the lines.

Proofreading Marks

- ⬭ spelling mistake
- ⌃ add something
- ⌐ take out something

We ride bicycles onthe street.
We wave to to all the friends we meet.
We hit puddles to make splashis.
And now andthen we have krashes.
We we jump dichtes in a bunch,
And eat sandwitches forlunch.
Even in the the hardest rains
We always stopto fix our chayns.

1. _____

2. _____

3. _____

4. _____

5. _____

Writing a Narrative Paragraph

Bicycles are not the only things that need special care. Write a paragraph that tells how to take care of something else, such as a pet or favorite toy. Use as many **list words** as you can. Remember to proofread your paragraph and fix any mistakes.

_____

_____

_____

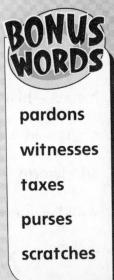

BONUS WORDS

pardons

witnesses

taxes

purses

scratches

Spelling Words in Action

When is it okay to "pig out"?

Pig Out

Most of the time, "pigging out" is considered bad manners and unhealthy. There is one day a year, however, when *not* pigging out is impolite. That day is March 1, National Pig Day.

Most **holidays** were started to recall historic events. This one, though, was begun by two sisters from Texas and North Carolina. These **ladies** shared a childhood fascination with pigs. They brought their love for pigs to **counties** everywhere when they had their Pig Day registered as a real holiday in 1972.

Today, across the **highways** and byways of our land, National Pig Day is celebrated by pig lovers. Some **communities** have pig **parties**. Others, like Davis, California, celebrate the holiday with all-day pig festivals. People are encouraged to dress up like pigs. If needed, guests can buy fake pig snouts, ears, and tails there. Guests can visit a pig petting zoo, go on pig rides, and make pig crafts. Some people "pig out" on special food like pig-shaped cookies and cakes. There are even pig **melodies** and pig cheers.

If you want to celebrate National Pig Day, try checking out your local library. Some **libraries** observe the day with an afternoon of pig **stories** and crafts. You could also make **copies** of your favorite pig pictures and pass them out to friends.

The singular form of each boldfaced word in the selection ends with the same letter. Which letter is it? How are the plurals spelled?

TIP

If a word ends in **y** preceded by a vowel, add **s** to make the plural.

holiday + **s** = holidays

If a word ends in **y** preceded by a consonant, change **y** to **i** and add **es**.

copy + **es** = copies

LIST WORDS

1. holidays
2. parties
3. stories
4. flies
5. birthdays
6. copies
7. duties
8. ladies
9. counties
10. valleys
11. groceries
12. hobbies
13. libraries
14. highways
15. batteries
16. injuries
17. cherries
18. melodies
19. surveys
20. communities

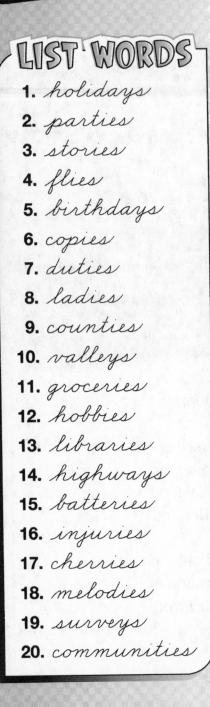

Forming Plurals of Words Ending in <u>y</u>

Complete each **list word** by writing **y** and adding **s** to make the plural, or by changing the **y** to **i** and adding **es** to make the plural.

1. grocer _____
2. fl _____
3. stor _____
4. dut _____
5. highwa _____
6. cop _____
7. birthda _____
8. hobb _____
9. batter _____
10. valle _____
11. holida _____
12. part _____
13. injur _____
14. surve _____
15. melod _____
16. communit _____
17. cherr _____
18. lad _____
19. count _____
20. librar _____

Complete the Paragraphs

Write a **list word** on each of the lines to complete the paragraphs.

Unusual Holidays

We all have our own _____ about the more usual _____.
Some people even consider their _____ to be holidays. There are
probably dozens of holidays, though, that you've never heard of. In fact, there is a
holiday for almost everything.

Every month has some kind of wacky holiday celebrated in _____
and _____ around the country. For example, did you know that the
second week in January is National Pizza Week? Better include some pizza fixings
in your _____ then! June 13 is National Juggling Day. Start
practicing to avoid any minor _____. If you like marshmallows, you'll
love National Toasted Marshmallow Day on August 30. Then, there's Miniature
Golf Day on September 21. It's never too early to practice hitting that golf ball
over those little hills and _____. _____ have shown that one
of the most popular holidays is September 22. That's the date to celebrate
Ice Cream Cone Day. Serve those cones with _____ on top!

Scrambled Words

What **list words** can you make from the letters in each group of words? Use each
letter once.

1. is, elf _____   **6.** a, sigh, why _____

2. sad, lie _____   **7.** bib, shoe _____

3. side, mole _____   **8.** us, tied _____

4. art, pies _____   **9.** rib, is, real _____

5. epic, so _____   **10.** a, bite, rest _____

Spelling and Writing

Proofreading

spelling mistake

capital letter

add something

The article below has eleven mistakes. Use the proofreading marks to fix each mistake. Then, write the misspelled **list words** correctly on the lines.

    have you ever heard storys about Turkey Trots One kind of Turkey Trot is a dance. Another is a race held around one of our most popular holidayes, Thanksgiving Day. Turkey Trots are held in communitees and countys around the country. They're usually planned like partees with plenty of running, food, and fun times. often, Turkey Trots are held to raise money for charities. The races are usually 5 or 10 kilometers. Afterall, we don't want any injurys. Ask around. see if there is a Turkey Trot near you.

1. _____

2. _____

3. _____

4. _____

5. _____

6. _____

Writing a Persuasive Paragraph

What event or day do you think should be celebrated? Use the **list words** to write a paragraph to convince people that your holiday is important. Use as many **list words** as you can. Remember to proofread your paragraph and fix any mistakes.

_____

_____

_____

_____

_____

BONUS WORDS

grizzlies

universities

deliveries

convoys

essays

Spelling Words in Action

How much do you really know about teeth?

A Toothy Story

Many kinds of animals have **teeth**, but some do not. Birds, toads, turtles, and some kinds of insects and whales are toothless. The shape and size of an animal's teeth depend chiefly on what kind of food the animal eats.

Sheep, **oxen**, **bison**, **buffaloes**, and **moose** are plant-eaters. They have very broad, flat teeth to chew, crush, and mash the twigs, **leaves**, and grasses they eat. Meat-eaters, such as dogs, cats, tigers, and wolves, have several long, pointed teeth that are very sharp. They use them to rip and tear at the bodies of their prey. People eat everything from **loaves** of bread to salads and meat. That is why people have some teeth that are sharp and some that are broad and flat.

Some animals have teeth that grow continuously, such as elephants' tusks. Beavers, rats, and rabbits also have teeth that grow throughout their **lives**. They must chew constantly to keep their teeth worn down.

Many fish and most reptiles have teeth that are about the same size and shape and that are only used for catching prey. Sharks have teeth that are as sharp as **knives**. They have many rows of teeth. When they lose a tooth, the one in back of it takes its place.

Look back at the boldfaced words. Notice that all the words are plurals. What is the singular form of each word?

Spelling Practice

TIP

Most words ending in **f/fe** change the **f/fe** to **v** and add **es** to make plurals.
calf—calves   knife—knives
A few words ending in **f** just add **s**.
chief—chiefs   hoof—hoofs
Words ending in **o** add **s** or **es**.
buffalo—buffaloes
Irregular plurals change their spelling or stay the same.
mouse—mice   sheep—sheep

LIST WORDS

1. teeth
2. mice
3. women
4. knives
5. leaves
6. halves
7. loaves
8. lives
9. calves
10. moose
11. sheep
12. oxen
13. yourselves
14. geese
15. chiefs
16. buffaloes
17. handkerchiefs
18. scarves
19. hoofs
20. bison

Writing Irregular Plurals

Write the **list word** that is the plural form of each word given.

1. hoof _____   13. moose _____

2. knife _____   14. mouse _____

3. sheep _____   15. loaf _____

4. chief _____   16. goose _____

5. ox _____   17. scarf _____

6. half _____   18. tooth _____

7. bison _____   19. calf _____

8. leaf _____   20. woman _____

9. life _____

10. handkerchief _____

11. buffalo _____

12. yourself _____

Comparing Words

The first two underlined words in each sentence are related. Write a **list word** that has the same relationship to the third underlined word.

1. <u>Feet</u> are to <u>people</u> as _____ are to <u>horses</u>.

2. <u>Patties</u> are to <u>hamburgers</u> as _____ are to <u>bread</u>.

3. <u>Walk</u> is to <u>legs</u> as <u>chew</u> is to _____.

4. <u>Men</u> are to <u>boys</u> as _____ are to <u>girls</u>.

5. <u>Scissors</u> are to <u>paper</u> as _____ are to <u>meat</u>.

6. <u>Belts</u> are to <u>waists</u> as _____ are to <u>necks</u>.

7. <u>Hay</u> is to <u>horses</u> as <u>cheese</u> is to _____.

8. <u>Captains</u> are to <u>police</u> as _____ are to <u>firemen</u>.

9. <u>Napkins</u> are to <u>hands</u> as _____ are to <u>noses</u>.

Riddle

Read each definition clue. Write **list words** in the spaces. Then, use the numbered letters to solve the riddle.

1. parts of a whole
   __ __ __ __ __ __

     8

2. young cows or bulls
   __ __ __ __ __ __

   1

3. birds that swim
   __ __ __ __ __

   7

4. members of the ox family
   __ __ __ __ __ __

 5   2

5. your own selves
   __ __ __ __ __ __ __ __ __ __

         6   9

6. animals related to deer
   __ __ __ __ __

 4

7. wild oxen
   __ __ __ __ __ __ __ __ __

   3   10

Riddle: What is most useful when it is used up?

Answer: __ __ __ __ __ __ __ __ __ __

      1 2   3 4 5 6 7 8 9 10

Lesson 27 • Irregular Plurals **111**

Spelling and Writing

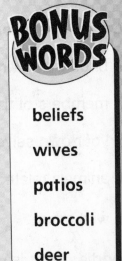

Proofreading

Proofreading Marks

⬭ spelling mistake

∧ add something

ℓ take out something

This informational article has nine mistakes. Use the proofreading marks to fix each mistake. Then, write the misspelled **list words** correctly on the lines.

Have you ever wondered what the difference was between an animal's horns and antlers? Goats, sheeps, cattle, oxes, and buffalos have horns. Horns can appear on both male and female animals. Horns are made of bone and are covered by a tough layer of skin. They grow out of the the animal's skull and may curve, but they do not branch. Horned animals have one set of horns for their entire lifes.

Deer, mooses, and elk have antlers. Antlers usually appear only on male animals. The animal loses its antlers every year. That leavs it to grow back a new set inthe spring. Like horns, antlers grow from the animal's skull. Antlers can can grow quite large and often form many branches.

1. _____

2. _____

3. _____

4. _____

5. _____

6. _____

Writing a Persuasive Paragraph

Write a paragraph that tells why teeth that never stop growing might help or harm an animal. Use as many **list words** as you can. Remember to proofread your paragraph and fix any mistakes.

_____

_____

_____

_____

_____

BONUS WORDS

beliefs

wives

patios

broccoli

deer

Spelling Words in Action

What is a geoglyph?

Grand Designs

Let's imagine that we are flying high over the deserts of southern Peru. Looking toward the ground, we see giant drawings covering the desert floor. **We're** looking at what are called the Nazca Lines. The shapes these lines create can only be seen from the air. One of the largest drawings is that of a monkey that reminds us of a **child's** drawing. No child drew this, though. The monkey is 350 feet long! **How's** it possible?

These pictures in the sand, called geoglyphs, were made by the Nazca people about 1,000 to 2,000 years ago. Geoglyphs also exist in **Arizona's** deserts and in other places around the world. They are made by moving the **desert's** dark stones to reveal the lighter soil underneath. The Nazca Lines include pictures of many kinds of plants and animals. There is a 150-foot spider, a 165-foot hummingbird, and a pelican that's over 900 feet long. There are also flowers, a **person's** hand, and different geometric shapes.

Wouldn't you like to know why the Nazca made these lines? So would scientists, but **they'll** have to wait a while longer as science **hasn't** yet found the answer. There is no real evidence because there is so little left of the Nazca culture.

Look back at the boldfaced words. Notice that each word has an apostrophe. Can you identify which words are possessives and which words are contractions?

113

TIP

Use an apostrophe to show where letters have been left out in a contraction.

she will—she'll

how is—how's

Use an apostrophe and s to show singular ownership.

the bike of my uncle—my uncle's bike

LIST WORDS

1. she'll
2. wouldn't
3. they'll
4. how's
5. let's
6. where's
7. we're
8. desert's
9. person's
10. sister's
11. bicycle's
12. Arizona's
13. child's
14. aunt's
15. cousin's
16. Florida's
17. uncle's
18. doctor's
19. hasn't
20. season's

Using an Apostrophe

Write the **list words** that are contractions using the word <u>is</u>.

1. _____ 2. _____

Write the **list words** that are contractions using the word <u>not</u>.

3. _____ 4. _____

Write the **list words** that are contractions using the word <u>will</u>.

5. _____ 6. _____

Write the **list word** that is a contraction using the word <u>are</u>.

7. _____

Write the **list word** that is a contraction using the word <u>us</u>.

8. _____

Write the **list words** that show ownership.

9. _____ 10. _____

11. _____ 12. _____

13. _____ 14. _____

15. _____ 16. _____

17. _____ 18. _____

19. _____ 20. _____

Missing Words

Write the **list word** that best completes each sentence.

1. The hat that the child owns is the _____ hat.

2. The clothes of my sister are my _____ clothes.

3. The house of my aunt is my _____ house.

4. <u>They will</u> means the same as the contraction _____.

5. The nickname of Arizona is _____ nickname.

6. <u>Let us</u> means the same as the contraction _____.

7. <u>Has not</u> means the same as the contraction _____.

8. The name of the person is the _____ name.

9. The office belonging to the doctor is the _____ office.

10. <u>Where is</u> means the same as the contraction _____.

11. The lakes of Florida are _____ lakes.

12. The first snowfall of the season is the _____ first snowfall.

13. The father of my cousin is my _____ father.

Puzzle

Fill in the crossword puzzle by writing a **list word** to answer each clue. The apostrophes have been filled in for you.

ACROSS

1. how is
4. belonging to a bicycle
5. we are
6. of the desert

DOWN

2. she will
3. of the uncle

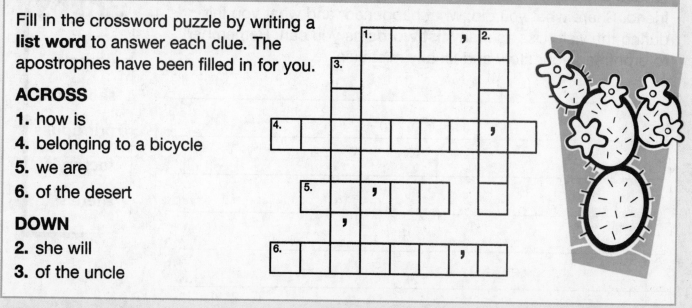

Spelling and Writing

Proofreading

Proofreading Marks

˅ add apostrophe

∧ add something

≡ capital letter

This article has eleven mistakes. Use the proofreading marks to fix each mistake. Then, write the **list words** correctly on the lines.

Wouldnt you know it, arizona was a big surprise I went to visit my cousins ranch near flagstaff. I asked, "Wheres the desert?" He said, "Below us. Flagstaff is too high for a desert climate. We're in forests where each seasons weather is different." What a beautiful place It should be on every persons list of places to go. some people like Florida's palm trees. I, however, like Arizonas pine trees.

1. _____   2. _____

3. _____   4. _____

5. _____   6. _____

Writing a Story

Write a short story about a time when you visited a relative or friend. Share what you did, what happened, and what you felt during the visit. Use as many **list words** as you can. Remember to proofread your story and fix any mistakes.

_____

_____

_____

_____

_____

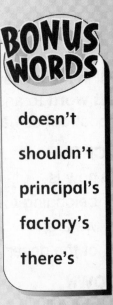

BONUS WORDS

doesn't

shouldn't

principal's

factory's

there's

Spelling Words in Action

What fabric never goes out of style?

Durable Denim

There is a kind of fabric that never goes out of style. Almost everyone has worn it at least once. Some people wear it every day. It's denim. This sturdy cloth has been meeting **families'** clothing needs for more than a hundred years. Every family **members'** clothing can be made from it.

In 1873, Levi Strauss and Jacob Davis patented the process of using rivets in making **men's** work clothes. Strauss used denim for the fabric because it was durable, comfortable, and looked good, and then he added rivets to the pockets and other stress points. This kept the pants from ripping when worn by workers such as miners.

Jeans today are often made of denim. Denim is used not only for men's clothing, but women's and **children's** clothing as well. In fact, denim is a cloth that can be used to make almost anything. It can be used for **passengers'** luggage, **hostesses'** uniforms, **umpires'** caps, and children's shoes. **Dresses'** styles have been based on the popularity of denim. Even **governments'** highest leaders have been seen wearing this common fabric. Despite the passage of over a hundred years, denim is also still the center of Levi Strauss's **businesses'** success.

Look back at the boldfaced words. Notice that all the words are plural. How is the possessive of each word formed?

LIST WORDS

1. passengers'
2. armies'
3. families'
4. thieves'
5. ranches'
6. benches'
7. umpires'
8. airlines'
9. dresses'
10. hostesses'
11. banjos'
12. pianos'
13. men's
14. children's
15. bodies'
16. daisies'
17. televisions'
18. members'
19. governments'
20. businesses'

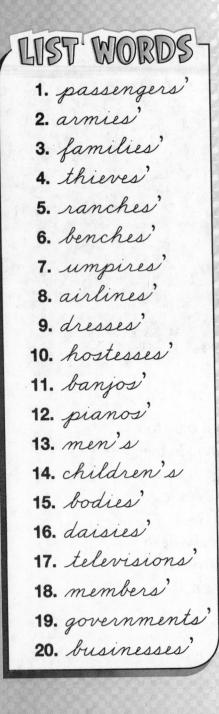

Forming Plural Possessives

Write each **list word** that is formed by adding an apostrophe and **s** to a plural word.

1. _____ 2. _____

Write each **list word** that is formed by adding just an apostrophe to a plural word.

3. _____ 4. _____

5. _____ 6. _____

7. _____ 8. _____

9. _____ 10. _____

11. _____ 12. _____

13. _____ 14. _____

15. _____ 16. _____

17. _____ 18. _____

19. _____ 20. _____

Possessives

The **list word** in each sentence needs an apostrophe. Circle the **list word**, and then write it correctly on the line.

1. All of the passengers meals were served hot. _____

2. Both umpires decisions are final. _____

3. Both businesses workers put in long hours. _____

4. The 50 members dues are paid every March. _____

5. The thieves names were in the newspaper. _____

6. The daisies petals were yellow and white. _____

7. All the benches seats had good cushions. _____

8. The two ranches cattle roam the open fields. _____

9. The four hostesses uniforms are exactly alike. _____

10. Our families homes are next to each other. _____

Word Search

Ten **list words** are hidden in the puzzle, but the apostrophes are missing. The words go across, up, down, backward, and diagonally. Circle each word. Then, write the words with apostrophes to show their plural possessives.

1. _____ 2. _____

3. _____ 4. _____

5. _____ 6. _____

7. _____ 8. _____

9. _____ 10. _____

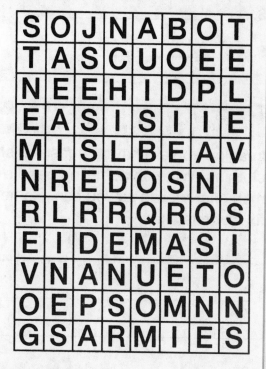

Spelling and Writing

Proofreading

Proofreading Marks

↧ add apostrophe

⌃ add something

／ make small letter

Find the twelve mistakes in the article below. Use the proofreading marks to fix each mistake. Then, write the **list words** correctly on the lines.

Thousands of years ago, Only the Chinese knew that silkworms spin the silk threads needed for making silk fabric. For a long time, government members efforts to guard thissecret worked. When other Countries discovered the wonderful cloth, they wanted to make it themselves. Some travelers discovered howto sneak Silkworms out of China. The thieves idea was to carry the creatures out inthe hollows of bamboo canes. The idea worked! Soon, other countries could Make silk fabric and produce mens, women's, and childrens clothing. Many families wardrobes could now include this fabric.

1. _____   2. _____

3. _____   4. _____

5. _____

Writing an Advertisement

Imagine you are having a fashion show to exhibit the latest casual clothing. Write an ad telling people what you're showing. Use as many **list words** as you can. Remember to proofread your ad and fix any mistakes.

_____

_____

_____

_____

BONUS WORDS

diaries'

fish's

classes'

spies'

species'

Lessons 25–29 • Review

Lesson
30

In lessons 25 through 29, you have learned how to spell plural words, irregular plurals, contractions, and possessives.

Check Your Spelling Notebook

Look at the words in your spelling notebook. Which words for lessons 25 through 29 did you have the most trouble with? Write them here.

_____

_____

Practice writing your troublesome words with a partner. Form the letters of each word using clay. Your partner can spell the word aloud as you form the letters.

Lesson 25

TIP Most plurals are formed by adding **s** to the singular form, as in <u>chains</u>. If a word ends in **x**, **ss**, **sh**, or **ch**, add **es** to form the plural, as in <u>foxes</u> and <u>bosses</u>.

Write a **list word** to match each definition.

List Words
axes
waxes
matches
sandwiches
eyelashes
sashes
ditches
flashes
churches
paces

1. bright bursts of light _____

2. cloths worn at waists _____

3. sticks to light a fire _____

4. hairs on eyelids _____

5. tools to chop wood _____

6. holes in the ground _____

7. meals between bread _____

8. makes surfaces shiny _____

9. places of worship _____

10. steps taken _____

121

TIP If a word ends in **vowel–y**, add **s**, as in <u>valleys</u>. If it ends in **consonant–y**, change **y** to **i** and add **es**, as in <u>duties</u>.

Write a **list word** to complete each sentence.

List Words

holidays
flies
groceries
libraries
batteries
injuries
cherries
melodies
surveys
communities

1. _____ loan books.

2. _____ are common insects.

3. School is closed on _____.

4. Portable radios run on _____.

5. I made a pie with fresh _____.

6. _____ are made up of families.

7. Don sang three new _____.

8. We were told to fill out _____.

9. Helmets have prevented _____.

10. Those _____ will feed us for a week.

TIP If a word ends in **f** or **fe**, usually change the **f** or **fe** to **v** and add **es**, as in <u>scarves</u>. Some words change their vowel sound or spelling to make the plural form, as in <u>teeth</u>. Others have the same form for singular and plural, as in <u>bison</u>.

List Words

mice
knives
halves
calves
sheep
oxen
geese
chiefs
buffaloes
hoofs

Write the **list words** in alphabetical order.

1. _____

2. _____

3. _____

4. _____

5. _____   6. _____

7. _____   8. _____

9. _____   10. _____

TIP Use apostrophes in contractions, as in <u>where's</u> and <u>wouldn't</u>. Singular possessives and those made from irregular plurals take **'s**, as in <u>sister's</u> and <u>child's</u>.

List Words

she'll
they'll
we're
bicycle's
Arizona's
cousin's
Florida's
uncle's
doctor's
hasn't

Write the **list word** that is part of each word given.

1. has _____
2. Arizona _____
3. bicycle _____
4. cousin _____
5. she _____

6. Florida _____
7. we _____
8. uncle _____
9. doctor _____
10. they _____

TIP Form the possessive of a plural word that ends in **s** by adding an apostrophe, as in <u>dresses'</u>. Plural words that do not end in s add **'s**, as in <u>women's</u>.

List Words

passengers'
families'
umpires'
airlines'
hostesses'
banjos'
men's
children's
members'
businesses'

Circle the correct form of the **list word** in each group. Then, write the **list word** on the line.

1. banjose'   banjos' _____
2. businesses'   businesses's _____
3. mens'   men's _____
4. hostesse's   hostesses' _____
5. umpires's   umpires' _____
6. members'   members's _____
7. children's   childrens' _____
8. families's   families' _____
9. passengers'   passengers's _____
10. airlines'   airlineses' _____

Show What You Know

One word is misspelled in each set of **list words**. Fill in the circle next to the **list word** that is spelled incorrectly.

1. ○ pianos' ○ surveyes ○ desert's ○ sheep ○ paces
2. ○ kisses ○ uncle's ○ banjoes' ○ loaves ○ hobbies
3. ○ hasn't ○ mice ○ shoes ○ ladies ○ goverments'
4. ○ eyelashes ○ benches' ○ flies ○ wheres ○ yourselves
5. ○ lives ○ how's ○ storys ○ foxes ○ children's
6. ○ clashes ○ valleyes ○ child's ○ men's ○ handkerchiefs
7. ○ buffalos ○ dresses' ○ Florida's ○ ashes ○ highways
8. ○ churches ○ librarys ○ oxen ○ sister's ○ armies'
9. ○ aunt's ○ waxes ○ dutys ○ geese ○ businesses'
10. ○ bicycle's ○ batteries ○ chiefs ○ daisys' ○ toothbrushes
11. ○ axes ○ teeth ○ we're ○ chaines ○ passengers'
12. ○ leaves ○ copies ○ airlines' ○ person's ○ birthdaies
13. ○ matches ○ parties ○ women ○ theyll ○ televisions'
14. ○ Arizona's ○ bosses ○ injurys ○ moose ○ hostesses'
15. ○ bodies' ○ ditches ○ scarfes ○ she'll ○ melodies
16. ○ let's ○ counties ○ hoofs ○ thiefs' ○ sandwiches
17. ○ wouldnt ○ sashes ○ umpires' ○ halves ○ communities
18. ○ flashes ○ season's ○ ranchs' ○ bison ○ groceries
19. ○ members' ○ crashes ○ calfs ○ doctor's ○ holidays
20. ○ splashes ○ cousin's ○ cherrys ○ knives ○ families'

Spelling Words in Action

How can you get people interested in a community project?

Let's Play

Does your community have a playground? If not, maybe it's time to create one! To start, first you need to **convince** people that you're serious about building a playground. Talk to lots of people and get them interested in your idea.

Of course, you'll need a place to **construct** the playground. Look for a vacant lot. Maybe there's an old playground that needs to be **returned** to its original purpose. Check out public parks, too, because there might be some extra space there that's just right for a playground.

It costs money to build a playground, so raising money is important. **Conduct** interviews with **nonprofit** groups in your community. Give them a **preview** of your ideas, and then see if they are interested in donating money. Hold fund-raising events, such as fairs, art shows, and bake sales. **Report** to local government officials and see if they can help.

It's usually a good **precaution** to hire professionals to help design and build the playground. There are organizations that do just that. They take **control** and work with local volunteers to help build the playground. Using volunteers gets everyone in the community involved. Suddenly, the playground is much less **impersonal**. It belongs to everybody.

> **Say the boldfaced words. These words have word parts called prefixes added to the front of the words. Can you name the prefix in each word?**

TIP

A prefix is a word part that is added to the beginning of a root or base word to make a new word. Every prefix has a meaning, and it changes the meaning of the root or base word.

pre = <u>before</u>, as in <u>preview</u>

re = <u>again</u> or <u>back</u>, as in <u>refills</u>

im and non = <u>not</u>, as in <u>imperfect</u>

con = <u>with</u> or <u>together</u>, as in <u>construct</u>

LIST WORDS

1. nonsense
2. prepaid
3. control
4. returned
5. impractical
6. nonstop
7. conduct
8. preview
9. report
10. imperfect
11. nonprofit
12. refills
13. construct
14. immovable
15. precaution
16. predict
17. convince
18. impersonal
19. impure
20. reaction

Adding Prefixes

Write each **list word** under the correct heading.

words with the prefix **pre**

1. _____   2. _____

3. _____   4. _____

words with the prefix **im**

5. _____   6. _____

7. _____   8. _____

9. _____

words with the prefix **non**

10. _____   11. _____

12. _____

words with the prefix **re**

13. _____   14. _____

15. _____   16. _____

words with the prefix **con**

17. _____   18. _____

19. _____   20. _____

Antonyms

Write the **list word** that means the opposite of the word or words given.

1. personal _____

2. movable _____

3. sense _____

4. with stops _____

5. perfect _____

6. for profit _____

7. practical _____

8. pure _____

9. destruct _____

10. put in doubt _____

Scrambled Words

What **list word** can you make from the letters in each word or group of words? Use each letter once.

1. duct, con _____

2. a, coin, erupt _____

3. corn, lot _____

4. pear, dip _____

5. fell, sir _____

6. rev, wipe _____

7. act, no, ire _____

8. top, err _____

9. reed, runt _____

10. drip, etc. _____

11. a, lone, prism _____

12. lamb, movie _____

13. umpire _____

14. print, of, no _____

15. if, me, crept _____

16. arctic, am, lip _____

Spelling and Writing

Proofreading Marks

- ⬭ spelling mistake
- ℓ take out something
- ⊙ add period

This informational article has ten mistakes. Use the proofreading marks to fix each mistake. Then, write the misspelled **list words** correctly on the lines.

Over a hundred years ago, the the idea of a playground would have been noncense Children played in yards, vacant lots, or in the streets. By the 1900s, however, it was easier to convinse people that there was a need for playgrounds For one thing, playing in in the streets was becoming dangerous and impracticle due to the nostop traffic. By 1899, the city of Boston had built a number of sandlots for small children to play in. Soon, other cities followed Boston's example. Simple sandlots gave way to to more elaborate playgrounds. Today, many cities and towns construkt community playgrounds for everyone to enjoy.

1. _____   2. _____

3. _____   4. _____

5. _____

Writing a News Story

Imagine that your community has just opened a new community playground. Write a news story about the event. Try to use as many **list words** as you can. Remember to proofread your story and fix any mistakes.

_____

_____

_____

BONUS WORDS

nonfiction

contact

preset

recount

impatient

Spelling Words in Action

How can you avoid catching a cold?

Don't Catch It!

With all the advances in medicine, doctors **admit** that they still haven't found a cure for the common cold. This **unpleasant** illness affects more people than any other disease. Each year, North Americans spend over a billion dollars to battle colds. There are ways people can **defend** themselves, though. Those who **explore** these options know in **advance** that the common cold will likely never be completely avoided.

Colds are not caused by going out in the rain or getting chilled. Although many will **disagree**, people rarely catch colds just by being near someone who is sneezing or coughing. Cold viruses almost always travel from the nose of an infected person to his or her hands. From there, they go to anything the person touches. If someone else touches the same object and then touches his or her nose or eyes, the virus can infect that person.

Here's some good **advice** so you won't be **unprepared**. Wash your hands often, and try not to touch your face. It's also **unwise** to touch things people with colds have touched. The common cold will never be **unknown**. With your help, it could become a little less common!

Take a look at the boldfaced words in the selection. What prefixes do you find?

TIP

Each prefix below has a meaning, and it changes the meaning of the base word or root that it is added to.

ex = <u>out of</u> or <u>from</u>, as in <u>express</u>

de = <u>down</u> or <u>away from</u>, as in <u>defend</u>

dis and **un** = <u>not</u> or <u>the opposite of</u>, as in <u>unclear</u>

ad = <u>to</u>, <u>at</u>, or <u>toward</u>, as in <u>advice</u>

LIST WORDS

1. express
2. design
3. unknown
4. admit
5. unclear
6. explore
7. disagree
8. defend
9. unreal
10. adventure
11. unwise
12. disclose
13. advice
14. excuse
15. disinterested
16. dishonest
17. unprepared
18. unpleasant
19. advance
20. adverb

Identifying Prefixes

Write each **list word** under the correct heading.

words with the prefix **un**

1. _____   2. _____

3. _____   4. _____

5. _____   6. _____

words with the prefix **ex**

7. _____   8. _____

9. _____

words with the prefix **dis**

10. _____   11. _____

12. _____   13. _____

words with the prefix **ad**

14. _____   15. _____

16. _____   17. _____

18. _____

words with the prefix **de**

19. _____   20. _____

Comparing Words

The first two underlined words in each sentence are related. Write a **list word** that has the same relationship to the third underlined word.

1. <u>Adjective</u> is to <u>noun</u> as _____ is to <u>verb</u>.

2. <u>Fair</u> is to <u>unfair</u> as honest is to _____.

3. <u>Backward</u> is to <u>behind</u> as <u>forward</u> is to _____.

4. <u>Unlike</u> is to <u>like</u> as _____ is to <u>agree</u>.

5. <u>Involved</u> is to <u>interested</u> as <u>uninvolved</u> is to _____.

6. <u>Say</u> is to <u>speak</u> as _____ is to <u>declare</u>.

7. <u>True</u> is to <u>untrue</u> as <u>real</u> is to _____.

8. <u>Happy</u> is to <u>unhappy</u> as <u>pleasant</u> is to _____.

9. <u>Clever</u> is to <u>smart</u> as _____ is to <u>foolish</u>.

Word Building

Add and subtract letters to form **list words**.

1. unknot – t + wn = _____

2. slice – sl + adv = _____

3. desire – re + gn = _____

4. admire – re + t = _____

5. amuse – am + exc = _____

6. resend – r + d – s + f = _____

7. reappear – re + un – app + cl = _____

8. repose – re + dis – p + cl = _____

9. replace – re + ex – ac + or = _____

10. invention – in + ad – ion + ure = _____

Spelling and Writing

Proofreading Marks

- ⬭ spelling mistake
- ¶ indent paragraph
- ⌃ add something

The article below has nine mistakes. Use the proofreading marks to fix each mistake. Then, write the misspelled **list words** correctly on the lines.

Having a cold is certainly unpleesant—especially if you are unprepaired for that sudden sneeze. Here's some good advise: "Keep a handkerchief close by."
Handkerchiefs havebeen used for a long time. In the first century B.C., they were madefrom linen. Later on, in the Far East, silk was used. In the 1600s, handkerchiefs of every size shape, and dezine could be found. Some had lace and buttons. Imagine using a handkerchief decorated with gemstones! Toward the 1800s, people became disintarested in these fancy pieces of cloth and began to use tissues.

1. _____   2. _____

3. _____   4. _____

5. _____

Writing an Informative Paragraph

What should people do to avoid getting a cold? Write a paragraph telling people what they can do to protect themselves from catching cold viruses. Use as many **list words** as you can. Remember to proofread your paragraph and fix any mistakes.

_____

_____

_____

_____

BONUS WORDS

- define
- unrelated
- disgrace
- advantage
- exchange

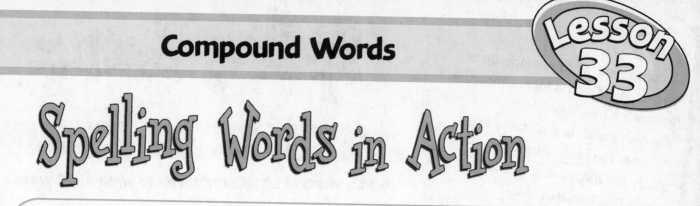

Spelling Words in Action

What was a frontier school like?

School Days

Imagine getting up 4:00 a.m. to do chores, which might include chopping wood, carrying water, or milking cows. Then, you eat **breakfast** and get ready for school. There are no cars, buses, or even a **sidewalk**. Instead, you walk miles on a dirt trail. You take along a **knapsack**.

The **schoolhouse** is a one-room log cabin with a dirt floor. If you are lucky, there are windows. There is a cast-iron stove in the middle of the room for warmth. Wooden shelves fastened to the walls serve as desks. **Everybody** sits at the shelves on three-legged stools or on long wooden benches. Students of different ages and grades are all mixed together.

There are no blackboards, books, paper, or pencils. **Therefore**, you brought what you needed from home. When you finish one lesson, you erase your slate and start again. At recess, boys and girls play separately **outdoors**. The boys play **horseshoes** while the girls play jump rope. After school, you start the trip home. There isn't much **homework** because you have more chores to do.

Considering the hardships, though, frontier children often did an **outstanding** job of learning the three R's—reading, 'riting, and 'rithmetic.

Take a look at the boldfaced words. What two words make up each word?

133

LIST WORDS

1. northwest
2. outdoors
3. everybody
4. teaspoon
5. waterfall
6. downtown
7. schoolhouse
8. southeast
9. supermarket
10. therefore
11. homework
12. sidewalk
13. breakfast
14. outstanding
15. overcoat
16. typewriter
17. horseshoes
18. toothache
19. aircraft
20. knapsack

Forming Compound Words

Add a word to each word given to write a **list word**.

1. knap _____
2. out _____
3. down _____
4. north _____
5. air _____
6. over _____
7. tea _____
8. home _____
9. every _____
10. tooth _____
11. out _____
12. type _____
13. horse _____
14. break _____
15. water _____
16. there _____
17. school _____
18. super _____
19. south _____
20. side _____

Puzzle

Write the **list word** that matches each clue. Then, read down the shaded boxes to solve the riddle.

1. a walkway next to the street

2. work done at home

3. a machine that makes printed letters

4. business section of a city

5. as a result

6. a nylon, canvas, or leather bag

7. water that falls from a steep height

8. a place to learn

Riddle: What did the king find on the stairs?

Answer: His ___ ___ ___ ___ ___ ___ ___ ___

Classification

Write the **list word** that belongs in each group.

1. lunch, dinner, _____

2. west, southwest, _____

3. great, terrific, _____

4. cup, tablespoon, _____

5. saddle, reins, _____

6. store, shop, _____

7. all, everyone, _____

8. jacket, parka, _____

9. east, northeast, _____

10. helicopter, plane, _____

11. headache, earache, _____

12. open air, outside, _____

Spelling and Writing

Proofreading

The journal entry below has twelve mistakes. Use the proofreading marks to fix each mistake. Then, write the misspelled **list words** correctly on the lines.

Proofreading Marks

⬭ spelling mistake

⊙ add period

/ make a small letter

November 23rd—I got up at 4 o'clock this morning It was my turn to carry water and collect firewood. It was really cold outdors. I'm lucky I have a warm overcote to wear. Mom made a really good Pancake breakfest Then I left for school. Dad hooked up the horses and took me in the Carriage. The horses have special horsehoes so they don't slip in the snow The Schoolhoose is about 4 miles northewest of here. It was still cold when I got there, but it warmed up quickly.

1. _____

2. _____

3. _____

4. _____

5. _____

6. _____

Writing a Comparison

Imagine your class was transported to frontier times. Write about how it would be the same and different from life today. Use as many **list words** as you can. Remember to proofread your comparison and fix any mistakes.

_____

_____

_____

BONUS WORDS

taxpayer

easygoing

sweatshirt

breakdown

westward

Lesson 34

Spelling Words in Action

Why was the Pony Express in business for only two years?

The Mail Must Go Through!

It's been over a hundred years since the Pony Express stopped delivering mail. The Express was started in 1860 between Missouri and California. Riders made the **difficult journey** on horseback. They had to be **cautious**, and both rider and horse often got **weary** during the long ride. To help, relay stations were set up ten to fifteen miles apart. Riders would pick up fresh horses at each station. The **lengthy** trip took eight days. Because it was so **expensive**, the Pony Express had only a brief life. Railroads could offer cheaper rates and deliver the mail more **rapidly**. As a result, after only two years, the Pony Express went out of business.

However, in 1983 in California, an **enormous** mudslide closed the road to several mountain towns. The only way mail could be delivered was by horseback, so the Express was back in business! Each morning, the postmaster gave the first rider a pouch of mail. It took up to thirteen **sturdy** riders to make the long trip. Altogether, about 62 riders helped out. Eventually, the road was **repaired**, but for a brief time the Pony Express was back!

Look back at the boldfaced words in the selection. Can you name the word that means almost the same as <u>trip</u>? Can you name the word that means the opposite of <u>easy</u>?

Spelling Practice

LIST WORDS

1. difficult
2. tender
3. lengthy
4. sturdy
5. expensive
6. repaired
7. enormous
8. journey
9. weary
10. tense
11. cautious
12. sorrow
13. vague
14. ancient
15. courage
16. drowsy
17. disbelief
18. current
19. descend
20. rapidly

Writing Synonyms and Antonyms

Write the **list word** that best completes each sentence.

1. A hard problem is _____.

2. A long book is _____.

3. A huge elephant is _____.

4. A sleepy baby is _____.

5. A costly ring is _____.

6. Sadness is also _____.

7. A nervous person is _____.

8. A long trip is a _____.

9. A brave person has _____.

10. A fixed watch is _____.

11. Go slowly, not _____.

12. Don't be tough, be _____.

13. Climb up, don't _____.

14. Be energetic, not _____.

15. A modern desk is not _____.

16. A weak floor is not _____.

17. A clear idea is not _____.

18. It isn't trust, it's _____.

19. Reckless people aren't _____.

20. A past issue is not _____.

Puzzle

Fill in the crossword puzzle by writing a **list word** to answer each clue. Write antonyms across, and write synonyms down.

ACROSS (antonyms)
3. clear
6. happiness
9. broken
11. fear
12. modern
13. short

DOWN (synonyms)
1. recent
2. strong
4. nervous
5. costly
7. tired
8. hard
10. trip

Dictionary

Write the **list word** for each sound-spelling given.

1. (ē nôr′məs) _____

2. (kô′shəs) _____

3. (dis bə lēf′) _____

4. (dē send′) _____

5. (drou′zē) _____

6. (sär′ō) _____

7. (ten′dər) _____

8. (rap′id lē) _____

In a dictionary, a **sound-spelling** appears after each entry word. It tells how to pronounce the word.

weary (wir′ ē)

Spelling and Writing

Proofreading

There are eleven mistakes in this diary entry. Use the proofreading marks to fix each mistake. Then, write the misspelled **list words** correctly on the lines.

Proofreading Marks

⬭   spelling mistake

⌄   add apostrophe

℮   take out something

September 23, 1847

   This juorney seems more lengthey than I thought it would be be. Emmas horse has tennder feet and may have to to be left behind. Johns wagon has been repairred, but the delay was espensive. We cant waste any more time because winter is rapidley approaching.

1. _____ 2. _____

3. _____ 4. _____

5. _____ 6. _____

Writing an Advertisement

Pony Express riders faced many dangers on their long rides. Write a newspaper ad asking for riders to sign up. Include special skills a Pony Express rider might need. Use as many **list words** as you can. Remember to proofread your ad and fix any mistakes.

_____

_____

_____

_____

_____

_____

BONUS WORDS

smooth

regular

familiar

intelligent

brilliant

Spelling Words in Action

Who holds the record for the world's tallest hairstyle?

A Hairy Tale

It may seem like a tall **tale**, but **who's** to say it isn't true? According to Guinness World Records®, in 1997 Hoo Sateow became the holder of the record for the longest hair in the world. Hoo's **hair** measured almost 17 ft. long. Hoo washes it once a year with detergent and normally wears it wound up on his head. He says, "It keeps my head nice and warm."

For humans, hair is mostly decorative, but for many animals, hair can be an important tool for survival. Whiskers on animals such as cats and dogs are a kind of hair that responds to the **sense** of touch. They help the animals feel **their** way through narrow or dark places.

There are many animals **whose** hair serves as insulation, not only for the animals themselves, but also for their young. For example, the polar bear has a thick coat of fur that keeps it warm. A mother **hare** (rabbit) makes a nest of her own hair **which** shelters and protects her young. Hair is also used as protection from enemies. A porcupine's quills are a type of hair. A porcupine uses its **tail** to stick the quills into the bodies of attackers.

Look back at the boldfaced words. Which words sound the same, but have different spellings and meanings? Do you know another word that sounds the same as <u>sense</u> or <u>which</u>?

141

Spelling Practice

LIST WORDS

1. tale
2. tail
3. heel
4. heal
5. peace
6. piece
7. plain
8. plane
9. there
10. their
11. sense
12. scents
13. which
14. witch
15. whose
16. who's
17. break
18. brake
19. hair
20. hare

Identifying Homonyms

Write the **list words** that rhyme with each underlined word given.

<u>take</u>

1. _____

2. _____

<u>mail</u>

3. _____

4. _____

<u>tents</u>

5. _____

6. _____

<u>bear</u>

7. _____

8. _____

9. _____

10. _____

<u>chain</u>

11. _____

12. _____

<u>shoes</u>

13. _____

14. _____

<u>feel</u>

15. _____

16. _____

<u>pitch</u>

17. _____

18. _____

<u>grease</u>

19. _____

20. _____

Missing Words

Write two **list words** that are homonyms to complete each sentence.

1. The white _____ of the _____ matched the color of the snow.

2. _____ the lucky person _____ ticket won the prize?

3. The bike won't stop if you _____ the _____.

4. _____ seats for the game are over _____.

5. Soaking my hurt _____ should help it _____.

6. The _____ flew over the vast western _____.

7. One folk _____ tells how the bear lost its _____.

8. There was _____ after each child found a puzzle _____.

Homonym Search

There are five pairs of **list word** homonyms hidden in the puzzle. They go across, up, down, or diagonally. Circle each homonym. Then, write each homonym pair on the lines.

1. _____

2. _____

3. _____

4. _____

5. _____

6. _____

7. _____

8. _____

9. _____

10. _____

Spelling and Writing

Proofreading

There are ten mistakes in this article. Use the proofreading marks to fix each mistake. Then, write the correct **list words** on the lines.

Proofreading Marks

⬭ spelling mistake

≡ capital letter

⌃ add something

This tail of the history of the beard will raise your hare. did you know that at one time, all men wore beards Then, Alexander the Great thought it made scents for soldiers to shave there beards so enemies could not grab them. Did you know that the Vandyke beard, witch was pointed, was popular in the 1600s In the 1830s in america, most men did not wear beards. Joseph Palmer, who's beard was bushy, was jailed for wearing one.

1. _____   2. _____

3. _____   4. _____

5. _____   6. _____

Writing a Paragraph

Do you think hair fashions are funny, great, or not a subject you think about? Write your opinion in a paragraph, and state your reasons. Use as many **list words** as you can. Remember to proofread your paragraph and fix any mistakes.

_____

_____

_____

_____

_____

BONUS WORDS

flew

flue

flu

knead

need

In lessons 31–35, you have learned how to spell words with prefixes, compound words, and words that are synonyms, antonyms, and homonyms.

Check Your Spelling Notebook

Look at the words in your spelling notebook. Which words in lessons 31 through 35 did you have the most trouble with? Write them here.

_____

_____

Practice writing your troublesome words with a partner. Take turns dividing the words into syllables as your partner spells them aloud.

Lesson 31

TIP

pre = before, as in preview   **re** = again or back, as in refills
im = not, as in impure   **non** = not, as in nonprofit
con = with or together, as in control

List Words

nonsense
prepaid
impractical
nonstop
nonprofit
construct
immovable
predict
convince
reaction

Add a prefix to each word or word part to make a **list word**. Then, write the **list word**.

1. _____ movable   _____

2. _____ vince   _____

3. _____ sense   _____

4. _____ profit   _____

5. _____ action   _____

6. _____ stop   _____

7. _____ paid   _____

8. _____ struct   _____

9. _____ dict   _____

10. _____ practical   _____

Write a **list word** to match each definition.

List Words

express
design
unknown
admit
explore
disagree
adventure
unwise
excuse
unprepared

1. to be against an idea _____
2. not ready _____
3. not showing good sense _____
4. to state or say _____
5. decoration or pattern _____
6. to search carefully _____
7. to take or accept as true _____
8. undiscovered _____
9. to free from blame _____
10. an exciting experience _____

Combine each word in the first box with a word in the second box to make a compound **list word**. Then, write the **list word**.

List Words

outdoors
everybody
supermarket
sidewalk
breakfast
outstanding
typewriter
toothache
aircraft
knapsack

| out type every side super break out tooth air knap | doors fast standing body walk market writer ache sack craft |

1. _____   2. _____
3. _____   4. _____
5. _____   6. _____
7. _____   8. _____
9. _____   10. _____

TIP A **synonym** means the same or almost the same as another word. An **antonym** means the opposite or almost the opposite of another word.

List Words

lengthy
expensive
repaired
enormous
journey
cautious
vague
ancient
courage
descend

Write a **list word** to match each clue.

Synonyms

1. careful _____
2. bravery _____
3. fixed _____
4. voyage _____
5. old _____

Antonyms

6. go up _____
7. brief _____
8. cheap _____
9. small _____
10. clear _____

TIP **Homonyms** are words that sound alike, but have different meanings and spellings.

List Words

tale
tail
peace
piece
there
their
whose
who's
break
brake

Underline the **list word** that completes each sentence. Then, write that **list word** on the line.

1. The dog wagged its (tale, tail). _____
2. Grandma told us a (tale, tail). _____
3. (Whose, Who's) coat is this? _____
4. (Whose, Who's) the best singer? _____
5. I'd like a (peace, piece) of toast. _____
6. We work for world (peace, piece). _____
7. Please put my books (there, their). _____
8. Put (their, there) books on the table. _____
9. Use the (break, brake) to stop. _____
10. The cup could (break, brake). _____

Show What You Know

One word is misspelled in each set of **list words**. Fill in the circle next to the **list word** that is spelled incorrectly.

1. ○ nonsense ○ prepaid ○ returned ○ inpractical ○ control

2. ○ expres ○ design ○ unknown ○ heal ○ unclear

3. ○ northwest ○ outdoors ○ everybody ○ teespoon ○ waterfall

4. ○ difficult ○ tendar ○ lengthy ○ expensive ○ sturdy

5. ○ tale ○ report ○ heel ○ admitt ○ their

6. ○ nonstop ○ plane ○ preview ○ imperfact ○ tail

7. ○ explore ○ disagree ○ defend ○ advenjure ○ unreal

8. ○ downtown ○ schoolhouse ○ southeast ○ supermarket ○ therefour

9. ○ reparred ○ enormous ○ journey ○ weary ○ tense

10. ○ piece ○ plain ○ conduckt ○ there ○ peace

11. ○ nonprofit ○ scents ○ construct ○ precaution ○ imovable

12. ○ unwise ○ discloze ○ advice ○ disinterested ○ excuse

13. ○ homework ○ sidewalk ○ breakfest ○ outstanding ○ overcoat

14. ○ cawtious ○ sorrow ○ hair ○ ancient ○ courage

15. ○ brake ○ refils ○ which ○ current ○ whose

16. ○ predict ○ convince ○ impure ○ impersonel ○ reaction

17. ○ dishoness ○ unprepared ○ advance ○ unpleasant ○ adverb

18. ○ typewriter ○ horseshoes ○ toothach ○ aircraft ○ knapsack

19. ○ drowsy ○ disbelief ○ witch ○ decend ○ rapidly

20. ○ who's ○ breek ○ sense ○ vague ○ hare

Writing and Proofreading Guide

1. Choose a topic to write about.

2. Write your ideas. Don't worry about mistakes.

3. Now organize your writing so that it makes sense.

4. Proofread your work.

   Use these proofreading marks to make changes.

   ## Proofreading Marks

Mark	Meaning
⬭	spelling mistake
≡	capital letter
⊙	add period
⌃	add something
⌄	add apostrophe
ℒ	take out something
¶	indent paragraph
/	make small letter
⸌⸍	add quotation marks

   Isnt a (dolfin) one of the the most Intelligent sea mammals ?

5. Write your final copy.

   Isn't a dolphin one of the most intelligent sea mammals?

6. Share your writing.

Using Your Dictionary

The **Spelling Workout** Dictionary shows you many things about your spelling words.

The **entry word** listed in alphabetical order is the word you are looking up.

The **sound-spelling** or **respelling** tells how to pronounce the word.

The **part of speech** is given as an abbreviation.

im·prove (im proov′) **v. 1** to make or become better [Business has *improved*.] **2** to make good use of [She *improved* her spare time by reading.] —**im·proved**′, **im·prov′ing**

Sample sentences or **phrases** show how to use the word.

Other **forms** of the word are given.

The **definition** tells what the word means. There may be more than one definition.

Pronunciation Key

SYMBOL	KEY WORDS	SYMBOL	KEY WORDS	SYMBOL	KEY WORDS	SYMBOL	KEY WORDS
a	ask, fat	๐๐	look, pull	b	bed, dub	t	top, hat
ā	ape, date	yๆ	unite, cure	d	did, had	v	vat, have
ä	car, lot	o͞o	ooze, tool	f	fall, off	w	will, always
		yo͞o	cute, few	g	get, dog	y	yet, yard
e	elf, ten	ou	out, crowd	h	he, ahead	z	zebra, haze
er	berry, care			j	joy, jump		
ē	even, meet	u	up, cut	k	kill, bake	ch	chin, arch
		ʉ	fur, fern	l	let, ball	ŋ	ring, singer
i	is, hit			m	met, trim	sh	she, dash
ir	mirror, here	ə	a in ago	n	not, ton	th	thin, truth
ī	ice, fire		e in agent	p	put, tap	*th*	then, father
			e in father	r	red, dear	zh	s in pleasure
ō	open, go		i in unity	s	sell, pass		
ô	law, horn		o in collect				
oi	oil, point		u in focus				

An Americanism is a word or usage of a word that was born in this country. An open star (☆) before an entry word or definition means that the word or definition is an Americanism.

Aa

ab·sent (ab′sənt) **adj.** not present; away [No one in the class was *absent* that day.]

a·chieve (ə chēv′) **v.** **1** to do; succeed in doing; accomplish [She *achieved* a lot while she was mayor.] **2** to get or reach by trying hard; gain [He *achieved* his goal of graduating.] —**a·chieved′, a·chiev′ing**

ad·just (ə just′) **v.** **1** to change or move so as to make fit [You can *adjust* the piano bench to suit your size.] **2** to arrange the parts of; to make work correctly; regulate [My watch needs *adjusting*.] **3** to settle or put in order [We *adjust* our accounts at the end of the month.]

ad·mit (ad mit′) **v.** **1** to permit or give the right to enter [One ticket *admits* two people.] **2** to have room for [The hall *admits* 500 people.] **3** to take or accept as being true; confess [Lucy will not *admit* her mistake.] —**ad·mit′ted, ad·mit′ting**

a·dopt (ə däpt′) **v.** **1** to choose and take into one's family by a legal process [They *adopted* their daughter when she was four months old.] **2** to take and use as one's own [He *adopted* her teaching methods for his own classroom.] **3** to choose or follow [We must *adopt* a new plan of action.] —**a·dop′tion n.**

ad·vance (ad vans′) **v.** **1** to go or bring forward; move ahead [On first down they *advanced* the football two yards.] **2** to cause to happen earlier [The test date was *advanced* from May 10 to May 5.] —**ad·vanced′, ad·vanc′ing ◆n.** a moving forward or ahead; progress [new *advances* in science]

ad·van·tage (ad van′tij) **n.** a more favorable position; better chance [My speed gave me an *advantage* over them.]

ad·ven·ture (ad ven′chər) **n.** **1** an exciting and dangerous happening [He told of his *adventure* in the jungle.] **2** an unusual experience that is remembered [Going to a circus is an *adventure* for a child.]

ad·verb (ad′vurb) **n.** a word used with a verb, adjective, or another adverb to tell when, where, how, what kind, or how much [In the sentence, "She runs fast," the word "fast" is an *adverb*.]

ad·vice (ad vīs′) **n.** opinion given as to what to do or how to do something [We followed her *advice* in selecting a new home.]

af·fec·tion (ə fek′shən) **n.** fond or tender feeling; warm liking

af·ter (af′tər) **adv.** **1** behind; coming next [You go on ahead, and we'll follow *after*.] **2** following in time; later [They came at noon and left three hours *after*.] **◆prep. 1** behind [The soldiers marched one *after* the other.] **2** in search of [What are you *after*?] **3** later than [It's ten minutes *after* four.] **4** as a result of; because of [*After* what has happened, he won't go.]

air·craft (er′kraft) **n.** any machine or machines for flying [Airplanes, dirigibles, and helicopters are all *aircraft*.] —*pl.* **air′craft**

☆ **air·line** (er′līn) **n.** a system or company for moving freight and passengers by aircraft

al·low (ə lou′) **v.** **1** to let be done; permit; let [*Allow* us to pay. No smoking *allowed*.] **2** to let have [She *allows* herself no sweets.] **3** to let enter or stay [Dogs are not usually *allowed* on buses.] **4** to admit to be true or right [His claim for $50 was *allowed*.] —**al·lows′**

al·ly (al′ī) **n.** a country or person joined with another for a special purpose [England was our *ally* during World War II.] —*pl.* **al′lies**

al·pha·bet (al′fə bet) **n.** **1** the letters of a language, given in the regular order [The English *alphabet* goes from A to Z.] **2** any system of symbols used in writing [the Braille *alphabet*]

al·though (ôl thō′) **conj.** in spite of the fact that; even if; though: *sometimes spelled* **altho** [*Although* the sun is shining, it may rain later.]

al·ti·tude (al′tə to͞od′ *or* al′tə tyo͞od′) **n.** **1** height; especially, the height of a thing above the earth's surface or above sea level **2** a high place

a·mount (ə mount′) **v.** to add up; total [The bill *amounts* to $4.50.] **◆n. 1** the sum; total [The bill was $50, but he paid only half that *amount*.] **2** a quantity [a small *amount* of rain]

am·pli·fy (am′plə fī′) **v.** to make larger, stronger, louder, etc. —**am′pli·fies′, am′pli·fied′, am′pli·fy′ing**

an·cient (ān′chənt *or* ān′shənt) **adj.** **1** of times long past; belonging to the early history of people, before about 500 A.D. **2** having lasted a long time; very old [their *ancient* quarrel]

An·go·ra (aŋ gôr′ə) **n.** **1** a kind of cat with long, silky fur **2** a kind of goat with long, silky hair: this hair, called **Angora wool**, is used in making mohair **3** a long-eared rabbit (**Angora rabbit**) with long, silky hair: this hair is used to make a soft yarn which is woven into sweaters, mittens, etc.

an·gry (aŋ′grē) **adj.** **1** feeling or showing anger [*angry* words; an *angry* crowd] **2** wild and stormy [an *angry* sea] —**an′gri·er, an′gri·est**

aircraft

a	ask, fat
ā	ape, date
ä	car, lot
e	elf, ten
ē	even, meet
i	is, hit
ī	ice, fire
ō	open, go
ô	law, horn
oi	oil, point
o͞o	look, pull
o͞o	ooze, tool
ou	out, crowd
u	up, cut
ʉ	fur, fern
ə	a in ago
	e in agent
	e in father
	i in unity
	o in collect
	u in focus
ch	chin, arch
ŋ	ring, singer
sh	she, dash
th	thin, truth
th	then, father
zh	s in pleasure

an·swer (an′sər) *n.* **1** something said, written, or done in return to a question, argument, letter, action, etc.; reply; response [The only *answers* required for the test were "true" or "false." His *answer* to the insult was to turn his back.] **2** a solution to a problem, as in arithmetic ◆*v.* **1** to give an answer; reply or react, as to a question or action **2** to be responsible [You must *answer* for the children's conduct.]

Ant·arc·ti·ca (ant ärk′ti kə *or* ant är′ti kə) a large area of land, completely covered with ice, around the South Pole: *also called* **Antarctic Continent**

an·to·nym (an′tə nim) *n.* a word opposite in meaning to another word ["Sad" is an *antonym* of "happy."]

a·part·ment (ə pärt′mənt) *n.* a group of rooms, or a single large room, to live in: usually a single suite in a building (called an **apartment house**) of several or many suites

ap·pe·tiz·er (ap′ə tīz′ər) *n.* a small bit of a tasty food or a drink for giving one a bigger appetite at the beginning of a meal [Olives, tomato juice, etc. are used as *appetizers*.]

ap·ply (ə plī′) *v.* **1** to put or spread on [*Apply* glue to the surface.] **2** to put into use [*Apply* your knowledge to this problem.] **3** to work hard and steadily [He *applied* himself to his studies.] **4** to have to do with or be suitable to [This rule *applies* to all of us.] —**ap·plied′, ap·ply′ing**

ap·point (ə point′) *v.* **1** to fix or set; decide upon [Let's *appoint* a time for our meeting.] **2** to name or choose for an office or position [Federal judges are *appointed* by the President.] —**ap·point′ed**

ap·proach (ə prōch′) *v.* **1** to come closer or draw nearer [We saw three riders *approaching*. Vacation time *approaches*.] **2** to go to someone with a plan or request [Have you *approached* the bank about a loan?] ◆*n.* a coming closer or drawing nearer [The first robin marks the *approach* of spring.]

A·pril (ā′prəl) *n.* the fourth month of the year, which has 30 days; abbreviated **Apr.**

a·rith·me·tic (ə rith′mə tik′) *n.* the science or skill of using numbers, especially in adding, subtracting, multiplying, and dividing

Ar·i·zo·na (ar′ə zō′nə) a state in the southwestern part of the U.S.: abbreviated **Ariz., AZ**

ar·mor (är′mər) *n.* **1** covering worn to protect the body against weapons [The knight's suit of *armor* was made of metal plates.] **2** any covering that protects, as the shell of a turtle or the metal plates on a warship

ar·my (är′mē) *n.* **1** a large group of soldiers trained for war, especially on land; all the soldiers of a country **2** a large group of persons organized to work for some cause [the Salvation *Army*] **3** any large group of persons or animals [An *army* of workers was building the bridge.] —*pl.* **ar′mies**

ar·riv·al (ə rī′vəl) *n.* **1** the act of arriving [to welcome the *arrival* of spring] **2** a person or thing that has arrived [They are recent *arrivals* to the U.S. from South America.]

ar·rive (ə rīv′) *v.* **1** to come to a place after a journey [When does the bus from Chicago *arrive* here?] **2** to come [The time has *arrived* to say goodbye.] —**ar·rived′, ar·riv′ing**

art·ist (ärt′ist) *n.* **1** a person who works in any of the fine arts, especially in painting, drawing, sculpting, etc. **2** a person who does anything very well

ash·es (ash′əz) *pl.n.* the grayish powder or fine dust that is left after something has been burned

A·sia (ā′zhə) the largest continent, about 17,000,000 square miles in area: the Pacific Ocean is on its east and it is separated from northern Europe by the Ural Mountains

as·tro·naut (as′trə nôt *or* as′trə nät) *n.* a person trained to make rocket flights in outer space

as·tron·o·my (ə strän′ə mē) *n.* the science that studies the motion, size, and makeup of the stars, planets, comets, etc.

au·di·ence (ô′dē əns *or* ä′dē əns) *n.* **1** a group of people gathered together to hear and see a speaker, a play, a concert, etc. **2** all those people who are tuned in to a radio or TV program

aunt (ant *or* änt) *n.* **1** a sister of one's mother or father **2** the wife of one's uncle

Aus·tral·ia (ô strāl′yə *or* ä strāl′yə) **1** an island continent in the Southern Hemisphere, southeast of Asia **2** a country made up of this continent and Tasmania

au·thor (ôthər *or* ä′ther) *n.* a person who writes something, as a book or story [She is the *author* of many mystery stories.]

au·to·graph (ôt′ə graf) *n.* something written in a person's own handwriting, especially that person's name ◆*v.* to write one's name on [Please *autograph* this baseball.]

au·to·mat·ic (ôt′ə mat′ik *or* ät′ə mat′ik) *adj.* **1** done without thinking about it, as if mechanically or from force of habit; unconscious [Breathing is usually *automatic*.] **2** moving or working by itself [*automatic* machinery]

a·vi·a·tor (ā′vē āt′ər) *n.* a person who flies airplanes; pilot

a·while (ə hwīl′ *or* ə wīl′) *adv.* for a while; for a short time [Sit down and rest *awhile*.]

awk·ward (ôk′wərd *or* äk′wərd) *adj.* **1** not having grace or skill; clumsy; bungling [an *awkward* dancer; an *awkward* writing style] **2** hard to use or manage; not convenient [an *awkward* tool] **3** uncomfortable; cramped [sitting in an *awkward* position] **4** embarrassed or embarrassing [an *awkward* remark] —**awk′ward·ly** *adv.*

ax *or* **axe** (aks) *n.* a tool for chopping or splitting wood: it has a long wooden handle and a metal head with a sharp blade —*pl.* **ax′es**

bag·gage (bag′ij) *n.* the trunks, suitcases, etc. that a person takes on a trip; luggage

bait (bāt) *n.* **1** food put on a hook or trap to attract and catch fish or animals **2** anything used to tempt or attract a person ◆*v.* **1** to put bait on a hook or trap **2** to torment or tease by saying annoying or cruel things [They *baited* me by calling me "Fatty."]

bal·co·ny (bal′kə nē) *n.* **1** a platform with a low wall or railing, that juts out from the side of a building **2** an upper floor of rows of seats, as in a theater: it often juts out over the main floor —*pl.* **bal′co·nies**

bal·lot (bal′ət) *n.* **1** a piece of paper on which a person marks a choice in voting **2** the act or a way of voting

band·age (ban′dij) *n.* a strip of cloth, gauze, etc. used to cover a sore or wound ◆*v.* to bind or cover with a bandage; to bind up an injured part of the body —**band′aged, band′ag·ing**

☆ **ban·jo** (ban′jō) *n.* a stringed musical instrument with a long neck and a round body covered on top with tightly stretched skins: it has, usually, four or five strings that are plucked with the fingers or a pick —*pl.* **ban′jos** *or* **ban′joes**

ban·ner (ban′ər) *n.* **1** a piece of cloth with an emblem or words on it [The *banner* behind the President's desk bears the seal of the United States] **2** a flag [the Star-Spangled *Banner*] **3** a headline across a newspaper page ◆*adj.* top; leading [Our company had a *banner* year in sales.]

barge (bärj) *n.* a large boat with a flat bottom, for carrying goods on rivers or canals ◆*v.* to enter in a clumsy or rude way [They *barged* in without knocking.] —**barged, barg′ing**

ba·rom·e·ter (bə räm′ə tər) *n.* **1** an instrument that measures the pressure of the air around us: it is used in forecasting changes in the weather and finding the height above sea level **2** anything that shows changes in conditions [The stock market is a *barometer* of business.] —**bar·o·met·ric** (bar′ə met′rik) *adj.*

bar·rel (bar′əl) *n.* **1** a large, round container that has bulging sides and a flat top and bottom: usually made of wooden slats bound together by metal hoops **2** the amount a barrel will hold: the standard barrel in the U.S. holds 31 1/2 gallons (119.2275 liters) ◆*v.* to put in barrels —**bar′reled** *or* **bar′relled, bar′rel·ing** *or* **bar′rel·ling**

bask (bask) *v.* to warm oneself pleasantly [to *bask* in the sun]

bass (bas) *n.* a fish with spiny fins, found in both fresh and salt water and used for food —*pl.* **bass** *or* **bass′es**

bat·ter·y (bat′ər ē) *n.* an electric cell or a group of connected cells that furnishes an electric current [*Batteries* are used in automobiles and flashlights.] —*pl.* **bat′ter·ies**

be·gin (bē gin′) *v.* to start being, doing, acting, etc.; get under way [Work *begins* at 8:00 A.M. My cold *began* with a sore throat.] —**be·gan′, be·gun′, be·gin′ning**

be·gin·ning (bē gin′iŋ) *n.* a start or starting; first part or first action [We came in just after the *beginning* of the movie. Going to the dance together was the *beginning* of our friendship.]

be·lief (bē lēf′) *n.* a feeling that something is true or real; faith [You cannot destroy my *belief* in the honesty of most people.] —*pl.* **be·liefs**

be·lieve (bē lēv′) *v.* **1** to accept as true or real [Can we *believe* that story?] **2** to have trust or confidence [I know you will win; I *believe* in you.] **3** to suppose; guess —**be·lieved′, be·liev′ing** —**be·liev′a·ble** *adj.* —**be·liev′er** *n.*

bench (bench) *n.* **1** a long, hard seat for several persons, with or without a back **2** a strong table on which work with tools is done [a carpenter's *bench*] **3** the place where judges sit in a courtroom **4** a seat where sports players sit when not on the field —*pl.* **bench′es**

bend (bend) *v.* **1** to pull or press something hard or stiff into a curve or angle [*Bend* the branch down so we can reach the plums.] **2** to be curved in this way [The trees *bent* under the weight of the snow.] **3** to stoop [*Bend* over and touch your toes.] —**bent, bend′ing** ◆*n.* **1** the act of bending **2** a bent or curving part

ax

a	ask, fat
ā	ape, date
ä	car, lot
e	elf, ten
ē	even, meet
i	is, hit
ī	ice, fire
ō	open, go
ô	law, horn
oi	oil, point
o͝o	look, pull
o͞o	ooze, tool
ou	out, crowd
u	up, cut
ʉ	fur, fern
ə	a in ago
	e in agent
	e in father
	i in unity
	o in collect
	u in focus
ch	chin, arch
ŋ	ring, singer
sh	she, dash
th	thin, truth
th	then, father
zh	s in pleasure

153

bicycle

be·tween (bē twēn′) *prep.* **1** in the space, time, or degree that separates [a lake *between* the United States and Canada; office hours *between* one and five o'clock; a color *between* blue and green] **2** having to do with; involving [the war *between* the North and the South] **3** that connects [a road *between* Reno and Yuma; a bond *between* friends]

bev·er·age (bev′ər ij *or* bev′rij) *n.* any kind of drink (except water), as milk, coffee, or lemonade

bi·cy·cle (bī′si kəl) *n.* a vehicle to ride on that has two wheels, one behind the other: it is moved by foot pedals and steered by a handlebar ◆*v.* to ride a bicycle —**bi′cy·cled, bi′cy·cling**

birth·day (burth′dā) *n.* **1** the day on which a person is born or something is begun **2** the anniversary of this day

bi·son (bī′sən) *n.* a wild animal of the ox family, with a shaggy mane, short, curved horns, and a humped back: the American bison is often called a *buffalo* —*pl.* **bi′son**

blend (blend) *v.* **1** to mix different kinds together in order to get a certain flavor, color, etc. [to *blend* tea or paint] **2** to come together or mix so that the parts are no longer distinct [The sky *blended* with the sea at the horizon.] **3** to go well together; be in harmony [Her blue sweater *blends* well with her gray skirt.] ◆*n.* a mixture of different kinds [a *blend* of coffee] —**blend′ed, blend′ing**

☆ **bliz·zard** (bliz′ərd) *n.* a heavy snowstorm with very strong, cold winds

board (bôrd) *n.* **1** a long, flat, broad piece of sawed wood, used in building **2** a flat piece of wood or other hard material made for a special use [a checker*board*; a bulletin *board*; an ironing *board*] **3** a group of people who manage or control a business, school, department, etc. [*board* of education] ◆*v.* **1** to cover up with boards [The windows of the old house were *boarded* up.] **2** to get on a ship, airplane, bus, etc.

boast (bōst) *v.* **1** to talk about with too much pride and pleasure; praise too highly; brag [We tired of hearing him *boast* of his bravery.] **2** to be proud of having [Our city *boasts* a fine new zoo.] —**boast′ed**

bob (bäb) *v.* **1** to move with short, jerky motions [Our heads *bobbed* up and down as our car bounced over the ruts.] **2** to cut off short [to *bob* a dog's tail] —**bobbed, bob′bing** ◆*n.* **1** a short, jerky movement [She greeted us with a *bob* of her head.] **2** a style of short haircut for women or girls **3** a hanging weight at the end of a plumb line **4** a cork on a fishing line

bod·y (bäd′ē) *n.* **1** the whole physical part of a person or animal [Athletes have strong *bodies*.] **2** the main part of a person or animal, not including the head, legs, and arms [The boxer received many blows to the *body*.] **3** the main or central part of anything, as the trunk of a tree or the part of a car that holds the passengers —*pl.* **bod′ies**

boil (boil) *v.* **1** to bubble up and become steam or vapor by being heated [Water *boils* at 100°C.] **2** to heat a liquid until it bubbles up in this way [to *boil* water] **3** to cook in a boiling liquid [to *boil* potatoes] **4** to be stirred up, as with rage ◆*n.* the condition of boiling [Bring the soup to a *boil*.]

bomb (bäm) *n.* a hollow case filled with an explosive or a poisonous gas: bombs are blown up by a fuse or timing device or by being dropped or thrown against something with force

☆ **boss** (bôs *or* bäs) *n.* **1** a person who is in charge of workers, as an employer, a manager, or a supervisor **2** a person who controls a political group, as in a county —*pl.* **bosses** ◆*v.* to act as boss of

both·er (bäth′ər) *v.* **1** to annoy; cause worry or trouble to; pester [Does the noise *bother* you?] **2** to take the time or trouble [Don't *bother* to answer this letter.] ◆*n.* something that annoys or causes worry or trouble [Flies are a *bother*.]

bot·tle (bät′l) *n.* **1** a container, especially for liquids, usually made of glass or plastic: bottles generally have a narrow neck and no handles **2** the amount that a bottle holds [The baby drank a *bottle* of milk.] ◆*v.* **1** to put into a bottle or into bottles **2** to store under pressure in a tank [*bottled* gas] —**bot′tled, bot′tling**

bounce (bouns) *v.* **1** to hit against a surface so as to spring back; bound or rebound [to *bounce* a ball against a wall; to *bounce* up and down on a sofa] **2** to move suddenly; jump; leap [I *bounced* out of bed when the alarm went off.] —**bounced, bounc′ing** ◆*n.* **1** a springing or bounding; leap **2** the ability to bound or rebound [This ball has lost its *bounce*.]

bounc·ing (boun′siŋ) *adj.* big, healthy, strong, etc. [It's a *bouncing* baby boy.]

bou·quet (bōō kā′ *or* bō kā′) *n.* **1** a bunch of flowers **2** (bōō kā′) a fragrant smell

☆ **box·car** (bäks′kär′) *n.* a railroad car for carrying freight, with a roof and closed sides

brain (brān) *n.* **1** the gray and white tissue inside the skull of a person or of any animal with a backbone: it is the main part of the nervous system, by which one thinks and feels **2** *often* **brains**, *pl.* intelligence; understanding

brake (brāk) *n.* a device used to slow down or stop a car, machine, etc.: it is often a block or band that is pressed against a wheel or other moving part ◆*v.* to slow down or stop with a brake —**braked, brak´ing**

branch (branch) *n.* any part of a tree growing from the trunk or from a main limb

break (brāk) *v.* **1** to come or make come apart by force; split or crack sharply into pieces [*Break* an egg into the bowl. The rusty hinge *broke.*] **2** to force one's way [A firefighter *broke* through the door.] **3** to get out of working order; make or become useless [You can *break* your watch by winding it too tightly.] **4** to fail to carry out or follow [to *break* an agreement; to *break* the law] —**broke, bro´ken, break´ing** ◆*n.* **1** a broken place [The X-ray showed a *break* in the bone.] **2** an interruption [Recess is a relaxing *break* in our school day.]

break·down (brāk´doun) *n.* a failure to work properly [*breakdown* of a machine]

break·fast (brek´fəst) *n.* the first meal of the day ◆*v.* to eat breakfast

breeze (brēz) *n.* **1** a light and gentle wind **2** a thing easy to do; *used only in everyday talk* [The test was a *breeze.*] ◆*v.* to move or go quickly, briskly, etc.: *slang in this meaning* —**breezed, breez´ing**

brief (brēf) *adj.* **1** not lasting very long; short in time [a *brief* visit] **2** using just a few words; not wordy; concise [a *brief* news report] ◆*v.* to give the main points or necessary facts to [to *brief* pilots before a flight] —**brief´ly adv.** —**brief´ness n.**

bril·liant (bril´yənt) *adj.* **1** very bright; glittering or sparkling [the *brilliant* sun on the water] **2** outstanding or distinguished [a *brilliant* performance]

bring (briŋ) *v.* **1** to carry or lead here or to the place where the speaker will be [*Bring* it to my house tomorrow.] **2** to cause to happen or come [War *brings* death and hunger.]

broc·co·li (bräk´ə lē) *n.* a plant whose tender shoots and loose heads of tiny green buds are eaten as a vegetable

broil (broil) *v.* **1** to cook or be cooked close to a flame or other high heat [to *broil* steaks over charcoal] **2** to make or be very hot [a *broiling* summer day] ◆*n.* the act or state of broiling —**broil´ing**

broth·er (bru*th*´ər) *n.* **1** a boy or man as he is related to the other children of his parents **2** a person who is close to one in some way; especially, a fellow member of the same race, religion, club, etc. —*pl.* **broth´ers**

brought (brôt *or* brät) *past tense and past participle of* **bring**

buf·fa·lo (buf´ə lō´) *n.* a wild ox, sometimes tamed as a work animal, as the water buffalo of India: the American bison is also commonly called a *buffalo* —*pl.* **buf´fa·loes´** or **buf´fa·los´** or **buf´fa·lo´**

bump (bump) *v.* **1** to knock against something; hit with a jolt [The bus *bumped* the car ahead of it. Don't *bump* into the wall.] **2** to move with jerks or jumps; jolt [The car *bumped* over the railroad tracks.] ◆*n.* **1** a knock or blow; light jolt **2** a part that bulges out, causing an uneven surface **3** a swelling caused by a blow

bur·y (ber´ē) *v.* **1** to put a dead body into the earth, a tomb, or the sea [The Egyptians *buried* the pharaohs in pyramids.] **2** to cover up so as to hide [He *buried* his face in his hands.] **3** to put away and forget [Let's *bury* our feud.] **4** to put oneself deeply into [She *buried* herself in her work.] —**bur´ies, bur´ied, bur´y·ing**

busi·ness (biz´nəs) *n.* **1** what one does for a living; one's work or occupation [Shakespeare's *business* was writing plays.] **2** what one has a right or duty to do [You had no *business* telling her I was here.] **3** the buying and selling of goods and services; commerce; trade **4** a place where things are made or sold; store or factory [Nino owns three *businesses.*] —*pl.* **bus´i·ness·es**

but·ter·milk (but´ər milk) *n.* the sour liquid left after churning butter from milk

buy (bī) *v.* to get by paying money or something else [The Dutch *bought* Manhattan Island for about $24.] —**bought, buy´ing**

byte (bīt) *n.* a series of computer bits, usually eight, used as a single piece of information

Cc

cab·in (kab´in) *n.* **1** a small house built in a simple, rough way, usually of wood [Lincoln was born in a log *cabin.*] **2** a room on a ship, especially one with berths for sleeping **3** the space in an airplane where the passengers ride

☆**ca·boose** (kə bōōs´) *n.* a car for the crew on a freight train: it is usually the last car

cac·tus (kak´təs) *n.* a plant with fleshy stems that bear spines or scales instead of leaves: cactuses grow in hot, dry places and often have showy flowers —*pl.* **cac´tus·es** or **cac·ti** (kak´tī)

a	ask, fat
ā	ape, date
ä	car, lot
e	elf, ten
ē	even, meet
i	is, hit
ī	ice, fire
ō	open, go
ô	law, horn
oi	oil, point
ōō	look, pull
ōō	ooze, tool
ou	out, crowd
u	up, cut
ʉ	fur, fern
ə	a in ago
	e in agent
	e in father
	i in unity
	o in collect
	u in focus
ch	chin, arch
ŋ	ring, singer
sh	she, dash
th	thin, truth
th	then, father
zh	s in pleasure

cal·cu·la·tor (kal′kyōō lāt′ər) *n.* **1** a person who calculates **2** a machine that adds, subtracts, etc. rapidly, now often by electronic means

calf¹ (kaf) *n.* **1** a young cow or bull **2** a young elephant, whale, hippopotamus, seal, etc. **3** *a shorter word for* **calfskin** —*pl.* **calves**

calf² (kaf) *n.* the fleshy back part of the leg between the knee and the ankle —*pl.* **calves**

cam·el (kam′əl) *n.* a large, cud-chewing animal with a humped back, that is commonly used for riding and for carrying goods in Asian and North African deserts: when food and drink are scarce, it can keep going for a few days on the fat and water stored in its body tissue: the **Arabian camel** has one hump and the **Bac·tri·an** (bak′trē ən) **camel** has two

can·di·date (kan′di dāt′) *n.* a person who seeks, or who has been suggested for, an office or award [a *candidate* for mayor]

car·di·nal (kärd′n əl) *adj.* **1** of most importance; chief [The *cardinal* points of the compass are north, south, east, and west.] **2** bright red ◆☆*n.* an American songbird that is bright red and has a black face

car·go (kär′gō) *n.* the load of goods carried by a ship, airplane, truck, etc. —*pl.* **car′goes** or **car′gos**

car·ry (ker′ē) *v.* **1** to take from one place to another; transport or conduct [Please help me *carry* these books home. The large pipe *carries* water. Air *carries* sounds.] **2** to cause to go; lead [A love of travel *carried* them around the world.] **3** to bring over a figure from one column to the next in adding a row of figures —**car′ried, car′ry·ing**

car·ton (kärt′n) *n.* a box or other container made of cardboard, plastic, etc.

cast (kast) *v.* **1** to throw out or down; toss; fling; hurl [to *cast* stones into the water; to *cast* a line in fishing] **2** to deposit a ballot or vote ◆*n.* a stiff plaster form for keeping a broken arm or leg in place while it is healing —**cast, cast′ing**

catch·er (kach′ər *or* kech′ər) *n.* **1** one who catches ☆**2** in baseball, the player behind home plate, who catches pitched balls that are not hit away by the batter

cat·e·go·ry (kat′ə gôr′ē) *n.* a division of a main subject or group; class [Biology is divided into two *categories*, zoology and botany.] —*pl.* **cat′e·go′ries**

cause (kôz *or* käz) *n.* **1** a person or thing that brings about some action or result [A spark from the wire was the *cause* of the fire.] **2** a reason for some action, feeling, etc. [We had *cause* to admire the coach.] ◆*v.* to be the cause of; make happen; bring about [The icy streets *caused* some accidents.] —**caused, caus′ing** —**cause′less** *adj.*

cau·tious (kô′shəs *or* kä′shəs) *adj.* careful not to get into danger or make mistakes [a *cautious* chess player] —**cau′tious·ly** *adv.*

ceil·ing (sēl′iŋ) *n.* the inside top part of a room, opposite the floor

cel·e·ry (sel′ər ē) *n.* a plant whose crisp, long stalks are eaten as a vegetable

ce·ment (sə ment′) *n.* **1** a powder made of lime and clay, mixed with water and sand to make mortar or with water, sand, and gravel to make concrete: it hardens like stone when it dries **2** any soft substance that fastens things together when it hardens, as paste or glue ◆*v.* to fasten together or cover with cement [to *cement* the pieces of a broken cup]

cen·ter (sen′tər) *n.* **1** a point inside a circle or sphere that is the same distance from all points on the circumference or surface **2** the middle point or part; place at the middle [A vase of flowers stood at the *center* of the table.] ◆*v.* to place in or at the center [Try to *center* the design on the page.]

chain (chān) *n.* **1** a number of links or loops joined together in a line that can be bent [a *chain* of steel; a *chain* of daisies] **2 chains,** *pl.* anything that binds or holds someone prisoner, as bonds or shackles **3** a series of things joined together [a mountain *chain*; a *chain* of events] ◆*v.* **1** to fasten or bind with chains [The prisoner was *chained* to the wall.] **2** to hold down; bind [I was *chained* to my job.]

cham·pi·on (cham′pē ən′) *n.* a person, animal, or thing that wins first place or is judged to be best in a contest or sport [a tennis *champion*]

change (chānj) *v.* **1** to make or become different in some way; alter [Time *changes* all things. His voice began to *change* at the age of thirteen.] **2** to put or take one thing in place of another; substitute [to *change* one's clothes; to *change* jobs] **3** to give or take one thing in return for another; substitute [Let's *change* seats. Can you *change* this dollar bill for four quarters?] —**changed, chang′ing** ◆*n.* **1** the act of changing in some way [There will be a *change* in the weather tomorrow.] **2** something put in place of something else [a fresh *change* of clothing] **3** the money returned when one has paid more than the amount owed [If it costs 70 cents and you pay with a dollar, you get back 30 cents as *change*.]

chain

charge (chärj) *v.* **1** to load or fill [to *charge* a gun with ammunition] ☆**2** to supply with electrical energy [to *charge* a battery] **3** to give a task, duty, etc. to; make responsible for [The nurse was *charged* with the care of the child.] **4** to set as a price; ask for payment [Barbers once *charged* a quarter for a haircut. We do not *charge* for gift wrappings.] —**charged, charg´ing**

chat (chat) *v.* to talk in an easy, relaxed way —**chat´ted, chat´ting** ◆*n.* an easy, relaxed talk or conversation

cheat (chēt) *v.* to act in a dishonest or unfair way in order to get what one wants [to *cheat* on a test]

check (chek) *n.* **1** a test to find out if something is as it should be [Add the column of numbers again as a *check* on your answer.] **2** the mark √, used to show that something is right, or to call attention to something **3** a piece of paper telling how much one owes, as for a meal at a restaurant **4** a written order to a bank to pay a certain amount of money from one's account to a certain person **5** a pattern of small squares like a checkerboard; also, any of the squares in such a pattern ◆*v.* to prove to be right or find what is wanted by examining, comparing, etc. [These figures *check* with mine. *Check* the records for this information.] —**checked, check´ing**

cheer·ful (chir´fəl) *adj.* **1** full of cheer; glad; joyful [a *cheerful* smile] **2** bright and gay [a *cheerful* room] **3** willing; glad to help [a *cheerful* worker] —**cheer´ful·ly** *adv.* —**cheer´ful·ness** *n.*

chee·tah (chēt´ə) *n.* an animal found in Africa and southern Asia that is like the leopard but smaller: it can be trained to hunt

cher·ry (cher´ē) *n.* **1** a small, round fruit with sweet flesh covering a smooth, hard seed: cherries are bright red, dark red, or yellow **2** the tree that this fruit grows on **3** bright red —*pl.* **cher´ries**

Chi·ca·go (shi kä´gō) a city in northeastern Illinois

chick·en (chik´ən) *n.* **1** a common farm bird raised for its eggs and flesh; hen or rooster, especially a young one **2** the flesh of a chicken

chief (chēf) *n.* the leader or head of some group [an Indian *chief*; the *chief* of a hospital staff] —*pl.* **chiefs** ◆*adj.* **1** having the highest position [the *chief* foreman] **2** main; most important [Jill's *chief* interest is golf.]

chief·ly (chēf´lē) *adv.* most of all; mainly; mostly [A watermelon is *chiefly* water.]

child (chīld) *n.* **1** a baby; infant **2** a young boy or girl **3** a son or daughter [Their *children* are all grown up.] —*pl.* **chil´dren**

chil·dren (chil´drən) *n.* *plural of* **child**

chim·ney (chim´nē) *n.* **1** a pipe or shaft going up through a roof to carry off smoke from a furnace, fireplace, or stove: chimneys are usually enclosed with brick or stone **2** a glass tube around the flame of a lamp —*pl.* **chim´neys**

Chi·na (chī´nə) a country in eastern Asia: it has the most people of any country in the world

☆**chow·der** (chou´dər) *n.* a thick soup made of fish or clams with onions, potatoes, milk, or tomatoes, etc.

church (church) *n.* **1** a building for holding religious services, especially one for Christian worship **2** religious services [*Church* will be at 11 a.m. on Sunday.] —*pl.* **church´es**

cir·cle (sur´kəl) *n.* **1** a closed curved line forming a perfectly round, flat figure: every point on this line is the same distance from a point inside called the center **2** the figure formed by such a line **3** anything round like a circle or ring [a *circle* of children playing a game]

clap (klap) *v.* **1** to make the sudden, loud sound of two flat surfaces being struck together **2** to strike the palms of the hands together, as in applauding —**clapped, clap´ping** ◆*n.* **1** the sudden, loud sound of clapping [a *clap* of thunder] **2** a sharp blow; slap

clash (klash) *n.* **1** a loud, harsh noise, as of metal striking against metal with great force [the *clash* of a sword on a shield] **2** a sharp disagreement; conflict [a *clash* of ideas] —*pl.* **clash´es** ◆*v.* to strike with a clash [He *clashed* the cymbals together.]

clasp (klasp) *n.* **1** a fastening, as a hook or catch, for holding two things or parts together [The *clasp* on my pocketbook is loose.] **2** a holding in the arms; embrace **3** a holding with the hand; grip ◆*v.* to fasten with a clasp

class (klas) ☆a group of students meeting together to be taught [Half the *class* missed school today.] —*pl.* **clas·ses**

claw (klô *or* klä) *n.* **1** a sharp, curved nail on the foot of an animal or bird **2** a foot with such nails [The eagle holds its victims in its *claws*.] **3** the grasping part on each front leg of a lobster, crab, or scorpion

clean (klēn) *adj.* **1** without dirt or impure matter [*clean* dishes; *clean* oil] **2** without evil or wrongdoing [to lead a *clean* life] **3** neat and tidy [to keep a *clean* desk] ◆*v.* to make clean [Please *clean* the oven.] —**cleaned, clean´ing**

clerk (klurk) *n.* **1** an office worker who keeps records, types letters, etc. [Some *clerks*, as a *clerk* of courts or a city *clerk*, have special duties.] ☆**2** a person who sells in a store; salesperson

cherries

a	ask, fat
ā	ape, date
ä	car, lot
e	elf, ten
ē	even, meet
i	is, hit
ī	ice, fire
ō	open, go
ô	law, horn
oi	oil, point
oo	look, pull
o͞o	ooze, tool
ou	out, crowd
u	up, cut
u	fur, fern
ə	a in ago
	e in agent
	e in father
	i in unity
	o in collect
	u in focus
ch	chin, arch
ŋ	ring, singer
sh	she, dash
th	thin, truth
th	then, father
zh	s in pleasure

157

Cleve·land (klĕv′lənd) a city in northeastern Ohio

cli·mate (klī′mət) *n.* **1** the average weather conditions of a place over a period of years [Arizona has a mild, dry *climate*, but its weather last week was stormy.] **2** a region with particular weather conditions [They went south to a warmer *climate*.]

clo·ver (klō′vər) *n.* a low-growing plant with leaves in three parts and small, sweet-smelling flowers. Red *clover* is grown for fodder; white *clover* is often found in lawns

clue (klo͞o) *n.* a fact or thing that helps to solve a puzzle or mystery [Muddy footprints were a *clue* to the man's guilt.]

clum·sy (klum′zē) *adj.* not having good control in moving the hands or feet; awkward [The *clumsy* waiter dropped the dish.] —**clum′si·er, clum′si·est**

cock·pit (käk′pit) *n.* in a small airplane, the space where the pilot and passengers sit: in a large plane, it is the space for the pilot and copilot

col·an·der (kul′ən dər *or* käl′ən dər) *n.* a pan with holes in the bottom for draining off liquids, as in washing vegetables

cold (kōld) *adj.* **1** having a temperature much lower than that of the human body; very chilly; frigid [a *cold* day; a *cold* drink] **2** without the proper heat or warmth [Your bath will get *cold*.] **3** feeling chilled [If you are *cold*, put on your coat.] **4** without any feeling; unkind, unfriendly, or gloomy [a *cold* welcome; a *cold* stare] —**cold′er, cold′est**

col·lege (käl′ij) *n.* a school that one can go to after high school for higher studies

Co·lum·bus (kə lum′bəs) the capital of Ohio

comb (kōm) *n.* a thin strip of hard rubber, plastic, metal, etc. with teeth: a comb is passed through the hair to arrange or clean it, or is put in the hair to hold it in place ◆*v.* **1** to smooth, arrange, or clean with a comb **2** to search carefully through [I *combed* the house for that book.]

come (kum) *v.* **1** to move from "there" to "here" [*Come* to me. Will you *come* to our party?] **2** to arrive or appear [Help will *come* soon.] —**came, com′ing**

com·ing (kum′iŋ) *adj.* that will come; approaching; on the way [Let's go this *coming* Friday.] ◆*n.* arrival; approach [Cold mornings warn of the *coming* of winter.]

com·mon (käm′ən) *adj.* **1** belonging equally to each or all [The science club members share a *common* interest.] **2** belonging to all the people; public [a *common* park] **3** of, from, by, or to all [the *common* good] **4** often seen or heard; widespread; usual [Squirrels are *common* in these woods. That's a *common* saying.]

com·mu·ni·ty (kə myo͞o′ni tē) *n.* **1** all the people who live in a particular district, city, etc. [The new swimming pool is for the use of the entire *community*.] **2** a group of people living together and having similar interests and work [a college *community*] —*pl.* **com·mu′ni·ties**

☆**com·mut·er** (kə myo͞ot′ər) *n.* a person who travels daily by train, bus, car, etc. between home and work or school

com·pare (kəm per′) *v.* **1** to describe as being the same; liken [The sound of thunder can be *compared* to the roll of drums.] **2** to examine certain things in order to find out how they are alike or different [How do the two cars *compare* in size and price?] **3** to equal or come close to by comparison [Few dogs can *compare* with the Great Dane in size.] —**com·pared′, com·par′ing**

com·put·er (kəm pyo͞ot′ər) *n.* **1** a person who computes **2** an electronic device used as a calculator or to store and select data

con·duct (kän′dukt) *n.* the way one acts or behaves; behavior [The teacher praised the students for their good *conduct* in class.] ◆*v.* (kən dukt′) **1** to manage; direct; be the leader of [to *conduct* a meeting; to *conduct* an orchestra] **2** to behave [They *conducted* themselves like adults.] **3** to be a means for carrying; transmit [Copper *conducts* electricity.]

cone (kōn) *n.* a solid object that narrows evenly from a flat circle at one end to a point at the other

con·stel·la·tion (kän′stə lā′shən) *n.* a group of stars, usually named after something that it is supposed to suggest [Orion is a *constellation* seen in the winter sky.]

con·struct (kən strukt′) *v.* to make or build with a plan [to *construct* a house or a theory]

con·tact (kän′takt) *v.* to get in touch with; communicate with [*Contact* my cousin as soon as possible.]

con·test (kən test′) *v.* **1** to try to prove that something is not true, right, or lawful; dispute [to *contest* a will] **2** to fight for; struggle to win or keep [to *contest* a prize] ◆*n.* (kän′test) **1** a fight, struggle, or argument **2** a race, game, etc. in which there is a struggle to be the winner

con·ti·nent (kän′ti nənt) *n.* any of the main large land areas of the earth: the continents are Africa, Asia, Australia, Europe, North America, South America, and, sometimes, Antarctica —**the Continent**, all of Europe except the British Isles

con·tin·ue (kən tin′yoo) **v. 1** to keep on being or doing [The rain *continued* for five days.] **2** to stay in the same place or position [The chairman will *continue* in office for another year.] **3** to go on or start again after a stop; resume [After a sip of water, the speaker *continued*.] **4** to go on or extend; stretch —**con·tin′ued, con·tin′u·ing**

con·trol (kən trōl′) **v. 1** to have the power of ruling, guiding, or managing [A thermostat *controls* the heat.] **2** to hold back; curb [*Control* your temper!] —**con·trolled′, con·trol′ling** ◆**n.** power to direct or manage [He's a poor coach, with little *control* over the team.]

con·vince (kən vins′) **v.** to make feel sure; persuade [I'm *convinced* they are telling the truth.] —**con·vinced′, con·vinc′ing**

con·voy (kän′voi) **n.** a group of ships or vehicles traveling together in order to protect one another

cop·y (käp′ē) **n. 1** a thing made just like another; imitation or likeness [four carbon *copies* of a letter] **2** any one of a number of books, magazines, pictures, etc. with the same printed matter [a library with six *copies* of *Tom Sawyer*] **3** a piece of writing that is to be set in type for printing [Reporters must write clear *copy*.] —*pl.* **cop′ies** ◆**v. 1** to make a copy or copies of [*Copy* the questions that are on the chalkboard.] **2** to act or be the same as; imitate —**cop′ied, cop′y·ing**

cor·al (kôr′əl) **n. 1** a hard, stony substance made up of the skeletons of many tiny sea animals: reefs of coral are found in tropical seas **2** piece of coral ◆**adj. 1** made of coral **2** yellowish-red in color

cor·ner (kôr′nər) **n. 1** the place where two lines or surfaces come together to form an angle **2** the space between such lines or surfaces [a lamp in the *corner* of a room] **3** the place where two streets meet **4** a place or region; quarter [every *corner* of America]

cos·tume (käs′toom *or* käs′tyoom) **n. 1** the way or style of dressing of a certain place or time or for a certain purpose [a Japanese *costume*; an eighteenth-century *costume*; a riding *costume*] **2** clothing worn by an actor in a play or by a person at a masquerade [a pirate *costume*]

cot·tage (kät′ij) **n.** a small house [a peasant's *cottage*; a summer *cottage* at the beach]

cou·gar (koo′gər) **n.** a large animal of the cat family, with a slender, tan body and a long tail

cough (kôf *or* käf) **v. 1** to force air from the lungs with a sudden, loud noise, as to clear the throat **2** to get out of the throat by coughing [to *cough* up phlegm] ◆**n. 1** the act or sound of coughing **2** a condition of coughing often [I have a bad *cough*.]

coun·ty (koun′tē) **n.** ☆**1** in the United States, any of the sections into which a state is divided: each county has its own officials **2** any of the districts into which Great Britain and Ireland are divided —*pl.* **coun′ties**

cou·ple (kup′əl) **n.** two things of the same kind that go together; pair [a *couple* of bookends]

cour·age (kur′ij) **n.** the quality of being able to control one's fear and so to face danger, pain, or trouble willingly; bravery

cous·in (kuz′ən) **n. 1** the son or daughter of one's uncle or aunt: *also called* **first cousin.** You are a *second cousin* to the children of your parents' first cousins, and you are a *first cousin once removed* to the children of your first cousins. **2** a distant relation

crack (krak) **v. 1** to make or cause to make a sudden, sharp noise, as of something breaking [The lion tamer *cracked* his whip.] **2** to break or split, with or without the parts falling apart [The snowball *cracked* the window. *Crack* the coconut open.] **3** to become harsh or change pitch suddenly [Her voice *cracked* when she sang the highest note.]

craft (kraft) **n. 1** special skill or ability **2** work that takes special skill, especially with the hands [the *craft* of weaving] **3** the members of a skilled trade **4** skill in fooling or tricking others; slyness

crash (krash) **v. 1** to fall, hit, or break with force and with a loud, smashing noise **2** to fall to the earth so as to be damaged or smashed [The airplane *crashed*.] ◆**n. 1** a loud, smashing noise **2** the crashing of a car, airplane, etc.

cray·on (krā′ən *or* krā′än) **n.** a small stick of chalk, charcoal, or colored wax, used for drawing or writing ◆**v.** to draw with crayons

cra·zy (krā′zē) **adj.** mentally ill; insane —**cra′zi·er, cra′zi·est**

cream (krēm) **n. 1** the oily, yellowish part of milk that rises to the top and contains the butterfat **2** any food that is made of cream or is like cream [ice *cream*] **3** a smooth, oily substance used to clean and soften the skin

creep (krēp) **v. 1** to move along with the body close to the ground, as a baby on hands and knees **2** to move in a slow or sneaking way [The cars *crept* along in the heavy traffic. The thieves *crept* into the store at night.] **3** to come on almost without being noticed [Old age *crept* up on her.] —**crept, creep′ing**

crept (krept) **v.** *past tense and past participle of* **creep**

cries (krīz) **1** *the form of the verb* **cry** *used in the present with* he, she, *or* it **2** *the plural of the noun* **cry**

a	ask, fat
ā	ape, date
ä	car, lot
e	elf, ten
ē	even, meet
i	is, hit
ī	ice, fire
ō	open, go
ô	law, horn
oi	oil, point
oo	look, pull
oo	ooze, tool
ou	out, crowd
u	up, cut
ʉ	fur, fern
ə	a in ago
	e in agent
	e in father
	i in unity
	o in collect
	u in focus
ch	chin, arch
ŋ	ring, singer
sh	she, dash
th	thin, truth
th	then, father
zh	s in pleasure

crime (krīm) **n.** **1** the doing of something that is against the law; serious wrongdoing that breaks the law **2** an evil or foolish act; sin [It would be a *crime* to waste this food.]

cruise (krōōz) **v.** **1** to sail or drive about from place to place, as for pleasure or in searching for something **2** to move smoothly at a speed that is not strained [The airplane *cruised* at 300 miles per hour.] —**cruised, cruis′ing** ◆**n.** a ship voyage from place to place for pleasure

crumb (krum) **n.** **1** a tiny piece broken off, as of bread or cake **2** any bit or scrap [*crumbs* of knowledge]

crunch (krunch) **v.** **1** to chew with a noisy, crackling sound [to *crunch* raw carrots] **2** to grind or move over with a noisy, crushing sound [The wheels *crunched* the pebbles in the driveway.]

crush (krush) **v.** **1** to press or squeeze with force so as to break, hurt, or put out of shape [She *crushed* the flower in her hand. His hat was *crushed* when he sat on it.] **2** to grind or pound into bits [This machine *crushes* rocks.] **3** to bring to an end by force; subdue; suppress [The government *crushed* the revolt.] ◆**n.** a crushing or squeezing; strong pressure

cry (krī) **v.** **1** to make a loud sound with the voice; call out or shout [Lou *cried* out in fright when a face appeared at the window.] **2** to show sorrow, pain, etc. by sobbing or shedding tears **3** to say loudly; shout; exclaim ["Help! Help!" the victim *cried*.] —**cried, cry′ing** ◆**n.** **1** a loud sound made by the voice; shout or call [I heard your *cry* for help.] **2** a fit of sobbing and weeping [I had a good *cry* and fell asleep.] **3** the sound an animal makes [the *cry* of a lost sheep] —*pl.* **cries**

cry

cube (kyōōb) **n.** **1** a solid with six square sides, all the same size **2** anything with more or less this shape [an ice *cube*] **3** the result got by multiplying a number by itself and then multiplying the product by the same number [The *cube* of 3 is 27 (3 × 3 × 3 = 27).] ◆**v.** to cut into cubes [I *cubed* the fruit for salad.] —**cubed, cub′ing**

curb (kurb) **n.** **1** a chain or strap passed around a horse's jaw and attached to the bit: it holds back the horse when the reins are pulled **2** anything that checks or holds back [Fear of punishment is often a *curb* to wrongdoing.] **3** the stone or concrete edging along a street ◆**v.** to hold back; keep in check [to *curb* one's appetite]

curl·y (kur′lē) **adj.** full of curls [*curly* hair] —**curl′i·er, curl′i·est**

cur·rent (kur′ənt) **adj.** **1** of the present time; now going on; most recent [the *current* decade; *current* events] **2** commonly known, used, or accepted [*current* gossip; a belief *current* in earlier times] ◆**n.** **1** a flow of water or air in a definite direction; stream **2** the flow of electricity in a wire or other conductor **3** the general movement or drift, as of opinion —**cur′rent·ly adv.**

Dd

dair·y (der′ē) **n.** **1** a building where milk and cream are kept and butter and cheese are made **2** a farm (**dairy farm**) on which milk, butter, cheese, etc. are produced **3** a store that sells milk, butter, cheese, etc. —*pl.* **dair′ies**

dai·sy (dā′zē) **n.** ☆**1** a common plant with flowers that have white or pink petals around a yellow center **2** such a flower —*pl.* **dai′sies**

dam·age (dam′ij) **n.** injury or harm to a person or thing that results in a loss of health, value, and so on [A poor diet can cause *damage* to your heart.]

danc·er (dan′sər) **n.** a person who dances

daugh·ter (dôt′ər *or* dät′ər) **n.** a girl or woman as she is related to a parent or to both parents

dawn (dôn *or* dän) **v.** **1** to begin to grow light as the sun rises [Day is *dawning*.] **2** to come into being; begin to develop [With the discovery of electricity, a new age *dawned*.] **3** to begin to be understood or felt [The meaning suddenly *dawned* on me.] ◆**n.** **1** the beginning of day; daybreak **2** the beginning of anything [the *dawn* of the space age]

de·ceive (dē sēv′) **v.** to make someone believe what is not true; fool or trick; mislead [The queen *deceived* Snow White by pretending to be her friend.]

de·cide (dē sīd′) **v.** **1** to choose after some thought; make up one's mind [I can't *decide* what suit to wear.] **2** to end a contest or argument by giving one side the victory; settle [A jury will *decide* the case.] —**de·cid′ed, de·cid′ing**

deer (dir) **n.** a swift-running, hoofed animal —*pl.* **deer** or **deers**

de·fend (dē fend′) **v.** **1** to keep safe from harm or danger; guard; protect [She learned karate to *defend* herself.] **2** to uphold something that is under attack; especially, to be the lawyer for a person accused or sued in a law court

de·fine (dē fin′) **v.** to tell the meaning or meanings of; explain [The dictionary *defines* "deficient" as "not having enough."]

de·lay (dē lā´) *v.* to put off to a later time; postpone [The bride's illness will *delay* the wedding.]

de·liv·er·y (dē liv´ər ē) *n.* the act of transferring or distributing [daily *deliveries* to customers] —*pl.* **de·liv´er·ies**

den·tist (den´tist) *n.* a doctor whose work is preventing and taking care of diseased or crooked teeth, or replacing them with artificial teeth

de·ny (dē nī´) *v.* 1 to say that something is not true or right; contradict [They *denied* that they had broken the window.] 2 to refuse to grant or give [We were *denied* permission to see the movie.] —**de·nies´, de·nied´, de·ny´ing**

de·scend (dē send´) *v.* 1 to move down to a lower place [to *descend* from a hilltop; to *descend* a staircase] 2 to become lesser or smaller [Prices have *descended* during the past month.] 3 to come from a certain source [They are *descended* from pioneers.]

des·ert (dez´ərt) *n.* a dry sandy region with little or no plant life ◆*adj.* 1 of or like a desert 2 wild and not lived in [a *desert* island]

de·sign (dē zīn´) *v.* 1 to think up and draw plans for [to *design* a new model of a car] 2 to arrange the parts, colors, etc. of [Who *designed* this book?] 3 to set apart for a certain use; intend [This chair was not *designed* for hard use.] ◆*n.* 1 a drawing or plan to be followed in making something [the *designs* for a house] 2 the arrangement of parts, colors, etc.; pattern or decoration [the *design* in a rug] 3 a plan or purpose [It was my *design* to study law.]

de·stroy (dē stroi´) *v.* to put an end to by breaking up, tearing down, ruining, or spoiling [The flood *destroyed* 300 homes.] —**de·stroyed´, de·stroy´ing**

di·a·ry (dī´ə rē) *n.* a record written day by day of some of the things done, seen, or thought by the writer —*pl.* **di´a·ries**

die (dī) *v.* 1 to stop living; become dead 2 to stop going, moving, acting, etc. [The motor sputtered and *died*.] 3 to lose force; become weak, faint, etc. [The sound of music *died* away.] 4 to want greatly: *used only in everyday talk* [She's *dying* to know my secret.] —**died, dy´ing**

di·et (dī´ət) *n.* 1 what a person or animal usually eats or drinks; usual food [Rice is a basic food in the *diet* of many Asian people.] 2 a special choice as to kinds and amounts of food eaten, as for one's health or to gain or lose weight [a sugar-free *diet*; a reducing *diet*] ◆*v.* to eat certain kinds and amounts of food, especially in order to lose weight

dif·fer·ent (dif´ər ənt *or* dif´rənt) *adj.* 1 not alike; unlike [Cottage cheese is quite *different* from Swiss cheese.] 2 not the same; separate; distinct [There are three *different* colleges in the city.] 3 not like most others; unusual [Their house is really *different*.] —**dif´fer·ent·ly** *adv.*

dif·fi·cult (dif´i kult) *adj.* 1 hard to do, make, or understand; that takes much trouble, thought, or skill [This arithmetic problem is *difficult*.] 2 hard to please; not easy to get along with [a *difficult* employer]

dim (dim) *v.* to make or grow somewhat dark [Cars approaching each other should *dim* their headlights.] —**dimmed, dim´ming**

dirt·y (dʉrt´ē) *adj.* 1 having dirt on or in it; not clean; soiled 2 foul or indecent; not nice; mean [a *dirty* trick] —**dirt´i·er, dirt´i·est** ◆*v.* to make or become dirty; soil —**dirt´ied, dirt´y·ing** —**dirt´i·ness** *n.*

dis·a·gree (dis´ə grē´) *v.* 1 to differ in opinion; often, to quarrel or argue [to *disagree* on politics] 2 to be different; differ [His story of the accident *disagreed* with hers.] —**dis´a·greed´, dis´a·gree´ing**

dis·ap·point (dis´ə point´) *v.* to fail to give or do what is wanted, expected, or promised; leave unsatisfied [I am *disappointed* in the weather. You promised to come, but *disappointed* us.]

dis·be·lief (dis´bə lēf´) *n.* the state of not believing; lack of belief [The guide stared at me in *disbelief*.]

dis·close (dis klōz´) *v.* 1 to bring into view; uncover [I opened my hand and *disclosed* the new penny.] 2 to make known; reveal [to *disclose* a secret] —**dis·closed´, dis·clos´ing**

dis·grace (dis grās´) *n.* loss of favor, respect, or honor; dishonor; shame [in *disgrace* for cheating]

dis·hon·est (dis än´əst) *adj.* not honest; lying, cheating, stealing, etc. —**dis·hon´est·ly** *adv.* —**dis·hon´es·ty** *n.*

dis·in·ter·est·ed (dis in´trəs təd) *adj.* 1 not having a selfish interest in the matter; impartial [A *disinterested* judge picked the winner.] 2 not interested; uninterested: *an older meaning that is being used again*

dis·loy·al (dis loi´əl) *adj.* not loyal or faithful; faithless —**dis·loy´al·ty** *n.*

dis·play (di splā´) *v.* 1 to put or spread out so as to be seen; exhibit [to *display* a collection of stamps] 2 to do something that is a sign or example of; show; reveal [to *display* one's courage] ◆*n.* a displaying or showing; exhibition [a *display* of jewelry; a *display* of strength]

ditch (dich) *n.* a long, narrow opening dug in the earth, as for carrying off water; trench [a *ditch* along the road] —*pl.* **ditch´es** ◆*v.* 1 to dig a ditch in or around 2 to throw into a ditch

a	ask, fat
ā	ape, date
ä	car, lot
e	elf, ten
ē	even, meet
i	is, hit
ī	ice, fire
ō	open, go
ô	law, horn
oi	oil, point
ᴏᴏ	look, pull
ᴏᴏ	ooze, tool
ou	out, crowd
u	up, cut
ʉ	fur, fern
ə	a in ago
	e in agent
	e in father
	i in unity
	o in collect
	u in focus
ch	chin, arch
ŋ	ring, singer
sh	she, dash
th	thin, truth
th	then, father
zh	s in pleasure

161

eagle

doc·tor (däk′tər) *n.* **1** a person trained to heal the sick; especially, a physician or surgeon **2** a person who has received the highest degree given by a university [*Doctor* of Philosophy] ◆*v.* to try to heal [to *doctor* oneself]

does·n't (duz′ənt) *contraction* does not

dol·lar (däl′ər) *n.* ☆**1** a U.S. coin or piece of paper money, equal to 100 cents: the dollar is our basic unit of money; its symbol is $ **2** a unit of money in certain other countries, as Canada

dol·phin (dôl′fin) *n.* a water animal related to the whale but smaller: the common dolphin has a long snout and many teeth

☆**down·town** (doun′toun) *adj., adv.* in or toward the lower part or the main business section of a city or town ◆*n.* this section of a city or town

drag (drag) *v.* **1** to pull in a slow, hard way, especially along the ground; haul [He *dragged* the sled up the hill.] **2** to be pulled along the ground, floor, etc. [Her skirt *dragged* in the mud.] **3** to move or pass too slowly [Time *dragged* as we waited for recess.] **4** to search for something in a river, lake, etc. by dragging a net or hooks along the bottom —**dragged, drag′ging**

draw (drô *or* drä) *v.* to make a picture or design with a pencil, pen, or chalk —**drew** (drōō), **draw′ing**

draw·ing (drô′iŋ *or* drä′iŋ) *n.* **1** the making of pictures, designs, etc., as with a pencil or pen **2** such a picture, design, etc. **3** a lottery

drawn (drôn *or* drän) *past participle of* **draw**

dream (drēm) *n.* **1** a series of thoughts, pictures, or feelings that passes through the mind of a sleeping person **2** a pleasant idea that one imagines or hopes for; daydream [to have *dreams* of glory] ◆*v.* **1** to have a dream or dreams **2** to imagine as possible; have any idea of [I wouldn't *dream* of going without you.] —**dreamed** or **dreamt** (dremt), **dream′ing** —**dream′er** *n.*

dress (dres) *n.* **1** the common outer garment worn by girls and women: it is usually of one piece with a skirt **2** clothes in general [native *dress*; formal *dress*] —*pl.* **dress′es** ◆*v.* **1** to put clothes on; clothe **2** to put medicine and bandages on a wound or sore **3** to make ready for use; prepare [to *dress* a chicken; to *dress* leather] ◆*adj.* worn on formal occasions [a *dress* suit]

drive (drīv) *v.* to control the movement of an automobile, horse and wagon, bus, or other vehicle [She *drives* a school bus.] —**drove, driv′ing**

drop (dräp) *n.* **1** a bit of liquid that is rounded in shape, as when falling [*drops* of rain] **2** anything like this in shape [a chocolate *drop*] **3** a very small amount [He hasn't a *drop* of courage.] ◆*v.* **1** to fall or

let fall in drops [Tears *dropped* from the actor's eyes.] **2** to fall or let fall [Ripe fruit *dropped* from the trees. He *dropped* his lunch in the mud.] —**dropped** or *sometimes* **dropt, drop′ping**

drown (droun) *v.* to die from being under water, where the lungs can get no air [to fall overboard and *drown*] —**drowned, drown′ing**

drow·sy (drou′zē) *adj.* **1** sleepy or half asleep **2** making one feel sleepy [*drowsy* music] —**drow′si·er, drow′si·est** —**drow′si·ly** *adv.* —**drow′si·ness** *n.*

dry (drī) *adj.* **1** not under water [*dry* land] **2** not wet or damp; without moisture **3** having little or no rain or water [a *dry* summer] **4** with all its water or other liquid gone [a *dry* fountain pen; *dry* bread; a *dry* well] —**dri′er, dri′est** —**dried, dry′ing** —**dry′ly** *adv.* —**dry′ness** *n.*

dues (dōōz *or* dyōōz) *n.* money paid regularly for being a member of a club or institution [The *dues* are $25 per month.]

dusk (dusk) *n.* the dim part of twilight that comes before the dark of night

du·ty (dōōt′ē *or* dyōōt′ē) *n.* **1** what a person should do because it is thought to be right, just, or moral [It is the *duty* of every citizen to vote.] **2** any of the things that are done as part of a person's work [the *duties* of a secretary] —*pl.* **du′ties**

ea·gle (ē′gəl) *n.* a large, strong bird that captures and eats other birds and animals and has sharp eyesight: the **bald eagle** is the symbol of the United States

ear·ly (ʉr′lē) *adv., adj.* **1** near the beginning; soon after the start [in the *early* afternoon; *early* in his career] **2** before the usual or expected time [The bus arrived *early*.] —**ear′li·er, ear′li·est** —**ear′li·ness** *n.*

ear·muffs (ir′mufs) *pl.n.* cloth or fur coverings worn over the ears to keep them warm in cold weather

east·ern (ēs′tərn) *adj.* **1** in, of, or toward the east [the *eastern* sky] **2** from the east [an *eastern* wind] **3** Eastern, of the East

eas·y (ē′zē) *adj.* **1** not hard to do, learn, get, etc. [an *easy* job; an *easy* book] **2** without worry, pain, or trouble [an *easy* life] **3** restful or comfortable [an *easy* chair] —**eas′i·er, eas′i·est**

eas·y·go·ing (ē′zē gō′iŋ) *adj.* not worried, rushed, or strict about things

edge (ej) *n.* **1** the sharp, cutting part [the *edge* of a knife] **2** the line or part where something begins or ends; border or margin [the *edge* of a plate; the *edge* of the forest] **3** the brink [on the *edge* of disaster] —**edged, edg´ing**

ed·i·tor (ed´it ər) *n.* **1** a person who edits ☆**2** the head of a department of a newspaper, magazine, etc.

eight·een (ā´tēn´) *n., adj.* eight more than ten; the number 18

el·e·phant (el´ə fənt) *n.* a huge animal with a thick skin, two ivory tusks, and a long snout, or trunk: it is found in Africa and India and is the largest of the four-legged animals

e·lev·en (ē lev´ən) *n., adj.* one more than ten; the number 11

em·broi·der (em broi´dər) *v.* to stitch designs on cloth with a needle and thread [Hal *embroidered* his initials on his shirt.]

e·mer·gen·cy (ē mur´jən sē) *n.* a sudden happening that needs action or attention right away [the *emergency* created by a hurricane] —*pl.* **e·mer·gen·cies**

em·ploy (em ploi´) *v.* **1** to hire and pay for the work or services of; have working for one [That company *employs* 50 people.] **2** to use [The baby *employed* clever tricks to get attention.] ◆*n.* the condition of being employed [Chan is no longer in our *employ*.]

emp·ty (emp´tē) *adj.* **1** having nothing or no one in it; not occupied; vacant [an *empty* jar; an *empty* house] —**emp´ti·er, emp´ti·est** ◆*v.* **1** to make or become empty [The auditorium was *emptied* in ten minutes.] **2** to take out or pour out [*Empty* the dirty water in the sink.] **3** to flow out; discharge [The Amazon *empties* into the Atlantic.] —**emp´tied, emp´ty·ing** —**emp´ti·ly** *adv.* —**emp´ti·ness** *n.*

en·e·my (en´ə mē) *n.* a person, group, or country that hates another or fights against another; foe —*pl.* **en´e·mies**

en·er·gy (en´ər jē) *n.* **1** power to work or be active; force; vigor [Eleanor Roosevelt was a woman of great *energy*.] **2** the power of certain forces in nature to do work [Electricity and heat are forms of *energy*.] **3** resources, as coal, oil, etc., used to produce such power; also, the supply of such resources that can be got [an *energy* shortage] —*pl.* **en´er·gies**

e·nor·mous (ē nôr´məs) *adj.* much larger than usual; huge [an *enormous* stadium] —**e·nor´mous·ly** *adv.* —**e·nor´mous·ness** *n.*

e·nough (ē nuf´) *adj.* as much or as many as needed or wanted; sufficient [There is *enough* food for all.] ◆*n.* the amount needed or wanted [I have heard *enough* of that music.] ◆*adv.* **1** as much as needed; to the right amount [Is your steak cooked *enough*?] **2** fully; quite [Oddly *enough*, she never asked me.]

en·ter·tain (en tər tān´) *v.* to keep interested and give pleasure to [She *entertained* us by playing the organ.]

e·qual (ē´kwəl) *adj.* **1** of the same amount, size, or value [The horses were of *equal* height.] **2** having the same rights, ability, or position [All persons are *equal* in a court of law in a just society.] ◆*n.* any person or thing that is equal [As a sculptor, she has few *equals*.] ◆*v.* to be equal to; match [His long jump *equaled* the school record. Six minus two *equals* four.] —**e´qualed** or **e´qualled, e´qual·ing** or **e´qual·ling** —**e´qual·ly** *adv.*

e·qua·tor (ē kwāt´ər) *n.* an imaginary circle around the middle of the earth, at an equal distance from the North Pole and South Pole

er·ror (ar´ər) *n.* **1** a belief, answer, act, etc. that is untrue, incorrect, or wrong mistake [an *error* in multiplication] **2** a play by a baseball fielder which is poorly made, but which would have resulted in an out if it had been properly made

es·say (es´ā) *n.* a short piece of writing on some subject, giving the writer's personal ideas

Eu·rope (yoor´əp) the continent between Asia and the Atlantic Ocean

ev·er·y·bod·y (ev´rē bäd´ē *or* ev´rē bud´ē) *pron.* every person; everyone [*Everybody* loves a good story.]

ex·change (eks chānj´) *v.* to give in return for something else; trade [She *exchanged* the bicycle for a larger one.] —**ex·changed´, ex·chang´ing**

ex·cuse (ek skyooz´) *v.* **1** to be a proper reason or explanation for [That was a selfish act that nothing will *excuse*.] **2** to think of a fault or wrongdoing as not important; overlook; forgive; pardon [Please *excuse* this interruption.] **3** to allow to leave or go [You may be *excused* from the table.] —**ex·cused´, ex·cus´ing** ◆*n.* (ek skyoos´) a reason given to explain some action or behavior; apology [Ignorance of the law is no *excuse* for wrongdoing.]

ex·er·cise (ek´sər sīz) *n.* **1** active use of the body in order to make it stronger or healthier [Long walks are good outdoor *exercise*.] **2** *usually* **exercises**, *pl.* a series of movements done regularly to make some part of the body stronger or to develop some skill [These *exercises* will strengthen your legs.] **3** a problem to be studied and worked on by a student in order to get more skill [piano *exercises*] ◆*v.* to put into use or do certain regular movements, in order to develop or train [*Exercise* your weak ankle. I *exercise* every morning.] —**ex´er·cised, ex´er·cis·ing**

a	ask, fat
ā	ape, date
ä	car, lot
e	elf, ten
ē	even, meet
i	is, hit
ī	ice, fire
ō	open, go
ô	law, horn
oi	oil, point
σσ	look, pull
ōō	ooze, tool
ou	out, crowd
u	up, cut
ʉ	fur, fern
ə	a in ago
	e in agent
	e in father
	i in unity
	o in collect
	u in focus
ch	chin, arch
ŋ	ring, singer
sh	she, dash
th	thin, truth
th	then, father
zh	s in pleasure

163

ex·pen·sive (ek spen′siv) *adj.* costing much; having a high price [She wears *expensive* clothes.] —**ex·pen′sive·ly** *adv.*

ex·plore (ek splôr′) *v.* **1** to travel in a region that is unknown or not well known, in order to find out more about it [to *explore* a wild jungle] **2** to look into or examine carefully [to *explore* a problem] —**ex·plored′, ex·plor′ing** —**ex′plo·ra′tion** *n.* —**ex·plor′er** *n.*

ex·press (ek spres′) *v.* **1** to put into words; state [It is hard to *express* my feelings.] **2** to give or be a sign of; show [a frown that *expressed* doubt] ☆**3** to send goods by a fast way ✦*adj.* taking the shortest and fastest route; not making many stops [an *express* train or bus]

ex·tend (ek stend′) *v.* to make longer; stretch out [Careful cleaning *extends* the life of a rug.]

ex·tinct (ek stiŋkt′) *adj.* **1** no longer living; having died out [Dinosaurs are *extinct.*] **2** no longer burning or active [an *extinct* volcano]

ex·tin·guish·er (ek stiŋ′gwish ər) *n.* a person or thing that extinguishes; especially, a device for putting out a fire by spraying a liquid or gas on it

eye·lash (ī′lash) *n.* **1** any of the hairs that grow along the edge of the eyelid **2** a fringe of these hairs —*pl.* **eye′lash·es**

Ff

fa·ble (fā′bəl) *n.* **1** a very short story that teaches a lesson: it is usually about animals who act and talk like people [Aesop's *fable* "The Grasshopper and the Ant" teaches the need to work hard and be thrifty.]

fac·to·ry (fak′tər ē *or* fak′trē) *n.* a building or group of buildings where products are made by machinery —*pl.* **fac′to·ries**

fair (fer) *adj.* **1** beautiful [your *fair* city] **2** light in color; blond [*fair* hair; *fair* skin] **3** clear and sunny [*fair* weather] **4** just and honest; according to what is right [a *fair* price; *fair* play] —**fair′ness** *n.*

fame (fām) *n.* the condition of being well known or much talked about; great reputation [Marie Curie's scientific research brought her much *fame.*]

fa·mil·iar (fə mil′yər) *adj.* friendly; intimate; well-acquainted [a *familiar* face in the crowd]

fam·i·ly (fam′ə lē) *n.* **1** a group made up of two parents and all of their children **2** the children alone [a widow who raised a large family] **3** a group of people who are related by marriage or a common ancestor; relatives; clan —*pl.* **fam′i·lies**

fan·cy (fan′sē) *n.* the power of picturing in the mind things that are not real, especially in a light and playful way; imagination ["Alice's Adventures in Wonderland" is the product of Lewis Carroll's *fancy.*] —*pl.* **fan′cies** ✦*adj.* **1** having much design and decoration; not plain; elaborate [a *fancy* tie] **2** of better quality than the usual; special [a *fancy* grade of canned pears] —**fan′ci·er, fan′ci·est** ✦*v.* to have a liking for [He *fancies* Swiss chocolate.] —**fan′cied, fan′cy·ing**

far·ther (fär *th*ər) *the comparative of* **far** ✦*adj.* more distant [My home is *farther* from school than yours.] ✦*adv.* at or to a greater distance [I can swim *farther* than you can.]

fault (fôlt) *n.* **1** a thing that keeps something from being perfect; defect; flaw [His main *fault* is that he's lazy.] **2** an error; mistake **3** blame; responsibility [It isn't my *fault* that we're late.]

fawn (fôn *or* fän) *n.* a young deer, less than one year old

fear·less (fir′ləs) *adj.* having no fear; not afraid; brave —**fear′less·ly** *adv.*

feath·er (fe*th*′ər) *n.* any of the parts that grow out of the skin of birds, covering the body and filling out the wings and tail: feathers are soft and light —**feath′er·y** *adj.*

fend·er (fen′dər) *n.* ☆**1** a metal piece over the wheel of a car to keep off splashing mud **2** a metal piece at the front of a locomotive to throw off things that are hit

field (fēld) *n.* **1** a wide piece of open land without many trees; especially, a piece of land for growing crops, grazing animals, etc. **2** a piece of land having a special use or producing a certain thing [a landing *field*; an oil *field*] **3** an area where games or athletic events are held; also, the part of such an area where such events as high jump, long jump, pole vault, shot put, etc. are held ✦*v.* to stop or catch and return a batted ball

fight (fīt) *v.* to use fists, weapons, or other force in trying to beat or overcome someone or something [to *fight* a war] —**fought, fight′ing**

film (film) *n.* **1** a thin skin or coating [a *film* of ice on the pond] **2** a sheet or roll of material covered with a chemical substance that is changed by light, used for taking photographs or making movies **3** a movie

fin·ish (fin′ish) *v.* **1** to bring or come to an end; complete or become completed [Did you *finish* your work? The game *finished* early.] **2** to give final touches to; perfect [We *finished* the room by putting up molding.] **3** to use up; consume completely [*Finish* your milk.] ◆*n.* the kind of surface a thing has [an oil *finish* on wood] —**fin′ish·ing**

fish (fish) *n.* an animal that lives in water and has a backbone, fins, and gills for breathing [The aquarium exhibits many *fishes*.] —*pl.* **fish** (or when different kinds are meant **fish′es**)

fla·min·go (flə min′gō) *n.* a wading bird that has a very long neck and legs, and pink or red feathers: it lives in tropical regions —*pl.* **fla·min′gos** or **fla·min′goes**

flash (flash) *v.* **1** to send out a short and bright burst of light [Electric signs *flashed* all along the street.] **2** to sparkle or gleam [Her eyes *flashed* with anger.] **3** to come, move, or send swiftly or suddenly [The train *flashed* by. The news was *flashed* to Paris by radio.] ◆*n.* a short burst of light or of something bright [a *flash* of lightning; a *flash* of wit, hope, etc.] —*pl.* **flash′es**

fleet¹ (flēt) *n.* **1** a group of warships under one command [our Pacific *fleet*] **2** any group of ships, trucks, buses, etc. moving together or under one control

fleet² (flēt) *adj.* moving swiftly; swift

flew (flo͞o) *past tense of* **fly¹**

flies (flīz) **1** *the form of the verb* **fly¹**, *used in the present with* he, she, *or* it **2** *the plural of* **fly¹** *and* **fly²**

flight (flīt) *n.* **1** the act or way of flying or moving through space **2** a trip through the air, as by an airplane, bird, etc. [a 500-mile *flight*] **3** a group of things flying together [a *flight* of wild swans]

Flor·i·da (flôr′i də) a state in the southeastern part of the United States: abbreviated **Fla.**, **FL**

flu (flo͞o) *n.* a disease caused by a virus, like a bad cold only more serious

flue (flo͞o) *n.* a tube, pipe, or shaft through which smoke, steam, or hot air can escape [the *flue* in a chimney]

fly¹ (flī) *v.* **1** to move through the air by using wings, as a bird **2** to travel or carry through the air, as in an aircraft **3** to pilot an aircraft **4** to wave or float in the air, or cause to float in the air, as a flag or kite **5** to move swiftly [The door *flew* open. Time *flies*.] —**flew, flown, fly′ing** ◆*n.* a baseball batted high in the air inside the foul lines —*pl.* **flies**

fly² (flī) *n.* **1** a flying insect having one pair of wings, as the housefly and gnat: some insects with two pairs of wings are called flies, as the mayfly **2** an object used in fishing, made of bright feathers, silk, etc. tied to a fishhook to look like a fly —*pl.* **flies**

folk (fōk) *n.* people or persons [The farmer disliked city *folk*. *Folks* differ in customs.] —*pl.* **folk** or **folks** ◆*adj.* of the common people [a *folk* saying]

folk tale a story made and handed down by word of mouth among the common people: *also* **folk story**

fol·low·ing (fä′lō iŋ) *adj.* going or coming after; next after [the *following* week] ◆*n.* people who follow; followers ◆*prep.* after [*Following* dinner we played cards.]

fond (fänd) *v.* loving and tender; affectionate [*fond* parents]

fool·ish (fo͞ol′ish) *adj.* without good sense; silly —**fool′ish·ly** *adv.* —**fool′ish·ness** *n.*

force (fôrs) *n.* **1** power or energy that can do or make something [Electricity is a powerful natural *force*. The *force* of the high winds broke the windows.] **2** power or strength used against a person or thing [The police used *force* to scatter the crowd.] **3** the power to cause motion or to stop or change motion [the *force* of gravity] ◆*v.* **1** to make or do something by using strength or power of some kind [You shouldn't *force* a child to eat. The blizzard *forced* us to stay home.] **2** to break open or through by using strength [He *forced* the lock with a pick.] —**forced, forc′ing**

fore·head (fôr′hed *or* fär′hed) *n.* the part of the face above the eyebrows

forth (fôrth) *adv.* **1** forward or onward [She never left the house from that day *forth*.] **2** out, into view [The bears came *forth* from their den.]

fought (fôt *or* fät) *past tense and past participle of* **fight**

fox (fäks) *n.* **1** a wild animal of the dog family, with pointed ears, a bushy tail, and usually, reddish-brown fur —*pl.* **fox** or **fox′es**

France (frans) a country in western Europe

fraud (frôd *or* fräd) *n.* **1** a cheat, trick, or lie; dishonesty **2** a person who cheats or is not what he or she pretends to be

fray (frā) *v.* to wear down so as to become ragged and have loose threads showing [a coat *frayed* at the elbows]

free·dom (frē′dəm) *n.* **1** the condition of being free; liberty; independent **2** a being able to use or move about as one wishes [Has your dog been given *freedom* of the house?]

freight·er (frāt′ər) *n.* a ship for freight

front (frunt) *n.* **1** the part that faces forward; most important side [The *front* of a house usually faces the street.] **2** the part ahead of the rest; first part; beginning [That chapter is toward the *front* of the book.] **3** outward look or behavior [I put on a bold *front* in spite of my fear.] **4** the land alongside a lake, ocean, street, etc. [docks on the water*front*]

fox

a	ask, fat
ā	ape, date
ä	car, lot
e	elf, ten
ē	even, meet
i	is, hit
ī	ice, fire
ō	open, go
ô	law, horn
oi	oil, point
o͞o	look, pull
o͞o	ooze, tool
ou	out, crowd
u	up, cut
ʉ	fur, fern
ə	a in ago
	e in agent
	e in father
	i in unity
	o in collect
	u in focus
ch	chin, arch
ŋ	ring, singer
sh	she, dash
th	thin, truth
th	then, father
zh	s in pleasure

165

glove

fron·tier (frun tir′) *n.* **1** the line or border between two countries ☆**2** the part of a settled country that lies next to a region that is still a wilderness **3** any new field of learning or any part of it still to be explored [the *frontiers* of medicine]

fry (frī) *v.* to cook in hot fat over direct heat —**fried, fry′ing** ◆*n.* ☆**1** a kind of picnic at which food is fried and eaten [a fish *fry*] **2 fries,** *pl.* things fried, as potatoes —*pl.* **fries**

fun·ny (fun′ē) *adj.* **1** causing smiles or laughter; amusing; comical **2** odd or unusual; *used only in everyday talk* [It's *funny* that he's late.] —**fun′ni·er, fun′ni·est** ◆☆*n.* usually **funnies,** *pl.* comic strips; *used only in everyday talk* —*pl.* **fun′nies** —**fun′ni·ness** *n.*

gal·ax·y (gal′ək sē) *often* **Galaxy,** *another name for* **Milky Way** ◆*n.* **1** any vast group of stars **2** a group of very famous people —*pl.* **gal′ax·ies**

gal·ley (gal′ē) *n.* **1** large, low ship of long ago, having both sails and many oars: the oars were usually rowed by slaves or prisoners in chains **2** the kitchen of a ship —*pl.* **gal′leys**

gal·lon (gal′ən) *n.* a measure of liquids, equal to four quarts or eight pints: one gallon equals 3.785 liters

gar·bage (gär′bij) *n.* spoiled food or food waste that is thrown away

gasp (gasp) *v.* to breathe in suddenly [She *gasped* in sudden surprise.]

gath·er (ga*th*′ər) *v.* **1** to bring or come together in one place or group [The child *gathered* her toys together. The families *gathered* for a reunion.] **2** to get or collect gradually; accumulate [to *gather* wealth; to *gather* one's strength; to *gather* news for a paper] **3** to pick or glean [to *gather* crops]. —**gath′er·er** *n.*

gaunt (gônt *or* gänt) *adj.* **1** so thin that the bones show; worn and lean, as from hunger or illness **2** looking gloomy and deserted [the *gaunt,* rocky coast of the island] —**gaunt′ly** *adv.* —**gaunt′ness** *n.*

geese (gēs) *n. plural of* **goose**

gen·tle (jent′l) *adj.* **1** mild, soft, or easy; not rough [a *gentle* touch; a *gentle* scolding] **2** tame; easy to handle [a *gentle* horse] **3** gradual; not sudden [a *gentle* slope] —**gen′tler, gen′tlest** —**gen′tle·ness** *n.*

ge·og·ra·phy (jē ôg′rə fē *or* jē ä′grə fē) *n.* **1** the study of the surface of the earth and how it is divided into continents, countries, seas, etc.: geography also deals with the climates, plants, animals, minerals, etc. of the earth **2** the natural features of a certain part of the earth [the *geography* of Ohio] —**ge·og′ra·pher** *n.*

ger·bil *or* **ger·bille** (jʉr′bəl) *n.* an animal like a mouse but with very long hind legs: it is found in Africa and Asia

ghost (gōst) *n.* **1** a pale, shadowy form that some people think they can see and that is supposed to be the spirit of a dead person **2** a mere shadow or slight trace [not a *ghost* of a chance]

gift (gift) *n.* **1** something given to show friendship, thanks, support, etc.; a present [Christmas *gifts;* a *gift* of $5,000 to a museum] **2** a natural ability; talent [a *gift* for writing catchy tunes]

gi·raffe (ji raf′) *n.* a large animal of Africa that chews its cud: it has a very long neck and legs and a spotted coat, and is the tallest animal alive

give (giv) *v.* **1** to pass or hand over to another [*Give* me your coat and I'll hang it up.] **2** to hand over to another to keep; make a gift of [My uncle *gave* a book to me for my birthday.] **3** to cause to have [Music *gives* me pleasure.] **4** to be the source of; supply [Cows *give* milk.] —**gave, giv′en, giv′ing**

gla·cier (glā′shər) *n.* a large mass of ice and snow that moves very slowly down a mountain or across land until it melts: icebergs are pieces of a glacier that have broken away into the sea

glove (gluv) *n.* **1** a covering to protect the hand, with a separate part for each finger and the thumb [Surgeons wear rubber *gloves.* Padded *gloves* are worn in playing baseball.] **2** a padded mitt worn in boxing: *also* **boxing glove** ◆*v.* to put gloves on —**gloved, glov′ing**

glow (glō) *v.* **1** to give off light because of great heat; be red-hot or white-hot [embers *glowing* in a fire] **2** to give out light without flame or heat [Fireflies *glow* in the dark.]

glue (glōō) *n.* **1** a thick, sticky substance made by boiling animal hoofs and bones, used for sticking things together **2** any sticky substance like this ◆*v.* **1** to stick together with glue **2** to keep or hold without moving [The exciting movie kept us *glued* to our seats.] —**glued, glu′ing** —**glue′y** *adj.*

gnaw (nô *or* nä) *v.* to bite and wear away bit by bit with the teeth [The rat *gnawed* the rope in two. The dog *gnawed* on the bone.]

gob·ble (gäb'əl) *v.* to eat quickly and greedily [She *gobbled* half the pizza before I finished a single piece.] —**gob'bled, gob'bling**

goose (g$\overline{oo}$s) *n.* a waterfowl that is like a duck but has a larger body and a longer neck; especially, the female of this bird: the male is called a *gander* —*pl.* **geese**

gov·ern·ment (guv'ərn mənt) *n.* **1** control or rule, as over a country, city, etc. **2** a system of ruling or controlling [a centralized *government*; democratic *governments*] **3** all the people who control the affairs of a country, city, etc. [The French *government* moved to Vichy during World War II.] —☆**gov·ern·men'tal** *adj.*

grab (grab) *v.* **1** to seize or snatch suddenly **2** to take by force or in a selfish way —**grabbed, grab'bing** ◆*n.* **1** the act of grabbing [He made a *grab* for the handle.] **2** something grabbed

grace·ful (grās'fəl) *adj.* having grace, or beauty of form or movement —**grace'ful·ly** *adv.* —**grace'ful·ness** *n.*

gram (gram) *n.* the basic unit of weight in the metric system: it is the weight of one cubic centimeter of distilled water at 4°C; one gram equals about 1/28 of an ounce

graph (graf) *n.* a chart or diagram that shows the changes taking place in something, by the use of connected lines, a curve, etc. [a *graph* showing how sales figures vary during the year]

Greece (grēs) a country in southeastern Europe, on the Mediterranean

greed·y (grēd'ē) *adj.* wanting or taking all that one can get with no thought of what others need [The *greedy* girl ate all the cookies.] —**greed'i·er, greed'i·est** —**greed'i·ly** *adv.* —**greed'i·ness** *n.*

grid·dle (grid'əl) *n.* a heavy, flat, metal plate or pan for cooking pancakes, etc.

griz·zly (griz'lē) *n.* a large, ferocious bear found in western North America —*pl.* **griz'zlies**

groan (grōn) *v.* to make a deep sound showing sorrow, pain, annoyance, or disapproval [We *groaned* when our team lost.]

gro·cer·y (grō'sər ē) *n.* ☆**1** a store selling food and household supplies **2** groceries, *pl.* the goods sold by a grocer —*pl.* **gro·cer·ies**

guess (ges) *v.* **1** to judge or decide about something without having enough facts to know for certain [Can you *guess* how old he is?] **2** to judge correctly by doing this [She *guessed* the exact number of beans in the jar.] **3** to think or suppose [I *guess* you're right.] ◆*n.* a judgment formed by guessing; surmise [Your *guess* is as good as mine.]—**guess'er** *n.,* **guessed**

gulp (gulp) *v.* to swallow in a hurried or greedy way [She *gulped* her breakfast and ran to school.] —**gulped, gulp'ing**

hair (her) *n.* **1** any of the thin growths, like threads, that come from the skin of animals and human beings **2** the whole number of these growths that cover a person's head, the skin of an animal, etc. [I must comb my *hair*.]

half (haf) *n.* **1** either of the two equal parts of something [Five is *half* of ten.] **2** either of two almost equal parts: *thought by some people to be not a proper use* [Take the smaller *half* of the pie.] **3** a half hour [It is *half* past two.]—*pl.* **halves** ◆*adj.* being either of the two equal parts [a *half* gallon.]

half·way (haf'wā') *adj.* **1** at the middle between two points or limits [to reach the *halfway* mark] **2** not complete; partial [to take *halfway* measures] ◆*adv.* **1** to the midway point; half the distance [They had gone *halfway* home.] **2** partially [The house is *halfway* built.]

halt (hôlt) *n., v.* stop [I worked all morning without a *halt*. Rain *halted* the game.]

halves (havz) *n. plural of* **half**

ham·mer (ham'ər) *n.* **1** a tool for driving in nails, breaking stones, shaping metal, etc.: it usually has a metal head and a handle **2** a thing like this in shape or use, as the part that strikes against the firing pin of a gun or any of the parts that strike the strings of a piano ◆*v.* to hit with many blows [They *hammered* on the door with their fists.]

hand (hand) *n.* **1** the end of the arm beyond the wrist, including the palm, fingers, and thumb **2** any of the pointers on a clock or watch **3** a person hired to work with the hands [a farm *hand*; dock *hand*] **4** help [Give me a *hand* with this job.] **5** a clapping of hands; applause [Give the dancer a big *hand*.] ◆*v.* to give with the hand; pass [*Hand* me the book, please.]

hand·ker·chief (haŋ'kər chif) *n.* a small piece of cloth for wiping the nose, eyes, or face, or worn as a decoration —*pl.* **hand'ker·chiefs**

hand

a	ask, fat
ā	ape, date
ä	car, lot
e	elf, ten
ē	even, meet
i	is, hit
ī	ice, fire
ō	open, go
ô	law, horn
oi	oil, point
$\overline{oo}$	look, pull
$\overline{oo}$	ooze, tool
ou	out, crowd
u	up, cut
ʉ	fur, fern
ə	a in ago
	e in agent
	e in father
	i in unity
	o in collect
	u in focus
ch	chin, arch
ŋ	ring, singer
sh	she, dash
th	thin, truth
th	then, father
zh	s in pleasure

167

hap·py (hap'ē) *adj.* **1** feeling or showing pleasure or joy; glad; contented [a *happy* child; a *happy* song] **2** lucky; fortunate [The story has a *happy* ending.]
—**hap'pi·er, hap'pi·est** —**hap'pi·ly** *adv.*
—**hap'pi·ness** *n.*

har·bor (här'bər) *n.* **1** a place where ships may anchor and be safe from storms; port; haven **2** any place where one is safe; shelter ◆*v.* to shelter or hide [to *harbor* an outlaw]

hare (her) *n.* a swift animal with long ears, a split upper lip, large front teeth used for gnawing, and long, powerful hind legs: hares are related to rabbits but are usually larger

har·vest (här'vəst) *n.* the act or process of gathering a crop of grain, fruit, or vegetables when it becomes ripe

has·n't (haz'ənt) *contraction* has not

haunt (hônt *or* hänt) *v.* **1** to spend much time at; visit often [We like to *haunt* bookstores. A *haunted* house is one that is supposed to be visited by a ghost.] **2** to keep coming back to the mind [Memories *haunt* her.] ◆*n.* a place often visited [They made the library their *haunt*.]

heal (hēl) *v.* to get or bring back to good health or a sound condition; cure or mend [The wound *healed* slowly. Time *heals* grief.]

heart (härt) *n.* **1** the hollow muscle that gets blood from the veins and sends it through the arteries by squeezing together and expanding **2** the part at the center [*hearts* of celery; the *heart* of the jungle] **3** the main or most important part [Get to the *heart* of the matter.] **4** the human heart thought of as the part that feels love, kindness, pity, sadness, etc. [a tender *heart*; a heavy *heart*]

hearth (härth) *n.* the stone or brick floor of a fireplace

heav·y (hev'ē) *adj.* **1** hard to lift or move because of its weight; weighing very much [a *heavy* load] **2** weighing more than is usual for its kind [Lead is a *heavy* metal.] **3** larger, deeper, greater, etc. than usual [a *heavy* vote; a *heavy* sleep; a *heavy* blow]
—**heav'i·er, heav'i·est** ◆*adv.* in a heavy manner [*heavy*-laden]

heel (hēl) *n.* **1** the back part of the foot, below the ankle and behind the arch **2** that part of a stocking or sock which covers the heel **3** the part of a shoe that is built up to support the heel

herd (hurd) *n.* a number of cattle or other large animals feeding or living together [a *herd* of cows; a *herd* of elephants] ◆*v.* **1** to form into a herd, group, or crowd **2** to take care of a herd of animals

heel

her·on (her'ən) *n.* a wading bird with long legs, a long neck, and a long, pointed bill: herons live in marshes or along river banks

hes·i·tate (hez'i tāt') *v.* **1** to stop or hold back, as because of feeling unsure [Never *hesitate* to speak the truth. He *hesitated* at the door before entering.] **2** to feel unwilling [I *hesitate* to ask you for money.]
—**hes'i·tat·ed, hes'i·tat·ing**

high·way (hī'wā) *n.* a main road

hob·by (häb'ē) *n.* something that one likes to do, study, etc. for pleasure in one's spare time [Her *hobby* is collecting coins.]
—*pl.* **hob'bies**

hoe (hō) *n.* a garden tool with a thin, flat blade on a long handle: it is used for removing weeds, loosening the soil, etc. ◆*v.* to dig, loosen soil, etc. with a hoe
—**hoed, hoe'ing**

hol·i·day (häl'ə dā) *n.* **1** a day on which most people do not have to work, often one set aside by law [Thanksgiving is a *holiday* in all states.] **2** a religious festival; holy day [Easter is a Christian *holiday*.]

hol·low (häl'ō) *adj.* **1** having an empty space on the inside; not solid [a *hollow* log] **2** shaped like a bowl; concave **3** sunken in [*hollow* cheeks] —**hol'low·ness** *n.*

home·work (hōm'wurk) *n.* **1** lessons to be studied or schoolwork to be done outside the classroom **2** any work to be done at home

hom·o·nym (häm'ə nim) *n.* a word that is pronounced like another word, but has a different meaning and is usually spelled differently ["Bore" and "boar" are *homonyms*.]

hon·est (än'əst) *adj.* **1** that does not steal, cheat, or lie; upright or trustworthy [an *honest* person] **2** got in a fair way, not by stealing, cheating, or lying [to earn an *honest* living] **3** sincere or genuine [He made an *honest* effort.]

hoof (hoof *or* hoof) *n.* **1** the horny covering on the feet of cows, horses, deer, pigs, etc. **2** the whole foot of such an animal
—*pl.* **hoofs** or **hooves**

hor·ri·fy (hôr'ə fī) *v.* to fill with horror [He was *horrified* at the sight of the victims.] —**hor'ri·fied, hor'ri·fy·ing**

horse·shoe (hôrs' shoo) *n.* **1** a flat metal plate shaped like a U, nailed to a horse's hoof to protect it **2** anything shaped like this **3** **horseshoes,** *pl.* a game in which the players toss horseshoes at a stake in the ground

host·ess (hōs'təs) *n.* **1** a woman who has guests in her own home, or who pays for their entertainment away from home **2** a woman hired by a restaurant to welcome people and show them to their tables
—*pl.* **host'ess·es**

hour (our) *n.* **1** any of the 24 equal parts of a day; 60 minutes **2** a particular time [At what *hour* shall we meet?] **3** *often* hours, *pl.* a particular period of time [the dinner *hour*; the doctor's office *hours*]

how (hou) *adv.* **1** in what way [*How* do you start the motor? She taught him *how* to dance.] **2** in what condition [*How* is your mother today?] **3** for what reason; why [*How* is it that you don't know?]

how's (houz) *contraction* **1** how is **2** how has **3** how does

hum (hum) *v.* **1** to make a low, steady, buzzing sound like that of a bee or a motor **2** to sing with the lips closed, not saying the words —**hummed, hum′ming**

☆**hum·ming·bird** (hum′iŋ burd′) *n.* a tiny bird with a long, thin bill that it uses to suck nectar from flowers: its wings move very fast, with a humming sound, and it can hover in the air

hun·dred (hun′drəd) *n., adj.* ten times ten; the number 100

hur·ri·cane (hur′ə kān) *n.* a very strong windstorm, often with heavy rain, in which the wind blows in a circle at 73 or more miles per hour: hurricanes usually start in the West Indies and move northward

hur·ry (hur′ē) *v.* **1** to move, send, or carry quickly or too quickly [You fell because you *hurried*. A taxi *hurried* us home.] **2** to make happen or be done more quickly [Please try to *hurry* those letters.] **3** to try to make move or act faster [Don't *hurry* me when I'm eating.] —**hur′ried, hur′ry·ing**

hy·giene (hī′jēn) *n.* the practice of keeping clean [good personal *hygiene*]

Ii

i·de·a (ī dē′ə) *n.* **1** something one thinks, knows, imagines, feels, etc.; belief or thought **2** a plan or purpose [an *idea* for making money]

im·mov·a·ble (im mo͞ov′ə bəl) *adj.* **1** that cannot be moved; firmly fixed [The ancients thought the earth *immovable*.] **2** not changing; steadfast [an *immovable* purpose]

im·pa·tient (im pā′shənt) *adj.* not patient; not willing to put up with delay or annoyance [*impatient* customers standing in line]

im·per·fect (im pur′fikt) *adj.* **1** not perfect; having some fault or flaw **2** lacking in something; not complete; unfinished [an *imperfect* knowledge of Russian] —**im·per′fect·ly adv.**

im·per·son·al (im′pur′sən əl) *adj.* not referring to any particular person [The teacher's remarks about cheating were *impersonal* and meant for all the students.] —**im′per′son·al·ly adv.**

im·prac·ti·cal (im′prak′ti kəl) *adj.* not practical; not useful, efficient, etc.

im·pure (im pyo͞or′) *adj.* **1** not clean; dirty [Smoke made the air *impure*.] **2** mixed with things that do not belong [*impure* gold] **3** not decent or proper [*impure* thoughts]

in·de·pend·ent (in′dē pen′dənt) *adj.* **1** not ruled or controlled by another; self-governing [Many colonies became *independent* countries after World War II.] **2** not connected with others; separate [an *independent* grocer] **3** not influenced by others; thinking for oneself [an *independent* voter] —**in′de·pend′ent·ly adv.**

In·di·a (in′dē ə) **1** a large peninsula of southern Asia **2** a country in the central and southern part of this peninsula

in·ju·ry (in′jər ē) *n.* harm or damage done to a person or thing [*injuries* received in a fall; *injury* to one's good name] —*pl.* **in′ju·ries**

in·stant (in′stənt) *n.* a very short time; moment [Wait just an *instant*.]

in·stead (in sted′) *adv.* in place of the other; as a substitute [If you have no cream, use milk *instead*.]

in·tel·li·gent (in tel′ə jənt) *adj.* having or showing intelligence, especially high intelligence —**in·tel′li·gent·ly adv.**

is·land (ī′lənd) *n.* **1** a piece of land smaller than a continent and surrounded by water **2** any place set apart from what surrounds it [The oasis was an *island* of green in the desert.]

It·a·ly (it′l ē) a country in southern Europe, including the islands of Sicily and Sardinia

Jj

jag·uar (jag′wär) *n.* a large wildcat that looks like a large leopard: it is yellowish with black spots and is found from the southwestern U.S. to Argentina

Jan·u·ar·y (jan′yo͞o er′ē) *n.* the first month of the year, which has 31 days: abbreviated **Jan.**

Ja·pan (jə pan′) a country east of Korea, made up of many islands

jaw (jô *or* jä) *n.* **1** either of the two bony parts that form the frame of the mouth and that hold the teeth **2** either of two parts that close to grip or crush something

a	ask, fat
ā	ape, date
ä	car, lot
e	elf, ten
ē	even, meet
i	is, hit
ī	ice, fire
ō	open, go
ô	law, horn
oi	oil, point
o͝o	look, pull
o͞o	ooze, tool
ou	out, crowd
u	up, cut
ʉ	fur, fern
ə	a in ago
	e in agent
	e in father
	i in unity
	o in collect
	u in focus
ch	chin, arch
ŋ	ring, singer
sh	she, dash
th	thin, truth
th	then, father
zh	s in pleasure

[A vise and a pair of pliers have *jaws*.]
3 jaws, the mouth; also, the entrance of a canyon, valley, etc.

jog (jäg) *v.* **1** to give a little shake to; jostle or nudge [*Jog* him to see if he's awake.] **2** to shake up or rouse, as the memory or the mind —**jogged, jog´ging** ◆*n.* **1** a little shake or nudge **2** a jogging pace; trot —**jog´ger**

jog

jour·nal (jʉr´nəl) *n.* **1** a daily record of what happens, such as a diary [She kept a *journal* of her trip.] **2** a written record of what happens at the meetings of a legislature, club, etc. **3** a newspaper or magazine

jour·ney (jʉr´nē) *n.* a traveling from one place to another; trip —*pl.* **jour´neys** ◆*v.* to go on a trip; travel —**jour´neyed, jour´ney·ing**

judge (juj) *n.* **1** a public official with power to hear cases in a law court and decide what laws apply to them **2** a person chosen to decide the winner in a contest or to settle an argument ◆*v.* **1** to decide the winner of a contest or settle an argument [to *judge* a beauty contest] **2** to form an opinion on something [Don't *judge* by first impressions.] —**judged, judg´ing** —**judg´ship´** *n.*

juic·y (jōō´sē) *adj.* full of juice [a *juicy* plum] —**juic´i·er, juic´i·est**

Ju·ly (jōō lī´) *n.* the seventh month of the year, which has 31 days; abbreviated **Jul.**

June (jōōn) *n.* the sixth month of the year, which has 30 days; abbreviated **Jun.**

Kk

kay·ak (kī´ak) *n.* an Eskimo canoe made of a wooden frame covered with skins all around, except for an opening for the paddler

kelp (kelp) *n.* a brown seaweed that is large and coarse

kil·o·gram (kil´ə gram) *n.* a unit of weight, equal to 1,000 grams

kil·o·li·ter (kil´ə lēt´ər) *n.* a unit of volume, equal to 1,000 liters or one cubic meter

kiss (kis) *v.* **1** to touch with the lips as a way of showing love, respect, etc. or as a greeting **2** to touch lightly [Her bowling ball just *kissed* the last pin.] ◆*n.* a touch or caress with the lips —*pl.* **kiss´es**

knap·sack (nap´sak) *n.* a leather or canvas bag worn on the back, as by hikers, for carrying supplies

knead (nēd) *v.* to keep pressing and squeezing dough or clay to make it ready for use [to *knead* bread dough]

knife (nīf) *n.* **1** a tool having a flat, sharp blade set in a handle, used for cutting **2** a cutting blade that is part of a machine —*pl.* **knives** ◆*v.* to cut or stab with a knife —**knifed, knif´ing**

knives (nīvz) *n.* plural of **knife**

know (nō) *v.* **1** to be sure of or have the facts about [Do you *know* why grass is green? She *knows* the law.] **2** to be aware of; realize [He suddenly *knew* he would be late.] **3** to have in one's mind or memory [The actress *knows* her lines.] **4** to be acquainted with [I *know* your brother well.] —**knew, known, know´ing**

knowl·edge (nä´lij) *n.* the fact or condition of knowing [*Knowledge* of the crime spread through the town.]

known (nōn) *past participle of* **know**

knuck·le (nuk´əl) *n.* **1** a joint of the finger; especially, a joint connecting a finger to the rest of the hand **2** the knee or hock joint of a pig, calf, etc., used as food —◆☆*v.* **knuckle down**, to work hard —**knuckle under**, to give in

kook·a·bur·ra (kook´ə bʉr ə) *n.* an Australian bird related to the kingfisher: its cry sounds like someone laughing loudly

Ll

la·dy (lā´dē) *n.* **1** a woman, especially one who is polite and refined and has a sense of honor **2** a woman belonging to a family of high social standing, as the wife of a lord —*pl.* **la´dies**

land·ing (lan´diŋ) *n.* **1** a coming to shore or a putting on shore [the *landing* of troops] **2** a place where a ship can land; pier or dock **3** a platform at the end of a flight of stairs **4** a coming down after flying, jumping, or falling

late (lāt) *adj., n.* **1** happening or coming after the usual or expected time; tardy [*late* for school; a *late* train] **2** happening or appearing just before now; recent [a *late* news broadcast] —**lat´er** or **lat´ter, lat´est** or **last** ◆*adv.* **1** after the usual or expected time [Roses bloomed *late* last year.] **2** toward the end of some period [They came *late* in the day.] —**lat´er, lat´est** —**late´ness** *n.*

lat·i·tude (lat´ə tōōd or lat´ə tyōōd) *n.* **1** freedom from strict rules; freedom to do as one wishes [Our school allows some *latitude* in choosing courses.] **2** distance north or south of the equator, measured in degrees [Minneapolis is at 45 degrees north *latitude*.]

laugh (laf) **v. 1** to make a series of quick sounds with the voice that show one is amused or happy or, sometimes, that show scorn: one usually smiles or grins when laughing ◆**n.** the act or sound of laughing

launch (lônch *or* länch) **v. 1** to throw, hurl, or send off into space [to *launch* a rocket] **2** to cause to slide into the water; set afloat [to *launch* a new ship] **3** to start or begin [to *launch* an attack]

law·yer (lô′yər *or* lä′yər) **n.** a person whose profession is giving advice on law or acting for others in lawsuits

lead (lēd) **v. 1** to show the way for; guide [*Lead* us along the path. The lights *led* me to the house.] **2** to go or make go in some direction [This path *leads* to the lake. Drainpipes *lead* the water away.] **3** to be at the head of or be first [He *leads* the band. Their team was *leading* at the half.] —**led** (led), **lead′ing** ◆**n. 1** the first place or position [The bay horse is in the *lead*.] **2** a clue [The police followed up every *lead*.]

lead·ing (lē′diŋ) **adj. 1** that leads; guiding [A *leading* question guides one toward a certain answer.] **2** most important; playing a chief role [She played a *leading* part in our campaign.]

leaf (lēf) **n. 1** any of the flat, green parts growing from the stem of a plant or tree **2** a petal [a rose *leaf*] **3** a sheet of paper in a book [Each side of a *leaf* is a page.] —*pl.* **leaves**

learn (lɣrn) **v. 1** to get some knowledge or skill, as by studying or being taught [I have *learned* to knit. Some people never *learn* from experience.] **2** to find out about something; come to know [When did you *learn* of his illness?] **3** to fix in the mind; memorize [*Learn* this poem by tomorrow.] —**learned** (lɣrnd) *or* **learnt** (lɣrnt), **learn′ing** —**learn′er n.**

leash (lēsh) **n.** a strap or chain by which a dog, etc. is led or held —*pl.* **leash′es** ◆**v.** to put a leash on

leaves (lēvz) **n.** *plural of* **leaf**

leg·end (lej′ənd) **n. 1** a story handed down through the years and connected with some real events, but probably not true in itself [The story of King Arthur is a British *legend*.] **2** all such stories as a group [famous in Irish *legend*]

☆**length·y** (leŋkth′ē) **adj.** long or too long [a *lengthy* speech] —**length′i·er, length′i·est** —**length′i·ly adv.**

leop·ard (lep′ərd) **n. 1** a large, fierce animal of the cat family, having a tan coat with black spots: it is found in Africa and Asia **2** *another name for* **jaguar**

let's (lets) **contraction** let us

let·ter (let′ər) **n. 1** any of the marks used in writing or printing to stand for a sound of speech; character of an alphabet **2** a written message, usually sent by mail ◆**v.** to print letters by hand [Will you *letter* this poster?]

li·brar·y (lī′brer′ē) **n. 1** a place where a collection of books is kept for reading or borrowing **2** a collection of books —*pl.* **li′brar′ies**

life (līf) **n. 1** the quality of plants and animals that makes it possible for them to take in food, grow, produce others of their kind, etc. and that makes them different from rocks, water, etc. [Death is the loss of *life*.] **2** a living thing; especially, a human being [The crash took six *lives*.] —*pl.* **lives**

life·boat (līf′bōt) **n. 1** any of the small boats carried by a ship for use if the ship must be abandoned **2** a sturdy boat kept on a shore, for use in rescuing people in danger of drowning

lift (lift) **v. 1** to bring up to a higher place; raise [Please *lift* that box onto the truck.] **2** to rise or go up [Our spirits *lifted* when spring came.] ◆**n. 1** a ride in the direction one is going **2** a device for carrying people up or down a slope [a ski *lift*]

lis·ten (lis′ən) **v.** to pay attention in order to hear; try to hear [*Listen* to the rain. *Listen* when the counselor speaks.] —**lis′ten·er n.**

li·ter (lēt′ər) **n.** the basic unit of capacity in the metric system, equal to 1 cubic decimeter: a liter is equal to a little more than a quart in liquid measure and to a little less than a quart in dry measure

lives (līvz) **n.** *plural of* **life**

loaf (lōf) **n. 1** a portion of bread baked in one piece, usually oblong in shape **2** any food baked in this shape [a meat *loaf*] —*pl.* **loaves**

loan (lōn) **n. 1** the act of lending [Thanks for the *loan* of your pen.] **2** something lent, especially a sum of money ◆**v.** to lend, especially a sum of money or something to be returned —**loaned, loan′ing**

loaves (lōvz) **n.** *plural of* **loaf**

lo·cate (lō′kāt *or* lō kāt′) **v. 1** to set up or place; situate [Their shop is *located* in the new mall.] **2** to find out where something is [Have you *located* the gloves that you lost?] —**lo′cat·ed, lo′cat·ing**

lock (läk) **n. 1** a device for fastening a door, safe, etc. by means of a bolt: a lock can usually be opened only by a special key, etc. **2** an enclosed part of a canal, river, etc. with gates at each end: water can be let in or out of it to raise or lower ships from one level to another ◆**v.** to fasten or become fastened with a lock [I *locked* the door.] —**locked, lock′ing**

lock

a	ask, fat
ā	ape, date
ä	car, lot
e	elf, ten
ē	even, meet
i	is, hit
ī	ice, fire
ō	open, go
ô	law, horn
oi	oil, point
͞oo	look, pull
o͞o	ooze, tool
ou	out, crowd
u	up, cut
ɣ	fur, fern
ə	a in ago
	e in agent
	e in father
	i in unity
	o in collect
	u in focus
ch	chin, arch
ŋ	ring, singer
sh	she, dash
th	thin, truth
th	then, father
zh	s in pleasure

lo·co·mo·tive (lō'kə mō'tiv) *n.* a steam, electric, or diesel engine on wheels, that pulls or pushes railroad trains ◆*adj.* moving or able to move from one place to another

lodge (läj) *n.* **1** a place to live in; especially a small house for some special purpose [a hunting *lodge*] **2** the hut or tent of an American Indian ◆*v.* **1** to provide with a place to live or sleep in for a time [She agreed to *lodge* the strangers overnight.] **2** to come to rest and stick firmly [A fish bone *lodged* in her throat.] —**lodged, lodg'ing**

lone·ly (lōn'lē) *adj.* **1** unhappy because one is alone or away from friends or family [Billy was *lonely* his first day at camp.] **2** without others nearby; alone [a *lonely* cottage] **3** with few or no people [a *lonely* island] —**lone'li·er, lone'li·est** —**lone'li·ness** *n.*

love (luv) *n.* **1** a deep and tender feeling of fondness and devotion [parents' *love* for their children; the *love* of Romeo and Juliet] **2** a strong liking [a *love* of books] **3** a person that one loves [my own true *love*] ◆*v.* to feel love for [to *love* one's parents; to *love* all people] —**loved, lov'ing**

love·ly (luv'lē) *adj.* very pleasing in looks or character; beautiful [a *lovely* person] —**love'li·er, love'li·est**

loy·al (loi'əl) *adj.* **1** faithful to one's country [a *loyal* citizen] **2** faithful to one's family, duty, or beliefs [a *loyal* friend]

luck·y (luk'ē) *adj.* having good luck [She is *lucky* to go to Rome.] —**luck'i·er, luck'i·est**

lug·gage (lug'ij) *n.* the suitcases, trunks, etc. of a traveler; baggage

locomotive

Mm

mag·ni·fy (mag'nə fī') *v.* to make look or seem larger than is really so [to *magnify* an object with a lens] —**mag'ni·fied', mag'ni·fy'ing**

mam·mal (mam'əl) *n.* any warm-blooded animal with a backbone; female mammals have glands that produce milk for feeding their young —**mam·ma'li·an** (mə mā'lē ən) *adj., n.*

mam·moth (mam'əth) *n.* a type of large elephant that lived long ago: mammoths had a hairy skin and long tusks that curved upward ◆*adj.* very big; huge

man (man) *n.* an adult male human being **2** any human being; person ["that all *men* are created equal"] —*pl.* **men**

man·ag·er (man'ij ər) *n.* a person who manages a business, baseball team, etc.

man·a·tee (man'ə tē) *n.* a large animal that lives in shallow tropical waters and feeds on plants: it has flippers and a broad, flat tail; sea cow

March (märch) *n.* the third month of the year, which has 31 days: abbreviated **Mar.**

marsh·mal·low (märsh'mel'ō *or* märsh'mal'ō) *n.* a soft, white, spongy candy coated with powdered sugar

mas·cot (mas'kät) *n.* a person, animal, or thing thought to bring good luck by being present [Our team's *mascot* is the lion.]

match¹ (mach) *n.* **1** a slender piece of wood or cardboard having a tip coated with a chemical that catches fire when rubbed on a certain surface **2** a slowly burning cord or wick once used for firing a gun or cannon —*pl.* **match'es**

match² (mach) *n.* **1** two or more people or things that go well together [That suit and tie are a good *match*.] **2** a game or contest between two persons or teams [a tennis *match*]

mead·ow (med'ō) *n.* **1** a piece of land where grass is grown for hay **2** low, level grassland near a stream or lake

mean·ing (mēn'iŋ) *n.* what is meant; what is supposed to be understood; significance [She repeated her words to make her *meaning* clear. What is the *meaning* of this poem?] —**mean'ing·ful** *adj.*

meas·ure (mezh'ər) *v.* **1** to find out the size, amount, or extent of, as by comparing with something else [*Measure* the child's height with a yardstick. How do you *measure* a person's worth?] **2** to set apart or mark off a certain amount or length of [*Measure* out three pounds of sugar.] **3** to be of a certain size, amount, or extent [The table *measures* five feet on each side.] —**meas'ured, meas'ur·ing** ◆*n.* the size, amount, or extent of something, found out by measuring [The *measure* of the bucket is 15 liters.] **2** the notes or rests between two bars on a staff of music **3** rhythm or meter, as of a poem or song

meat (mēt) *n.* **1** the flesh of animals used as food: meat usually does not include fish and often does not include poultry **2** the part that can be eaten [the *meat* of a nut]

med·i·cine (med'ə sən) *n.* **1** any substance used in or on the body to treat disease, lessen pain, heal, etc. **2** the science of treating and preventing disease **3** the branch of this science that makes use of drugs, diet, etc., especially as separate from surgery

mel·o·dy (mel′ə dē) **n.** **1** an arrangement of musical tones in a series so as to form a tune; often, the main tune in the harmony of a musical piece [The *melody* is played by the oboes.] **2** any pleasing series of sounds [a *melody* sung by birds] —*pl.* **mel′o·dies**

mem·ber (mem′bər) **n.** **1** any of the persons who make up a church, club, political party, or other group **2** a leg, arm, or other part of the body

mem·o·ry (mem′ər ē) **n.** **1** the act or power of remembering [to have a good *memory*] **2** all that one remembers **3** something remembered [The music brought back many *memories*.] **4** the part of a computer that stores information —*pl.* **mem′o·ries**

men (men) **n.** *plural of* **man**

mend (mend) **v.** to put back in good condition; repair; fix [to *mend* a torn shirt] —**mend′ed, mend′ing**

men·u (men′yo͞o) **n.** a list of the foods served at a meal [a restaurant's dinner *menu*]

me·ter (mēt′ər) **n.** **1** a measure of length that is the basic unit in the metric system: one meter is equal to 39.37 inches **2** rhythm in poetry; regular arrangement of accented and unaccented syllables in each line **3** rhythm in music; arrangement of beats in each measure [Marches are often in 4/4 *meter*, with four equal beats in each measure.]

Mi·am·i (mī am′ē) a city on the southeastern coast of Florida

mice (mīs) **n.** *plural of* **mouse**

mi·cro·wave (mī′krō wāv′) **n.** any radio wave within a certain range, usually between 300,000 and 300 megahertz: those of a certain wavelength create great heat when they pass through substances such as food. A **microwave oven** uses these waves for fast cooking: others are used to transmit signals to and from communications satellites

mi·grate (mī′grāt) **v.** **1** to move from one place or country to another, especially in order to make a new home **2** to move from one region to another when the season changes, as some birds do in the spring and fall —**mi′grat·ed, mi′grat·ing** —**mi·gra′tion n.**

milk (milk) **n.** a white liquid formed in special glands of female mammals for suckling their young: the milk that is a common food comes from cows ◆**v.** to squeeze milk out from a cow, goat, etc. —**milk′er n.** —**milk′ing n.**

mil·li·gram (mil′i gram) **n.** a unit of weight, equal to one thousandth of a gram

mil·li·li·ter (mil′i lēt′ər) **n.** a unit of volume, equal to one thousandth of a liter

mil·li·me·ter (mil′i mēt′ər) **n.** a unit of measure, equal to one thousandth of a meter (.03937 inch)

min·er·al (min′ər əl) **n.** **1** a substance formed in the earth by nature; especially, a solid substance that was never animal or vegetable [Iron, granite, and salt are *minerals*. Coal is sometimes called a *mineral*, too.] **2** any of certain elements, as iron or phosphorus, needed by plants and animals

miss (mis) **v.** **1** to fail to hit, meet, reach, get, catch, see, hear, etc. [The arrow *missed* the target. We *missed* our plane. I *missed* you at the play last night.] **2** to let go by; fail to take [You *missed* your turn.] **3** to escape; avoid [He just *missed* being hit.] —**missed**

mol·lusk or **mol·lusc** (mäl′əsk) **n.** an animal with a soft body that is usually protected by a shell, as the oyster, clam, snail, etc.

☆**moose** (mo͞os) **n.** a large animal related to the deer, of the northern U.S. and Canada: the male has broad antlers with many points —*pl.* **moose**

moun·tain (mount′n) **n.** **1** a part of the earth's surface that rises high into the air; very high hill **2 mountains,** *pl.* a chain or group of such high hills

mouse (mous) **n.** **1** a small, gnawing animal found in houses and fields throughout the world —*pl.* **mice** (mīs) ☆**2** a small device moved by the hand, as on a flat surface, so as to make the cursor move on a computer terminal —*pl.* **mouses**

mov·er (mo͞ov′ər) **n.** a person or thing that moves; especially, ☆one whose work is moving people's furniture from one home to another

mug·ger (mug′ər) **n.** a person who assaults others, usually in order to rob them

mul·ti·ply (mul′tə plī) **v.** **1** to become more, greater, etc.; increase [Our troubles *multiplied*.] **2** to repeat a certain figure a certain number of times [If you *multiply* 10 by 4, or repeat 10 four times, you get the product 40.] —**mul′ti·plied, mul′ti·ply·ing**

mus·cle (mus′l) **n.** **1** the tissue in an animal's body that makes up the fleshy parts: muscle can be stretched or tightened to move the parts of the body **2** any single part or band of this tissue [The biceps is a *muscle* in the upper arm.] **3** strength that comes from muscles that are developed; brawn

mu·si·cal (myo͞o′zi kəl) **adj.** **1** of music or for making music [a *musical* score; a *musical* instrument] **2** like music; full of melody, harmony, etc. [Wind has a *musical* sound.] **3** fond of music or skilled in music —**mu′si·cal·ly adv.**

milk

a	ask, fat
ā	ape, date
ä	car, lot
e	elf, ten
ē	even, meet
i	is, hit
ī	ice, fire
ō	open, go
ô	law, horn
oi	oil, point
o͝o	look, pull
o͞o	ooze, tool
ou	out, crowd
u	up, cut
ʉ	fur, fern
ə	a in ago
	e in agent
	e in father
	i in unity
	o in collect
	u in focus
ch	chin, arch
ŋ	ring, singer
sh	she, dash
th	thin, truth
th	then, father
zh	s in pleasure

☆**musk·rat** (musk′rat) *n.* **1** a North American animal that is like a large rat: it lives in water and has glossy brown fur

mys·ter·y (mis′tər ē *or* mis′trə) *n.* **1** any event or thing that remains unexplained or is so secret that it makes people curious [That murder is still a *mystery*.] **2** a story or play about such an event [She read a murder *mystery*.] —*pl.* **mys′ter·ies**

need (nēd) *v.* to require; want [She *needs* a car.]

neigh·bor (nā′bər) *n.* **1** a person who lives near another **2** a person or thing that is near another [France and Spain are *neighbors*.] **3** another human being; fellow person ["Love thy *neighbor*."]

neph·ew (nef′yo͞o) *n.* **1** the son of one's brother or sister **2** the son of one's brother-in-law or sister-in-law

nerv·ous (nʉr′vəs) *adj.* feeling fear or expecting trouble [He is *nervous* about seeing the dentist.]

night·in·gale (nīt′n gāl) *n.* a small European thrush: the male is known for its sweet singing

noise (noiz) *n.* sound, especially a loud, harsh, or confused sound [the *noise* of fireworks; *noises* of a city street] —*pl.* **nois′es** ◆*v.* to make public by telling; spread [to *noise* a rumor about] —**noised, nois′ing**

nom·i·nate (näm′ə nāt) *v.* **1** to name as a candidate for an election [Each political party *nominates* a person to run for president.] **2** to appoint to a position [The president *nominates* the members of the Cabinet.] —**nom′i·nat·ed, nom′i·nat·ing**

non·fic·tion (nän′fik′shən) *n.* a piece of writing about the real world, real people, or true events, as a biography or history

non·prof·it (nän präf′it) *adj.* not intending to make a profit [a *nonprofit* hospital]

non·sense (nän′sens) *n.* **1** speech or writing that is foolish or has no meaning [I read the letter but it just sounded like *nonsense* to me.] **2** silly or annoying behavior [She is a teacher who will put up with no *nonsense* in the classroom.] ◆*interj.* how silly! how foolish! indeed not!

non·stop (nän′stäp′) *adj., adv.* without making a stop [to fly *nonstop* from New York to Seattle]

North America the northern continent in the Western Hemisphere: Canada, the United States, Mexico, and the countries of Central America are in North America

north·west (nôrth west′ *or* nôr west′) *n.* **1** the direction halfway between north and west **2** a place or region in or toward this direction ◆*adj.* **1** in, of, or toward the northwest [the *northwest* part of the county] **2** from the northwest [a *northwest* wind] ◆*adv.* in or toward the northwest [to sail *northwest*]

numb (num) *adj.* not able to feel, or feeling very little; deadened [My toes were *numb* with cold. He sat *numb* with grief.] ◆*v.* to make numb —**numb′ly** *adv.* **numb′ness** *n.*

nurse (nʉrs) *n.* a person who has been trained to take care of sick people and help doctors

nu·tri·ent (no͞o′trē ənt *or* nyo͞o′trē ənt) *adj.* nourishing ◆*n.* any of the substances in food that are needed for health, such as proteins, minerals, vitamins, etc.

o·cean·og·ra·phy (o′shən äg′rə fē) *n.* the science that studies the oceans and the animals and plants that live in them —**o′cean·og′ra·pher**

of·ten (ôf′ən *or* ôf′tən) *adv.* many times; frequently

o·pen (ō′pən) *adj.* not closed, shut, covered, or stopped up [*open* eyes; *open* doors; an *open* jar; an *open* drain] ◆*v.* **1** to make or become open, or no longer closed [Please *open* that trunk. The door suddenly *opened*.] **2** to begin or start [We *opened* the program with a song.] **3** to start operating [She *opened* a new store. School will *open* in September.] —**o′pened** —**o′pen·ly** *adv.* —**o′pen·ness** *n.*

op·er·a·tor (äp′ər āt ər) *n.* ☆**1** a person who operates a machine or device [a telephone *operator*] **2** an owner or manager of a factory, mine, etc.

or·gan (ôr′gən) *n.* **1** a musical instrument having sets of pipes that make sounds when keys or pedals are pressed to send air through the pipes; *also called* **pipe organ** **2** a part of an animal or plant that has some special purpose [The heart, lungs, and eyes are *organs* of the body.]

or·gan·i·za·tion (ôr′gə ni zā′shən) *n.* **1** the act of organizing or arranging **2** a group of persons organized for some purpose

or·gan·ize (ôr′gə nīz) *v.* to arrange or place according to a system [The library books are *organized* according to their subjects.] —**or′gan·ized, or′gan·iz·ing** —**or′gan·iz′er** *n.*

or·phan (ôr′fən) *n.* a child whose parents are dead or, sometimes, one of whose parents is dead ◆*adj.* **1** being an orphan [an *orphan* child] **2** of or for orphans [an *orphan* home] ◆*v.* to cause to become an orphan [children *orphaned* by war]

os·trich (äs′trich) *n.* a very large bird of Africa and southwestern Asia, with a long neck and long legs: it cannot fly, but runs swiftly

ot·ter (ät′ər) *n.* **1** a furry animal related to the weasel: it has webbed feet used in swimming and a long tail, and it eats small animals and fish

☆**out·doors** (out′dôrz′) *adv.* in or into the open; outside [We went *outdoors* to play.] ◆*n.* (out dôrz′) the world outside of buildings; the open air

out·fit (out′fit) *n.* the clothing or equipment used in some work, activity, etc. [a hiking *outfit*] ◆*v.* to supply with what is needed [Their store *outfits* campers.] —**out′fit·ted, out′fit·ting**

out·stand·ing (out′stan′diŋ) *adj.* that stands out as very good or important [an *outstanding* lawyer]

☆**o·ver·coat** (ō′vər kōt) *n.* a heavy coat worn outdoors in cold weather

ox (äks) *n.* **1** a castrated male of the cattle family, used for pulling heavy loads **2** any animal of a group that chew their cud and have cloven hoofs, including the buffalo, bison, etc. —*pl.* **ox·en** (äk′s′n)

Pp

pace (pās) *n.* **1** a step in walking or running **2** the length of a step or stride, thought of as about 30 to 40 inches **3** the rate of speed at which something moves or develops [The scoutmaster set the *pace* in the hike. Science goes forward at a rapid *pace*.] ◆*v.* **1** to walk back and forth across [While waiting for the verdict, I *paced* the floor nervously.] **2** to measure by paces [*Pace* off 30 yards.] —**paced, pac′ing** —**pac′er** *n.*

pad (pad) *n.* **1** anything made of or stuffed with soft material, and used to protect against blows, to give comfort, etc.; cushion [a shoulder *pad*; seat *pad*] **2** the under part of the foot of some animals, as the wolf, lion, etc. ◆*v.* to stuff or cover with soft material [*padded* the chair] —**pad′ded, pad′ding**

par·don (pärd′n) *n.* the act of forgiving or excusing —*pl.* **par′dons**

par·ty (pär′tē) *n.* **1** a gathering of people to have a good time [a birthday *party*] **2** a group of people who share the same political opinions and work together to elect certain people, to promote certain policies, etc. [the Republican *Party*] **3** a group of people working or acting together [a hunting *party*] —*pl.* **par′ties**

pas·sen·ger (pas′ən jər) *n.* a person traveling in a car, bus, plane, ship, etc., but not driving or helping to operate it

☆**pa·ti·o** (pat′ē ō *or* pät′ē ō) *n.* **1** in Spain and Spanish America, a courtyard around which a house is built **2** a paved area near a house, with chairs, tables, etc. for outdoor lounging, dining, etc. —*pl.* **pa′ti·os**

pa·trol (pə trōl′) *v.* to make regular trips around a place in order to guard it [The watchman *patrolled* the area all night.] —**pa·trolled′, pa·trol′ling**

peace (pēs) *n.* **1** freedom from war or fighting [a nation that lives in *peace* with all other nations] **2** law and order [The rioters were disturbing the *peace*.] **3** calm or quiet [to find *peace* of mind]

pen·cil (pen′səl) *n.* a long, thin piece of wood, metal, etc. with a center stick of graphite or crayon that is sharpened to a point for writing or drawing ◆*v.* to mark, write, or draw with a pencil —**pen′ciled** or **pen′cilled, pen′cil·ing** or **pen′cil·ling**

pen·guin (peŋ′gwin) *n.* a sea bird mainly of the antarctic region, with webbed feet and flippers for swimming and diving: penguins cannot fly

pen·in·su·la (pə nin′sə lə) *n.* a long piece of land almost completely surrounded by water [Italy is a *peninsula*.] —**pen·in′su·lar** *adj.*

per·ceive (pər sēv′) *v.* **1** to become aware of through one of the senses, especially through seeing [to *perceive* the difference between two shades of red] **2** to take in through the mind [I quickly *perceived* the joke.] —**per·ceived′, per·ceiv′ing**

perch (pʉrch) *n.* **1** a small fish living in lakes and streams: it is used for food **2** a similar saltwater fish —*pl.* **perch** or **perch′es**

per·fect (pʉr′fəkt) *adj.* complete in every way and having no faults or errors [a *perfect* test paper]

per·form·er (pər fôrm′ər) *n.* one who does something to entertain an audience [The *performer* sang and danced.]

per·fume (pʉr′fyo͞om *or* pər fyo͞om′) *n.* **1** a sweet smell; pleasing odor; fragrance [the *perfume* of roses] **2** a liquid with a

overcoat

a	ask, fat
ā	ape, date
ä	car, lot
e	elf, ten
ē	even, meet
i	is, hit
ī	ice, fire
ō	open, go
ô	law, horn
oi	oil, point
o͝o	look, pull
o͞o	ooze, tool
ou	out, crowd
u	up, cut
ʉ	fur, fern
ə	a in ago
	e in agent
	e in father
	i in unity
	o in collect
	u in focus
ch	chin, arch
ŋ	ring, singer
sh	she, dash
th	thin, truth
th	then, father
zh	s in pleasure

175

piano

pleasing smell, for use on the body, clothing, etc. ◆**v.** (pər fyo͞om′) to give a pleasing smell to, as with perfume —**per·fumed′, per·fum′ing**

per·son (pur′sən) **n.** a human being; man, woman, or child [every *person* in this room]

pet·ri·fy (pe′tri fī) **v. 1** to change into a substance like stone by replacing the normal cells with minerals [Trees buried under lava for a great many years can become *petrified.*] **2** to make unable to move or act, as because of fear or surprise —**pet′ri·fied, pet′ri·fy·ing**

phase (fāz) **n. 1** any of the sides or views of a subject by which it may be looked at, thought about, or shown [We discussed the many *phases* of the problem.] **2** any stage in a series of changes [Adolescence is a *phase* we all go through.] ◆**v.** —**phased, phas′ing**

☆**pho·ny** or **pho·ney** (fō′nē) **adj.** not real or genuine; fake; false —**pho′ni·er, pho′ni·est** ◆**n.** a person or thing that is not really what it is supposed to be —*pl.* **pho′nies** *this is a slang word*

pho·to (fōt′ō) **n.** *a shorter name for* **photograph**: *used only in everyday talk* —*pl.* **pho′tos**

pho·to·graph (fōt′ə graf) **n.** a picture made with a camera ◆**v. 1** to take a photograph of **2** to look a certain way in photographs [She *photographs* taller than she is.]

pho·tog·ra·pher (fə täg′rə fər) **n.** a person who takes photographs, especially for a living

phrase (frāz) **n.** a group of words that is not a complete sentence, but that gives a single idea, usually as a separate part of a sentence

pi·an·o (pē ä′nō) **n.** a large musical instrument with many wire strings in a case and a keyboard: when a key is struck, it makes a small hammer hit a string to produce a tone; **grand piano** and **upright** —*pl.* **pi·an′os**

pic·ture (pik′chər) **n.** a likeness of a person, thing, scene, etc. made by drawing, painting, or photography; also, a printed copy of this ◆**v. 1** to make a picture of **2** to show; make clear [Joy was *pictured* in her face.] **3** to describe or explain [Dickens *pictured* life in England.] **4** to form an idea or picture in the mind; imagine [You can *picture* how pleased I was!] —**pic′tured, pic′tur·ing**

pie (pī) **n.** a dish with a filling made of fruit, meat, etc., baked in a pastry crust

piece (pēs) **n. 1** a part broken or separated from a whole thing [The glass shattered and I swept up the *pieces.*] **2** a part or section of a whole, thought of as complete by itself [a *piece* of meat; a *piece* of land] **3** any one of a set or group of things [a dinner set of 52 *pieces*; a chess *piece*] ◆**v.** to join the pieces of, as in mending [to *piece* together a broken jug]

pine·ap·ple (pīn′ap′əl) **n. 1** a juicy tropical fruit that looks a little like a large pine cone **2** the plant it grows on, having a short stem and curved leaves with prickly edges

pi·o·neer (pī′ə nir′) **n.** ☆a person who goes before, opening up the way for others to follow, as an early settler or a scientist doing original work [Daniel Boone was a *pioneer* in Kentucky. Marie Curie was a *pioneer* in the study of radium.] ◆**v.** to act as a pioneer; open up the way for others [The Wright brothers *pioneered* in air travel.]

Pitts·burgh (pits′burg) a city in southwestern Pennsylvania

pit·y (pit′ē) **v.** to feel sorrow for another's suffering or trouble [to *pity* someone's misfortune] —**pit′ied, pit′y·ing**

plain (plān) **adj. 1** open; clear; not blocked [in *plain* view] **2** easy to understand; clear to the mind [The meaning is *plain.*] **3** simple; easy [I can do a little *plain* cooking.] —**plain′ly adv.** —**plain′ness n.**

plane¹ (plān) **adj. 1** flat; level; even ◆**n. 2** *a shorter form of* **airplane**

plane² (plān) **n.** a tool used by carpenters for shaving wood in order to make it smooth or level ◆**v.** to make smooth or level with a plane —**planed, plan′ing**

plat·form (plat′fôrm) **n.** a flat surface or stage higher than the ground or floor around it [a *platform* at a railroad station; a speaker's *platform*]

po·et·ry (pō′ə trē) **n. 1** the art of writing poems **2** poems [the *poetry* of Keats]

po·lit·i·cal (pə lit′i kəl) **adj. 1** having to do with government, politics, etc. [*political* parties] **2** of or like political parties or politicians [a *political* speech] —**po·lit′i·cal·ly adv.**

poll (pōl) **n. 1** a voting or listing of opinions by persons; also, the counting of these votes or opinions [A *poll* of our class shows that most of us want a party.] **2** the number of votes cast **3** a list of voters ☆**4 polls,** *pl.* a place where people go to vote

porch (pôrch) **n. 1** a covered entrance to a building, usually with a roof that is held up by posts **2** a room on the outside of a building, either open or enclosed by screens, etc.

por·poise (pôr′pəs) *n.* **1** a water animal that is like a small whale: it is dark above and white below and has a blunt snout **2** *another name for* **dolphin**

port·hole (pôrt′hōl) *n.* a small opening in a ship's side, as for letting in light and air

pow·er·ful (pou′ər fəl) *adj.* having much power; strong or influential [a *powerful* hand; a *powerful* leader] —**pow′er·ful·ly** *adv.*

prac·tice (prak′tis) *v.* **1** to do or carry out regularly; make a habit of [to *practice* what one preaches; to *practice* charity] **2** to do something over and over again in order to become skilled at it [She *practices* two hours a day on the piano.] **3** to work at as a profession or occupation [to *practice* medicine] —**prac′ticed, prac′tic·ing**

☆ **prai·rie** (prer′ē) *n.* a large area of level or rolling grassy land without many trees

praise (prāz) *v.* **1** to say good things about; give a good opinion of [to *praise* someone's work] **2** to worship, as in song [to *praise* God] —**praised, prais′ing**

pre·cau·tion (prē kô′shən *or* prē kä′shən) *n.* care taken ahead of time, as against danger, failure, etc. [She took the *precaution* of locking the door before she left.] —**pre·cau′tion·ar′y** *adj.*

pre·cip·i·ta·tion (prē sip′ə tā′shən) *n.* **1** a sudden bringing about of something [the *precipitation* of a cold by getting chilled] **2** sudden or reckless haste **3** rain, snow, etc. or the amount of this

pre·dict (prē dikt′) *v.* to tell what one thinks will happen in the future [I *predict* that you will win.] —**pre·dict′a·ble** *adj.* —**pre·dict′a·bil·i·ty** *adv.*

pre·fix (prē′fiks) *n.* a syllable or group of syllables joined to the beginning of a word to change its meaning: some common prefixes are *un-*, *non-*, *re-*, *anti-*, and *in-*

pre·paid (prē pād′) *past tense and past participle of* **prepay**

pre·pay (prē pā′) *v.* to pay for ahead of time [Postage is normally *prepaid*.] —**pre·paid′, pre·pay′ing**

pre·set (prē set′) *v.* to set or adjust ahead of time [He *presets* the oven so it will be ready for the cake.] —**pre·set′, pre·set′ting**

pret·ty (prit′ē) *adj.* **1** pleasant to look at or hear, especially in a delicate, dainty, or graceful way [a *pretty* girl; a *pretty* voice; a *pretty* garden] **2** fine; good; nice —**pret′ti·er, pret′ti·est**

pre·view (prē′vyo̅o̅) *n.* ☆a view or showing ahead of time; especially, a private showing of a movie before showing it to the public ◆*v.* to give a preview of

price (prīs) *n.* **1** the amount of money asked or paid for something; cost [What is the *price* of that coat?] **2** value or worth [a painting of great *price*] ◆*v.* to set the price of [The rug was *priced* at $40.] —**priced, pric′ing**

pride (prīd) *n.* **1** an opinion of oneself that is too high; vanity [Her *pride* blinded her to her own faults.] **2** proper respect for oneself; dignity; self-respect [He has too much *pride* to go begging.] **3** pleasure or satisfaction in something done, owned, etc. [We take *pride* in our garden.] **4** a person or thing that makes one proud [She is her father's *pride* and joy.] —**prid′ed, prid′ing**

prince (prins) *n.* a son or grandson of a king or queen

prin·ci·pal (prin′sə pəl) *n.* the head of a school

print·ing (print′iŋ) *n.* **1** the act of one that prints **2** the making of printed material, as books, newspapers, etc. **3** printed words —**print′er**

pro·ceed (prō sēd′) *v.* **1** to go on, especially after stopping for a while [After eating, we *proceeded* to the next town.] **2** to begin and go on doing something [I *proceeded* to build a fire.]

prod·uct (präd′əkt) *n.* **1** something produced by nature or by human beings [Wood is a natural *product*. A desk is a manufactured *product*.] **2** result [The story is a *product* of her imagination.] **3** a number that is the result of multiplying [28 is the *product* of 7 multiplied by 4.]

pro·gram (prō′gram) *n.* **1** the acts, speeches, or musical pieces that make up a ceremony or entertainment [a commencement *program*] **2** a scheduled broadcast on radio or TV

prom·ise (präm′is) *n.* **1** an agreement to do or not to do something; vow [to make and keep a *promise*] **2** a sign that gives reason for expecting success; cause for hope [She shows *promise* as a singer.] ◆*v.* to make a promise to [I *promised* them I'd arrive at ten.] —**prom′ised, prom′is·ing**

prompt (prämpt) *adj.* **1** quick in doing what should be done; on time [He is *prompt* in paying his bills.] **2** done, spoken, etc. without waiting [We would like a *prompt* reply.] ◆*v.* to urge or stir into action [Tyranny *prompted* them to revolt.] —**prompt′ly** *adv.* —**prompt′ness** *n.*

prop·er (präp′ər) *adj.* **1** right, correct, or suitable [the *proper* tool for this job; the *proper* clothes for a party] **2** not to be ashamed of; decent; respectable [*proper* manners] —**prop′er·ly** *adv.*

pro·tect (prō tekt′) *v.* to guard or defend against harm or danger; shield [armor to *protect* the knight's body] —**pro·tec′tor** *n.*

prince

a	ask, fat
ā	ape, date
ä	car, lot
e	elf, ten
ē	even, meet
i	is, hit
ī	ice, fire
ō	open, go
ô	law, horn
oi	oil, point
o̅o̅	look, pull
o̅o̅	ooze, tool
ou	out, crowd
u	up, cut
ʉ	fur, fern
ə	a in ago
	e in agent
	e in father
	i in unity
	o in collect
	u in focus
ch	chin, arch
ŋ	ring, singer
sh	she, dash
th	thin, truth
th	then, father
zh	s in pleasure

pro·te·in (prō′tēn) *n.* a substance containing nitrogen and other elements, found in all living things and in such foods as cheese, meat, eggs, beans, etc.: it is a necessary part of an animal's diet

pro·test (prō test′ *or* prō′test) *v.* **1** to speak out against; object [They joined the march to *protest* against injustice.] **2** to say in a positive way; insist [Bill *protested* that he would be glad to help.] ◆*n.* (prō′test) the act of protesting; objection [They ignored my *protest* and continued hammering.] —**pro·test′er** or **pro·tes′tor**

prove (prōōv) *v.* **1** to show that something is true or correct [She showed us the method of *proving* our arithmetic problems.] **2** to put to a test or trial; find out about through experiments [A *proving* ground is a place for testing new equipment, as aircraft.] **3** to turn out to be [Your guess *proved* right.] —**proved, proved** or **prov′en, prov′ing**

pub·lic (pub′lik) *adj.* of or having to do with the people as a whole [*public* opinion] ◆*n.* the people as a whole [what the *public* wants]

punc·tu·a·tion (puŋk′chōō ā′shən) *n.* **1** the use of commas, periods, etc. in writing [rules of *punctuation*] **2** punctuation marks [What *punctuation* is used to end sentences?]

purse (purs) *n.* a bag of leather or cloth used for carrying money, cosmetics, keys, and so on —*pl.* **purs′es**

☆**quit·ter** (kwit′ər) *n.* a person who quits or gives up too easily

rail·road (rāl′rōd) *n.* **1** a road on which there is a track made up of parallel steel rails along which trains run **2** a series of such roads managed as a unit, together with the cars, engines, stations, etc. that belong to it

rai·sin (rā′zən) *n.* a sweet grape dried for eating

rake (rāk) *n.* a tool with a long handle having a set of teeth or prongs at one end: it is used for gathering loose grass, leaves, etc. or for smoothing broken ground ◆*v.* to gather together or smooth as with a rake [to *rake* leaves; to *rake* a gravel path] —**raked, rak′ing**

☆**ranch** (ranch) *n.* a large farm, especially in the Western part of the United States, where cattle, horses, or sheep are raised —*pl.* **ranch′es** —**ranch′er** *n.* ◆*v.* to work on or manage a ranch

rap·id (rap′id) *adj.* very swift or quick [a *rapid* journey] ◆☆*n.* usually **rapids**, *pl.* a part of a river where the water moves swiftly —**rap′id·ly** *adv.*

reach (rēch) *v.* **1** to stretch out one's hand, arm, etc. [He *reached* up and shook the branch.] **2** to touch, as by stretching out [Can you *reach* the top shelf?] **3** to stretch out in time, space, amount, etc. [Her fame *reaches* into all parts of the world.] —**reach′es**

re·ac·tion (rē ak′shən) *n.* an action, happening, etc. in return or in response to some other action, happening, force, etc. [What was their *reaction* to your suggestion? A rubber ball bounces as a *reaction* to hitting the ground.]

rea·son (rē′zən) *n.* **1** something said to explain or try to explain an act, idea, etc. [Write the *reasons* for your answer.] **2** a cause for some action, feeling, etc.; motive [Noisy neighbors were our *reason* for moving.] **3** the power to think, get ideas, decide things, etc. [Human beings are the only creatures that truly have *reason*.]

re·ceipt (rē sēt′) *n.* **1** a receiving or being received [Upon *receipt* of the gift, she thanked him.] **2** a written statement that something has been received [My landlord gave me a *receipt* when I paid my rent.] **3 receipts**, *pl.* the amount of money taken in, as in a business

re·ceive (rē sēv′) *v.* **1** to take or get what has been given or sent to one [to *receive* a letter] **2** to meet with; be given; undergo [to *receive* punishment; to *receive* applause] **3** to find out about; learn [He *received* the news calmly.] **4** to greet guests and let them come in [Our hostess *received* us at the door.] —**re·ceived′, re·ceiv′ing**

re·count (rē kount′) *v.* to count again [You had better *recount* your change just to make sure.]

re·duce (rē dōōs′ *or* rē dyōōs′) *v.* **1** to make smaller, less, fewer, etc.; decrease [to *reduce* speed; to *reduce* taxes] **2** to loose weight, as by dieting **3** to make lower, as in rank or condition; bring down [to *reduce* a major to rank of captain; a family *reduced* to poverty] —**re·duced′, re·duc′ing** —**re·duc′er** *n.* —**re·duc′i·ble** *adj.*

reel (rēl) *n.* **1** a frame or spool on which film, fishing line, wire, etc. is wound **2** the amount of movie film, wire, etc. usually wound on one reel ◆*v.* to wind on a reel

re·fill (rē fil′) *v.* to fill again ◆*n.* (rē′fil) **1** something to replace the contents of a special container [a *refill* for a ball point pen] **2** any extra filling of a prescription for medicine —**re·fill′a·ble** *adj.*

re·frig·er·a·tor (ri frij′ər āt′ər) *n.* a box or room in which the air is kept cool to keep food, etc. from spoiling

re·fund (rē fund′) *v.* to give back money, etc.; repay [We will *refund* the full price if you are not satisfied.] ◆*n.* (rē′fund) the act of refunding or the amount refunded —**re·fund′a·ble** *adj.*

reg·is·ter (rej′is tər) *n.* **1** a record or list of names, events, or things; also, a book in which such a record is kept [a hotel *register*, *register* of accounts] **2** a device for counting and keeping a record of [a cash *register*] ◆*v.* ☆**1** to keep a record of in a register [to *register* a birth] **2** to put one's name in a register, as of voters

reg·u·lar (reg′yə lər) *adj.* formed or arranged in an orderly way; balanced [a face with *regular* features]

rein·deer (rān′dir) *n.* a large deer found in northern regions, where it is tamed and used for work or as food: both the male and female have antlers —*pl.* **rein′deer**

re·lief (rē lēf′) *n.* **1** a lessening of pain, discomfort, worry, etc. [This salve will give *relief* from itching.] **2** anything that lessens pain, worry, etc. or gives a pleasing change [It's a *relief* to get out of that stuffy hall.] **3** help given to poor people, to victims of a flood, etc.

re·ly (rē lī′) *v.* to trust or depend [You can *rely* on me to be on time.] —**re·lied′, re·ly′ing**

re·mem·ber (rē mem′bər) *v.* **1** to think of again [I suddenly *remembered* I was supposed to mow the lawn.] **2** to bring back to mind by trying; recall [I just can't *remember* your name.] **3** to be careful not to forget [*Remember* to look both ways before crossing.] —**re·mem′bered**

re·move (rē mo͞ov′) *v.* to move to another place; take away or take off [They *removed* their coats.]

re·pair (rē per′) *v.* **1** to put into good condition again; fix, mend [to *repair* a broken toy] **2** to set right; correct [to *repair* a mistake; to *repair* an injustice] ◆*n.* **1** the act of repairing **2** *usually* **repairs** *pl.* work done in repairing [to make *repairs* on a house] —**re·pair′a·ble** *adj.*

re·ply (rē plī′) *v.* to answer by saying or doing something [to *reply* to a question; to *reply* to the enemy's fire with a counterattack] —**re·plied′, re·ply′ing** ◆*n.* an answer —*pl.* **re·plies′**

re·port (rē pôrt′) *v.* **1** to tell about; give an account of [I *reported* on my trip to the Falls.] **2** to tell as news [the papers *reported* little damage as a result of the storm.] ◆*n.* an account of something, often one in written or printed form [a financial *report*]

☆**res·tau·rant** (res′tər ənt *or* res′tränt) *n.* a place where meals can be bought and eaten

re·turn (rē turn′) *v.* **1** to go or come back [When did you *return* from your trip?] **2** to bring, send, carry, or put back [Our neighbor *returned* the ladder.] **3** to pay back by doing the same [to *return* a visit; to *return* a favor] **4** to report back [The jury *returned* a verdict of "not guilty."]

rid·er (rīd′ər) *n.* a person who rides

rise (rīz) *v.* **1** to stand up or get up from a lying or sitting position [*rise* to greet the guests] **2** to get up after sleeping [She *rises* early.] —**rose** (rōz), **ris·en** (riz′ən), **ris′ing**

risk (risk) *n.* the chance of getting hurt, or of losing, failing, etc.; danger [He ran into the burning house at the *risk* of his life.] ◆*v.* to take the chance of [Are you willing to *risk* a fight for your beliefs?]

roast (rōst) *v.* **1** to cook with little or no liquid, as in an oven or over an open fire [to *roast* a chicken or a whole ox] **2** to dry or brown with great heat [to *roast* coffee] ◆*n.* a piece of roasted meat —**roast′ed**

ro·dent (rōd′nt) *n.* an animal having sharp front teeth for gnawing: rats, mice, rabbits, squirrels, woodchucks, and beavers are rodents

rough·ly (ruf′lē) *adv.* **1** in a rough manner **2** more or less; about [*Roughly* 50 people came to the party.]

roy·al·ty (roi′əl tē) *n.* **1** a royal person, or royal persons as a group [a member of British *royalty*] **2** the rank or power of a king or queen **3** royal quality or nature; nobility, splendor, etc. —*pl.* **roy′al·ties**

rude (ro͞od) *adj.* without respect for others; impolite [It was *rude* of them not to thank you.] —**rud′er, rud′est**

rule (ro͞ol) *n.* **1** a statement or law that is meant to guide or control the way one acts or does something [the *rules* of grammar; baseball *rules*] **2** a usual way of doing something, behaving, etc. [to make it a *rule* never to rush] **3** government or reign [the *rule* of Elizabeth I]

rodent

a	ask, fat
ā	ape, date
ä	car, lot
e	elf, ten
ē	even, meet
i	is, hit
ī	ice, fire
ō	open, go
ô	law, horn
oi	oil, point
o͝o	look, pull
o͞o	ooze, tool
ou	out, crowd
u	up, cut
u	fur, fern
ə	a in ago
	e in agent
	e in father
	i in unity
	o in collect
	u in focus
ch	chin, arch
ŋ	ring, singer
sh	she, dash
th	thin, truth
th	then, father
zh	s in pleasure

☆run·way (run′wā) *n.* a track or path on which something moves, as a paved strip on an airfield used by airplanes in taking off and landing

Ss

sauce pan

safe (sāf) *adj.* 1 free from harm or danger; secure [a *safe* hiding place; *safe* in bed] 2 not hurt or harmed [We emerged *safe* from the wreck.] 3 that can be trusted [a *safe* investment] —**saf′er, saf′est** —**safe′ly** *adv.*

sal·ad (sal′əd) *n.* any mixture of vegetables, fruits, fish, eggs, etc., with a dressing of oil, vinegar, spices, etc.: it is usually served cold, often on lettuce leaves

sand·wich (san′dwich *or* san′wich) *n.* slices of bread with a filling of meat, cheese, etc. between them —*pl.* **sand′wich·es** ◆*v.* to squeeze in [a shed *sandwiched* between two houses]

San Fran·cis·co (san′ fran sis′kō) a city on the coast of central California

sar·dine (sär dēn′) *n.* a small fish, as a young herring, preserved in oil and packed in cans

sash (sash) *n.* a band, ribbon, or scarf worn over the shoulder or around the waist —*pl.* **sash′es**

sat·el·lite (sat′l īt) *n.* 1 a heavenly body that revolves around another, larger one [The moon is a *satellite* of the earth.] 2 an artificial object put into orbit around the earth, the moon, or some other heavenly body

sat·is·fy (sat′is fī) *v.* 1 to meet the needs or wishes of; content; please [Only first prize will *satisfy* him.] 2 to make feel sure; convince [The jury was *satisfied* that he was innocent.] —**sat′is·fied, sat′is·fy·ing**

sauce (sôs *or* säs) *n.* 1 a liquid or soft dressing served with food to make it tastier [spaghetti with tomato *sauce*] ☆2 fruit that has been stewed [apple*sauce*]

sauce·pan (sôs′pan *or* s'äs′pan) *n.* a small metal pot with a long handle, used for cooking

sau·cer (sô′sər *or* sä′sər) *n.* a small, shallow dish, especially one for a cup to rest on

save (sāv) *v.* 1 to rescue or keep from harm or danger [He was *saved* from drowning.] 2 to keep or store up for future use [She *saved* her money for a vacation.] 3 to keep from being lost or wasted [Traveling by plane *saved* many hours.] —**saved, sav′ing** —**sav′er** *n.*

scale¹ (skāl) *n.* 1 a series of marks along a line, with regular spaces in between, used for measuring [A Celsius thermometer has a basic *scale* of 100 degrees.] 2 the way that the size of a map, model, or drawing compares with the size of the thing that it stands for [One inch on a map of this *scale* equals 100 miles of real distance.] 3 a series of steps or degrees based on size, amount, rank, etc. [A passing grade on this *scale* is 70.]

scale² (skāl) *n.* 1 any of the thin, flat, hard plates that cover and protect certain fish and reptiles 2 a thin piece or layer; flake [*scales* of rust in a water pipe] ◆*v.* to scrape scales from [to *scale* a fish] —**scaled, scal′ing**

scale³ (skāl) *n.* 1 either of the shallow pans of a balance 2 *often* **scales,** *pl.* the balance itself; also, any device or machine for weighing ◆*v.* to weigh —**scaled, scal′ing**

scare (sker) *v.* to make or become afraid; frighten —**scared, scar′ing** ◆*n.* a sudden fear; fright [The loud noise gave me quite a *scare.*]

scarf (skärf) *n.* 1 a long or broad piece of cloth worn about the head, neck, or shoulders for warmth or decoration 2 a long, narrow piece of cloth used as a covering on top of a table, bureau, etc. —*pl.* **scarfs** or **scarves** (skärvz)

scent (sent) *n.* 1 a smell; odor [the *scent* of apple blossoms] 2 the sense of smell [Lions hunt partly by *scent.*] 3 a smell left by an animal [The dogs lost the fox's *scent* at the river.]

school·house (skool′hous) *n.* a building used as a school

scout (skout) *n.* a soldier, ship, or plane sent to spy out the strength or movements of the enemy

scram·ble (skram′bəl) *v.* to climb or crawl in a quick, rough way [The children *scrambled* up the steep hill.] —**scram′bled, scram′bling**

scratch (skrach) *n.* 1 a mark or cut made in a surface by something sharp 2 a slight wound —*pl.* **scratch′es**

scrawl (skrôl) *v.* to write or draw in a hasty, careless way ◆*n.* careless or poor handwriting that is hard to read

screech (skrēch) *v.* to give a harsh, high shriek ◆*n.* a harsh, high shriek

screen (skrēn) *n.* 1 a mesh woven loosely of wires so as to leave small openings between them: screens are used in windows, doors, etc. to keep insects out. 2 a covered frame or curtain used to hide, separate, or protect 3 anything that hides, separates, or protects [a smoke *screen;* a *screen* of trees]

scrub (skrub) *v.* to clean or wash by rubbing hard [to *scrub* floors] —**scrubbed, scrub′bing** ◆*n.* the act of cleaning by rubbing hard

scur·ry (skʉr′ē) *v.* to run quickly; scamper —**scur′ried, scur′ry·ing** ◆*n.* the act or sound of running quickly

sea·son (sē′zən) *n.* **1** any of the four parts into which the year is divided: spring, summer, fall, or winter **2** a special time of the year [the Easter *season*; the hunting *season*] **3** a period of time [the busy *season* at a factory] ◆*v.* to add to or change the flavor of [to *season* meat with herbs]

Se·at·tle (sē at′l) a city in Washington

sea·weed (sē′wēd) *n.* any plant or plants growing in the sea, especially algae: there are some plants like these that grow in fresh water and are also called seaweed

seek (sēk) *v.* **1** to try to find; search for [to *seek* gold] **2** to try to get; aim at [to *seek* a prize] —**sought, seek′ing**

seize (sēz) *v.* **1** to take hold of in a sudden, strong, or eager way; grasp [to *seize* a weapon and fight; to *seize* an opportunity] **2** to capture or arrest, as a criminal **3** to take over as by force [The troops *seized* the fort. The city *seized* the property for nonpayment of taxes.] —**seized, seiz′ing**

sense (sens) *n.* **1** any of the special powers of the body and mind that let one see, hear, feel, taste, smell, etc. **2** a feeling or sensation [a *sense* of warmth; a *sense* of guilt] **3** an understanding or appreciation; special awareness [a *sense* of honor; a *sense* of beauty; a *sense* of rhythm; a *sense* of humor] **4** judgment or intelligence; reasoning [He showed good *sense* in his decision. There's no *sense* in going there late.]

serve (sʉrv) *v.* **1** to work for someone as a servant [I *served* in their household for ten years.] **2** to do services for; aid; help [She *served* her country well.] **3** to hold a certain office [She *served* as mayor for two terms.] **4** to offer or pass food, drink, etc. to [May I *serve* you some chicken?] —**served, serv′ing**

sev·en (sev′ən) *n., adj.* one more than six; the number 7

shake (shāk) *v.* to move quickly up and down, back and forth, or from side to side [She *shook* her head in disapproval.] —**shook, shak′en, shak′ing**

share (sher) *n.* a part that each one of a group gets or has [your *share* of the cake; my *share* of the blame] ◆*v.* **1** to divide and give out in shares [The owners *shared* the profits with their employees.] **2** to have a share of with others; have or use together [The three of you will *share* the back seat.] —**shared, shar′ing**

sharp (shärp) *adj.* **1** having a thin edge for cutting, or a fine point for piercing [a *sharp* knife; a *sharp* needle] **2** not gradual; abrupt [a *sharp* turn] **3** severe or harsh [a *sharp* reply] ◆*adv.* in a sharp manner; keenly, alertly, briskly, etc. [Look *sharp* when crossing streets.] —**sharp′ly** —**sharp′ness** *n.*

shawl (shôl) *n.* a large piece of cloth worn, especially by women, over the shoulders or head

sheep (shēp) *n.* an animal that chews its cud and is related to the goat: its body is covered with heavy wool and its flesh is used as food, called mutton —*pl.* **sheep**

shelf (shelf) *n.* a thin, flat length of wood, metal, etc. fastened against a wall or built into a frame so as to hold things [the top *shelf* of a bookcase] —*pl.* **shelves**

she'll (shēl) *contraction* **1** she will **2** she shall

shel·ter (shel′tər) *n.* a place or thing that covers or protects from the weather or danger [The *shelter* protected us from the rain.]

sher·bet (shʉr′bət) *n.* a frozen dessert of fruit juice, sugar, and water, milk, etc.

ship·ment (ship′mənt) *n.* **1** the shipping of goods by any means **2** the goods shipped

shoe (sho͞o) *n.* an outdoor covering for the foot, usually of leather ◆*v.* to furnish with shoes; put shoes on [to *shoe* a horse]

shore (shôr) *n.* **1** land at the edge of a sea or lake **2** land, not water [The retired sailor lives on *shore*.]

short·en (shôrt′n) *v.* to make or become short or shorter [to *shorten* a skirt]

should·n't (sho͝od′nt) *contraction* should not

shov·el (shuv′əl) *n.* **1** a tool with a broad scoop and a handle, for lifting and moving loose material **2** a machine with a part like a shovel, used for digging or moving large amounts of loose material [a steam *shovel*] ◆*v.* to lift and move with a shovel [to *shovel* coal] —**shov′eled** or **shov′elled, shov′el·ing** or **shov′el·ling**

show·er (shou′ər) *n.* **1** a short fall of rain or hail **2** a sudden, very full fall or flow, as of sparks, praise, etc. ☆**3** a bath in which the body is sprayed with fine streams of water: *the full name is* **shower bath**

shriek (shrēk) *n.* a loud, sharp, shrill cry; screech; scream ◆*v.* to cry out with a shrill cry [to *shriek* in terror]

shrimp (shrimp) *n.* a small shellfish with a long tail, used as food —*pl.* **shrimp** or **shrimps**

shut·tle (shut′əl) *n.* **1** a device in weaving that carries a thread back and forth between the threads that go up and down ☆**2** a bus, train, or airplane that makes frequent trips back and forth over a short route ◆*v.* to move rapidly to and fro —**shut′tled, shut′tling**

a	ask, fat
ā	ape, date
ä	car, lot
e	elf, ten
ē	even, meet
i	is, hit
ī	ice, fire
ō	open, go
ô	law, horn
oi	oil, point
o͝o	look, pull
o͞o	ooze, tool
ou	out, crowd
u	up, cut
ʉ	fur, fern
ə	a in ago
	e in agent
	e in father
	i in unity
	o in collect
	u in focus
ch	chin, arch
ŋ	ring, singer
sh	she, dash
th	thin, truth
th	then, father
zh	s in pleasure

181

slice

☆**side·walk** (sīd′wôk) *n.* a path for walking, usually paved, along the side of a street

si·lent (sī′lənt) *adj.* **1** not speaking or not talking much **2** with no sound or noise; noiseless [Find a *silent* place to study. We went to a *silent* movie.] **3** not spoken or told [*silent* grief; the *silent* "b" in "debt"] —**si′lent·ly** *adv.*

sing·er (siŋ′ər) *n.* **1** a person that sings **2** a bird that sings

sink (siŋk) *v.* to go or put down below the surface [The boat is *sinking*] —**sank** or **sunk, sink′ing**

sink·er (siŋk′ər) *n.* something that sinks, as a lead weight put on the end of a fishing line

sis·ter (sis′tər) *n.* **1** a girl or woman as she is related to the other children of her parents **2** a girl or woman who is close to one in some way; especially, a fellow member of the same race, religion, club, etc. **3** a nun

sit (sit) *v.* **1** to rest the weight of the body upon the buttocks or haunches [She is *sitting* on a bench. The dog *sat* still.] **2** to perch, rest, lie, etc. [A bird *sat* on the fence. Cares *sit* lightly on him.] —**sat, sit′ting**

sit·ting (sit′iŋ) *n.* **1** the act or position of one that sits, as for a picture **2** a meeting, as of a court or a council **3** a period of being seated [I read the book in one *sitting*.]

skat·er (skāt′ər) *n.* one who moves along on skates [The *skater* twirled on the ice.]

skill (skil) *n.* **1** ability that comes from training, practice, etc. [He plays the violin with *skill*.] **2** an art, craft, or science, especially one that calls for use of the hands or body [Weaving is a *skill* often taught to the blind.]

skim (skim) *v.* **1** to take off floating matter from the top of a liquid [to *skim* cream from milk; to *skim* molten lead] **2** to look through a book, magazine, etc. quickly without reading carefully **3** to glide lightly, as over a surface [bugs *skimming* over the water] —**skimmed, skim′ming**

☆**skunk** (skuŋk) *n.* **1** an animal having a bushy tail and black fur with white stripes down its back: it sprays out a very bad-smelling liquid when frightened or attacked

☆**sleigh** (slā) *n.* a carriage with runners instead of wheels, for travel over snow or ice ◆*v.* to ride in or drive a sleigh

slen·der (slen′dər) *adj.* small in width as compared with the length or height; long and thin [a *slender* woman]

slice (slīs) *n.* a thin, broad piece cut from something [a *slice* of cheese; a *slice* of bread] ◆*v.* **1** to cut into slices [to *slice* a cake] **2** to cut as with a knife [The plow *sliced* through the soft earth.] —**sliced, slic′ing** —**slic′er** *n.*

slip (slip) *v.* **1** to go or pass quietly or without being noticed; escape [We *slipped* out the door. It *slipped* my mind. Time *slipped* by.] **2** to pass slowly into a certain condition [to *slip* into bad habits] **3** to move, shift, or drop, as by accident [The plate *slipped* from my hand.] **4** to slide by accident [He *slipped* on the ice.] —**slipped, slip′ping**

slip·per (slip′ər) *n.* a light, low shoe that is usually worn while a person is relaxing at home

smooth (smo͞oth) *adj.* having an even or level surface, with no bumps or rough spots [*smooth* water on the lake]

snap (snap) *v.* to bite, grasp, or snatch suddenly [The frog *snapped* at the fly.] —**snapped, snap′ping**

sneeze (snēz) *v.* to blow out breath from the mouth and nose in a sudden way that cannot be controlled [My cold made me *sneeze*.] —**sneezed, sneez′ing**

soar (sôr) *v.* to rise or fly high into the air [The plane *soared* out of sight.]

sof·ten (sôf′ən *or* säf′ən) *v.* to make or become soft or softer —**sof′ten·er** *n.*

soft·ware (sôft′wer′ *or* säft′wer) *n.* the special instructions, information, etc. that make a computer operate

sol·id (säl′id) *adj.* **1** keeping its shape instead of flowing or spreading out like a liquid or gas; quite firm or hard [Ice is water in a *solid* form.] **2** filled with matter throughout; not hollow [a *solid* block of wood] **3** that has length, width, and thickness [A prism is a *solid* figure.] **4** strong, firm, sound, dependable, etc. [*solid* thinking; a *solid* building] —**sol′id·ly** *adv.*

sor·row (sär′ō) *n.* **1** a sad or troubled feeling; sadness; grief **2** a loss, death, or trouble causing such a feeling [Our grandmother's illness is a great *sorrow* to us.] ◆*v.* to feel or show sorrow [We are *sorrowing* over his loss.]

sort (sôrt) *n.* **1** a group of things that are alike in some way; kind; class [various *sorts* of toys] **2** quality or type [phrases of a noble *sort*] ◆*v.* to separate or arrange according to class or kind [*Sort* out the clothes that need mending.] —**sort′ed**

sought (sôt *or* sät) *v.* past tense and past participle of **seek**

sound (sound) *n.* **1** the form of energy that acts on the ears so that one can hear: sound consists of waves of vibrations carried in the air, water, etc. [In air, *sound* travels at a speed of about 332 meters per second, or 1,088 feet per second.] **2** anything that can be heard; noise, tone, etc. [the *sound* of bells] **3** any of the noises made in speaking [a vowel *sound*] ◆*v.* to make a sound [Your voice *sounds* hoarse.]

soup (sōōp) *n.* a liquid food made by cooking meat, vegetables, etc. as in water or milk

South America the southern continent in the Western Hemisphere —**South American** *adj., n*

south·east (sou th ēst′ *or* sou ēst′) *n.* 1 the direction halfway between south and east 2 a place or region in or toward this direction ◆*adj.* 1 in, of, or toward the southeast [the *southeast* part of the county] 2 from the southeast [a *southeast* wind] ◆*adv.* in or toward the southeast [to sail *southeast*]

south·ern (su th′ərn) *adj.* 1 in, of, or toward the south [the *southern* sky] 2 from the south [a *southern* wind]. 3 **Southern**, of the South

soy·bean (soi′bēn) *n.* 1 the seed, or bean, of a plant of Asia, now grown throughout the world: the beans are ground into flour, pressed for oil, etc. 2 the plant itself

space (spās) *n.* 1 the area that stretches in all directions, has no limits, and contains all things in the universe [The earth, the sun, and all the stars exist in *space*.] 2 the distance or area between things or inside of something, especially as used for some purpose [a closet with much *space*; parking *space*] 3 *a shorter name for* **outer space** ◆*v.* to arrange with spaces in between [The trees are evenly *spaced*.] —**spaced, spac′ing**

space·craft (spās′kraft′) *n.* any spaceship or satellite designed for use in outer space —*pl.* **space′craft′**

spare (sper) *v.* 1 to save or free from something [*Spare* us the trouble of listening to that story again.] 2 to get along without; give up [We can't *spare* the money or the time for a vacation trip.] —**spared, spar′ing** ◆*adj.* 1 kept for use when needed [a *spare* room; a *spare* tire] 2 not taken up by regular work or duties; free [*spare* time] —**spar′er, spar′est** ◆*n.* 1 an extra part or thing ☆2 in bowling, the act of knocking down all ten pins with two rolls of the ball —**spare′ly** *adv.*

spark (spärk) *n.* 1 a small bit of burning matter, as one thrown off by a fire 2 any flash of light like this [the *spark* of a firefly] 3 the small flash of light that takes place when an electric current jumps across an open space, as in a spark plug

spar·row (sper′ō) *n.* a small gray and brown songbird with a short beak: the common sparrow seen on city streets is the **English sparrow**

spe·cies (spē′shēz *or* spē′sēz) *n.* a group of plants or animals that are alike in certain ways [The lion and tiger are two different *species* of cat.] —*pl.* **spe′cies**

speed (spēd) *n.* 1 fast motion; swiftness 2 rate of motion; velocity [a *speed* of 10 miles per hour] 3 swiftness of any action [reading *speed*] ◆*v.* 1 to go or move fast or too fast [The arrow *sped* to its mark.] 2 to make go or move fast [He *sped* the letter on its way.] —**sped** or **speed′ed, speed′ing**

spend (spend) *v.* 1 to pay out or give up, as money, time, or effort [He *spent* $50 for food. Try to *spend* some time with me.] 2 to pass [She *spent* the summer at camp.] —**spent, spend′ing** —**spend′er** *n.*

spent (spent) *past tense and past participle of* **spend** ◆*adj.* tired out; used up

spice (spīs) *n.* any one of several vegetable substances used to give a special flavor or smell to food [Cinnamon, nutmeg, and pepper are kinds of *spices*.]

splash (splash) *v.* 1 to make a liquid scatter and fall in drops [to *splash* water or mud about] 2 to dash a liquid on, so as to wet or soil [The car *splashed* my coat.] ◆*n.* the act or sound of splashing —*pl.* **splash′es** —**splash′y** *adj.*

splen·did (splen′did) *adj.* very bright, brilliant, showy, or magnificent [a *splendid* gown]

splin·ter (splin′tər) *v.* to break or split into thin, sharp pieces [Soft pine *splinters* easily.] ◆*n.* a thin, sharp piece of wood, bone, etc. broken off

spoil (spoil) *v.* 1 to make or become useless, worthless, rotten, etc.; damage; ruin [Ink stains *spoiled* the paper. Illness *spoiled* my attendance record. Meat *spoils* fast in warm weather.] 2 to cause a person to ask for or expect too much by giving in to all of that person's wishes [to *spoil* a child] —**spoiled** or **spoilt, spoil′ing**

sponge (spunj) *n.* 1 a sea animal that is like a plant and grows fixed to surfaces under water 2 the light, elastic skeleton of such an animal, that is full of holes and can soak up much water: sponges are used for washing, bathing, etc. 3 any artificial substance like this, as of plastic or rubber, used in the same way ◆*v.* to wipe, clean, make wet, or soak up as with a sponge [to *sponge* up gravy with a crust of bread] —**sponged, spong′ing**

sport (spôrt) *n.* 1 active play, a game, etc. taken up for exercise or pleasure and, sometimes, as a profession [Football, golf, bowling, swimming, diving, etc. are *sports*.] 2 fun or play [They thought it was great *sport* to fool others on the telephone.]

sprain (sprān) *v.* to twist a muscle or ligament in a joint without putting the bones out of place [to *sprain* one's wrist] ◆*n.* an injury caused by this

sport

a	ask, fat
ā	ape, date
ä	car, lot
e	elf, ten
ē	even, meet
i	is, hit
ī	ice, fire
ō	open, go
ô	law, horn
oi	oil, point
ᴏᴏ	look, pull
ᴏᴏ	ooze, tool
ou	out, crowd
u	up, cut
ʉ	fur, fern
ə	a in ago
	e in agent
	e in father
	i in unity
	o in collect
	u in focus
ch	chin, arch
ŋ	ring, singer
sh	she, dash
th	thin, truth
th	then, father
zh	s in pleasure

sprin·kle (spriŋ′kəl) *v.* **1** to scatter in drops or bits [to *sprinkle* salt on an egg] **2** to scatter drops or bits on [to *sprinkle* a lawn with water] **3** to rain light —**sprin′kled, sprin′kling** ◆*n.* **1** the act of sprinkling **2** a light rain —**sprin′kler**

spy (spī) *n.* a person who watches others secretly and carefully —*pl.* **spies**

squall (skwôl) *n.* a short, violent windstorm, usually with rain or snow ◆*v.* to storm for a short time —**squall′y** *adj.*

stage (stāj) *n.* **1** a raised platform or other area on which plays, speeches, etc. are given **2** the profession of acting; the theater [He left the *stage* to write.] **3** *a shorter name for* **stagecoach 4** a period or step in growth or development [She has reached a new *stage* in her career.] ◆*v.* to present on a stage, as a play —**staged, stag′ing**

stamp (stamp) *v.* **1** to bring one's foot down with force ["No!" she cried, *stamping* on the floor.] **2** to beat, press, or crush as with the foot [to *stamp* out a fire; to *stamp* out a revolt] **3** to press or print marks, letters, a design, etc. on something [He *stamped* his initials on all his books.] ◆*n.* **1** a machine, tool, or die used for stamping **2** a small piece of paper printed and sold by a government for sticking on letters, packages, etc. as proof that postage or taxes were paid

stand (stand) *v.* **1** to be or get in an upright position on one's feet [*Stand* by your desk.] **2** to be or place in an upright position on its base, bottom, etc. [Our trophy *stands* on the shelf. *Stand* the broom in the corner.] **3** to put up with; endure; bear [The boss can't *stand* noise.] —**stood, stand′ing** ◆*n.* **1** an opinion, belief, or attitude [What is the senator's *stand* on higher taxes?] **2** *often* **stands**, *pl.* seats in rising rows, as in a stadium, from which to watch games, races, etc. **3** a booth or counter where goods are sold [a popcorn *stand*] **4** a rack, framework, etc. for holding something [a music *stand*]

stare (ster) *v.* to look steadily with the eyes wide open [to *stare* in curiosity] —**stared, star′ing**

starve (stärv) *v.* to die or suffer from lack of food [Many pioneers *starved* during the long winter.] —**starved, starv′ing**

sta·tion (stā′shən) *n.* **1** the place where a person or thing stands or is located, as one's post when on duty, a building for a special purpose, etc. [a sentry's *station*; a police *station*] **2** a regular stopping place, as for a bus or train; also, a building at such a place

☆**steam·boat** (stēm′bōt) *n.* a steamship, especially a small one

step (step) *v.* to move by taking a step or steps [We *stepped* into the car.] —**stepped, step′ping**

stern[1] (sturn) *adj.* strict or harsh; not gentle, tender, easy, etc. [*stern* parents; *stern* treatment] —**stern′ly** *adv.* —**stern′ness** *n.*

stern[2] (sturn) *n.* the rear end of a ship or boat

stick (stik) *n.* **1** a twig or branch broken or cut off **2** any long, thin piece of wood, with a special shape for use as a cane, club, etc. [a walking *stick*; a hockey *stick*] **3** a long, thin piece [a *stick* of celery; a *stick* of chewing gum] ◆*v.* **1** to press a sharp point into; pierce; stab [He *stuck* his finger with a needle.] **2** to fasten or be fastened as by pinning or gluing [I *stuck* my name tag on my coat. The stamp *sticks* to the paper.] —**stuck, stick′ing**

stiff (stif) *adj.* **1** that does not bend easily; firm [*stiff* cardboard] **2** not able to move easily [*stiff* muscles] **3** not relaxed; tense or formal [a *stiff* smile] —**stiff′ly** *adv.* —**stiff′ness** *n.*

stitch (stich) *n.* **1** one complete movement of a needle and thread into and out of the material in sewing **2** one complete movement done in various ways in knitting, crocheting, etc. **3** a loop made by stitching [Tight *stitches* pucker the cloth.] —*pl.* **stitches**

sto·ry[1] (stôr′ē) *n.* **1** a telling of some happening, whether true or made-up [the *story* of the first Thanksgiving] **2** a made-up tale, written down, that is shorter than a novel [the *stories* of Poe] —*pl.* **sto′ries**

sto·ry[2] (stôr′ē) *n.* the space or rooms making up one level of a building, from a floor to the ceiling above it [a building with ten *stories*] —*pl.* **sto′ries**

stove (stōv) *n.* a device for cooking or heating by the use of gas, oil, electricity, etc.

straight (strāt) *adj.* **1** having the same direction all the way; not crooked, curved, wavy, etc. [a *straight* line; *straight* hair] **2** upright or erect [*straight* posture] **3** level or even [a *straight* hemline] **4** direct; staying right to the point, direction, etc. [a *straight* course; a *straight* answer]

strange (strānj) *adj.* **1** not known, seen, or heard before; not familiar [I saw a *strange* person at the door.] **2** different from what is usual; peculiar; odd [wearing a *strange* costume] **3** not familiar; without experience [She is *strange* to this job.] —**strang′er, strang′est** —**strange′ly** *adv.*

straw (strô *or* strä) *n.* **1** hollow stalks, as of wheat or rye, after the grain has been threshed out: straw is used as stuffing or is woven into hats, etc. **2** a tube, as of plastic, used for sucking a drink

strength (streŋkth *or* streŋth) *n.* the quality of being strong; force; power [the *strength* of a blow]

stretch (strech) *v.* **1** to reach out or hold out, as a hand, object, etc. **2** to draw out to full length, to a greater size, to a certain distance, etc.; extend [She *stretched* out on the sofa. Will this material *stretch*? *Stretch* the rope between two trees. The road *stretches* for miles through the hills.] **3** to pull or draw tight; strain [to *stretch* a muscle]

strict (strikt) *adj.* **1** keeping to rules in a careful, exact way [a *strict* supervisor] **2** never changing; rigid [a *strict* rule] —**strict′ly** *adv.* —**strict′ness** *n.*

stuff (stuf) *n.* **1** what anything is made of; material; substance **2** a collection of objects, belongings, etc. [I emptied the *stuff* from my bag.] ◆*v.* **1** to fill or pack [pockets *stuffed* with candy] **2** to fill with seasoning, bread crumbs, etc. before roasting [to *stuff* a turkey] **3** to force or push [I *stuffed* the money in my wallet.]

stum·ble (stum′bəl) *v.* to trip or almost fall while walking or running [to *stumble* over a curb] —**stum′bled, stum′bling**

stur·dy (stʉr′dē) *adj.* strong and hardy [a *sturdy* oak] —**stur′di·er, stur′di·est** —**stur′di·ly** *adv.* —**stur′di·ness** *n.*

sub·trac·tion (səb trak′shən) *n.* the act of subtracting one part, number, etc. from another

☆**su·per·mar·ket** (so͞o′pər mär′kət) *n.* a large food store in which shoppers serve themselves from open shelves and pay at the exit

sup·ply (sə plī′) *v.* **1** to give what is needed; furnish [The camp *supplies* sheets and towels. The book *supplied* us with the facts.] **2** to take care of the needs of [to *supply* workers with tools] —**sup·plied′, sup·ply′ing** ◆*n.* **1** the amount at hand; store; stock [I have a small *supply* of money but a large *supply* of books.] **2** **supplies**, *pl.* things needed; materials; provisions [school *supplies*] —*pl.* **sup·plies**

sur·prise (sər prīz′) *v.* to cause to feel wonder by being unexpected [Her sudden anger *surprised* us.] —**sur·prised′, sur·pris′ing**

sur·pris·ing (sər prīz′iŋ) *adj.* causing surprise; strange —**sur·pris′ing·ly** *adv.*

sur·vey (sər vā′) *v.* **1** to look over in a careful way; examine; inspect [The lookout *surveyed* the horizon.] **2** to measure the size, shape, boundaries, etc. of a piece of land by the use of special instruments [to *survey* a farm] ◆*n.* (sʉr′vā) a general study covering the main facts or points [The *survey* shows that we need more schools. This book is a *survey* of American poetry.] —*pl.* **sur′veys**

sur·viv·al (sər vī′vəl) *n.* the act or fact of surviving, or continuing to exist [Nuclear war threatens the *survival* of all nations.]

swal·low (swä′lō) *v.* **1** to let food, drink, etc. go through the throat into the stomach **2** to move the muscles of the throat as in swallowing something [I *swallowed* hard to keep from crying.] **3** to take in; engulf [The waters of the lake *swallowed* him up.] —**swal·lowed′**

swamp (swämp) *n.* a piece of wet, spongy land; marsh; bog; *also called* ☆**swamp′land** —**swamp′y** *adj.*

sway (swā) *v.* **1** to swing or bend back and forth or from side to side [The flowers *swayed* in the breeze.] **2** to lean or go to one side; veer [The car *swayed* to the right on the curve.] **3** to change the thinking or actions of; influence [We will not be *swayed* by their promises.] —**sway′ing**

sweat (swet) *v.* **1** to give out a salty liquid through the pores of the skin; perspire [Running fast made me *sweat*.] —**sweat** *or* **sweat′ed, sweat′ing** ◆*n.* **1** the salty liquid given out through the pores of the skin

sweat shirt (swet shʉrt) *n.* a heavy, loose cotton shirt with long or short sleeves

swift (swift) *adj.* **1** moving or able to move very fast [a *swift* runner] **2** coming, happening, or done quickly [a *swift* reply] **3** acting quickly; prompt [They were *swift* to help us.] —**swift′ly** *adv.* —**swift′ness** *n.*

sword (sôrd) *n.* a weapon having a long, sharp blade, with a handle, or hilt, at one end

syl·la·ble (sil′ə bəl) *n.* **1** a word or part of a word spoken with a single sounding of the voice ["Moon" is a word of one *syllable*. "Moonlight" is a word of two *syllables*.] **2** any of the parts into which a written word is divided to show where it may be broken at the end of a line [The *syllables* of the entry words in this dictionary are divided by tiny dots.]

syn·o·nym (sin′ə nim) *n.* a word having the same or almost the same meaning as another ["Big" and "large" are *synonyms*.]

Tt

tail (tāl) *n.* **1** the part at the rear of an animal's body that sticks out beyond the backbone **2** any thing or part like this [the *tail* of a shirt; a pig*tail*] **3** the hind or last part [the *tail* of a parade] —*pl.* **tails** —**tail′less** *adj.*

tai·lor (tā′lər) *n.* a person who makes or repairs suits, coats, etc. ◆*v.* **1** to work as a tailor or make as a tailor does [suits *tailored* for stout people] **2** to make or change so as to fit a certain need [That movie was *tailored* to please children.]

a	ask, fat
ā	ape, date
ä	car, lot
e	elf, ten
ē	even, meet
i	is, hit
ī	ice, fire
ō	open, go
ô	law, horn
oi	oil, point
o͝o	look, pull
o͞o	ooze, tool
ou	out, crowd
u	up, cut
ʉ	fur, fern
ə	a in ago
	e in agent
	e in father
	i in unity
	o in collect
	u in focus
ch	chin, arch
ŋ	ring, singer
sh	she, dash
th	thin, truth
th	then, father
zh	s in pleasure

tale (tāl) *n.* a story, especially about things that are imagined or made up [The sitter read the child both folk *tales* and fairy *tales*.]

tar·dy (tär′dē) *adj.* not on time; late; delayed [to be *tardy* for class] —**tar′di·er, tar′di·est** —**tar′di·ly** *adv.* —**tar′di·ness** *n.*

tast·y (tās′tē) *adj.* tasting good; full of flavor [a *tasty* meal] —**tast′i·er, tast′i·est**

tax (taks) *n.* money that citizens and businesses must pay to help support a government —*pl.* **tax′es**

tax·pay·er (taks′pā ər) *n.* a person who pays a tax or taxes

teach·er (tēch′ər) *n.* a person who teaches, especially in a school or college

tea·spoon (tē′spσσn) *n.* **1** a spoon for stirring tea, coffee, etc. and eating some soft foods **2** *a shorter form of* **teaspoonful**

teeth (tēth) *n. plural of* **tooth**

tel·e·scope (tel′ə skōp) *n.* a device for making far-off things seem closer and larger, used especially in astronomy: it consists of one or more tubes containing lenses and, often, mirrors

tel·e·vi·sion (tel′ə vizhən) *n.* **1** a way of sending pictures through space by changing the light rays into electric waves which are picked up by a receiver that changes them back to light rays shown on a screen: the sound that goes with the picture is sent by radio at the same time **2** such a receiver, usually in a cabinet

tem·per·ate (tem′pər ət *or* tem′prət) *adj.* **1** using or showing temperance in one's actions, appetites, etc.; moderate [Although she was angry, she made a *temperate* reply.] **2** neither very hot nor very cold [a *temperate* climate] —**tem′per·ate·ly** *adv.*

ten·der (ten′dər) *adj.* **1** soft or delicate and easily chewed, cut, etc. [*tender* meat; *tender* blades of grass] **2** that is hurt or feels pain easily; sensitive [My sprained ankle still feels *tender*.] —**ten′der·ly** *adv.* —**ten′der·ness** *n.*

tense¹ (tens) *adj.* **1** stretched tight; taut [a *tense* rope; *tense* muscles] **2** feeling or showing nervous strain, anxious [a *tense* silence] **3** causing a nervous feeling [a *tense* situation] —**tens′er, tens′est** ◆*v.* to make or become tense; tighten, as muscles —**tensed, tens′ing** —**tense′ly** *adv.*

tense² (tens) *n.* any of the forms of a verb that show the time of the action or condition [Present, past, and future *tenses* of "sail" are "sail" or "sails," "sailed," and "will sail."]

☆**te·pee** (tē′pē) *n.* a tent made of animal skins and shaped like a cone, used by some Native Americans

ter·ri·to·ry (ter′ə tôr′ē) *n.* **1** the land ruled by a nation or state **2** **Territory**, a large division of a country or empire, that does not have the full rights of a province or state, as in Canada or Australia [the Northwest *Territories*] **3** any large stretch of land; region **4** the particular area chosen as its own by an animal or group of animals —*pl.* **ter′ri·to·ries**

thank·ful (thaŋk′fəl) *adj.* feeling or showing thanks; grateful

their (*th*er) *adj.* of them or done by them: *this possessive form of* **they** *is used before a noun and thought of as an adjective* [*their* house; *their* work]

there (*th*er) *adv.* **1** at or in that place [Who lives *there*?] **2** to, toward, or into that place [Go *there*.]

there·fore (*th*er′fôr) *adv.* for this or that reason; as a result of this or that; hence; *this word is often used as a conjunction* [We missed the bus; *therefore*, we were late.]

there's (*th*erz) *contraction* there is

these (*th*ēz) *pron., adj. plural of* **this**

they'll (*th*āl) *contraction* **1** they will **2** they shall

thief (thēf) *n.* a person who steals, especially secretly —*pl.* **thieves** (thēvz)

think (thiŋk) *v.* to use the mind; reason [*Think* before you act.] —**thought, think′ing**

this (*th*is) *pron.* **1** the person or thing mentioned or understood [*This* is Juan. *This* tastes good.] **2** the thing that is present or nearer [*This* is prettier than that.] **3** the fact, idea, etc. about to be told [Now hear *this*!] —*pl.* **these** (*th*ēz) ◆*adj.* **1** being the one that is mentioned or understood [Copy down *this* rule.] **2** being the one that is present or nearer [*This* house is newer than that one.] ◆*adv.* to such a degree; so [It was *this* big.]

thought¹ (thôt *or* *th*ät) *n.* **1** the act or process of thinking [When deep in *thought*, he doesn't hear.] **2** what one thinks; idea, opinion, plan, etc. [a penny for your *thoughts*]

thought² (thôt *or* *th*ät) *past tense and past participle of* **think**

thou·sand (thσu′zənd) *n., adj.* ten times one hundred; the number 1,000

thumb (thum) *n.* the short, thick finger nearest the wrist

thun·der (thun′dər) *n.* **1** the loud noise that comes after a flash of lightning: it is caused when the discharge of electricity disturbs the air **2** any loud, rumbling noise like this [We heard the *thunder* of stampeding cattle.]

Thurs·day (thʉrz′dē) *n.* the fifth day of the week

tight (tīt) *adj.* **1** put together firmly or closely [a *tight* knot] **2** fitting too closely [a *tight* shirt] **3** stretched and strained; taut [a *tight* wire; *tight* nerves] —**tight′ly** *adv.* —**tight′ness** *n.*

tim·id (tim′id) *adj.* feeling or showing fear or shyness

tip·toe (tip′tō) *n.* the tip of a toe ◆*v.* to walk on one's tiptoes in a quiet or careful way —**tip′toed, tip′toe·ing**

to·ma·to (tə māt′ō *or* tə mät′ō) *n.* a red or yellow, round fruit with a juicy pulp —*pl.* **to·ma′toes**

tooth (to͞oth) *n.* **1** any of the white, bony parts growing from the jaws and used for biting and chewing **2** any part more or less like a tooth, as on a saw, comb, gearwheel, etc. —*pl.* **teeth** (tēth) —**tooth′less** *adj.*

tooth·ache (to͞oth′āk) *n.* pain in or near a tooth

tooth·brush (to͞oth′brush) *n.* a small brush for cleaning the teeth —*pl.* **tooth′brush·es**

tor·na·do (tôr nā′dō) *n.* a high, narrow column of air that is whirling very fast: it is often seen as a slender cloud shaped like a funnel, that usually destroys everything in its narrow path —*pl.* **tor·na′does** or **tor·na′dos**

toss (tôs *or* täs) *v.* **1** to throw from the hand in a light, easy way [to *toss* a ball] **2** to throw about; fling here and there [The waves *tossed* the boat.] —**tossed**

tough (tuf) *adj.* **1** able to bend or twist without tearing or breaking [*tough* rubber] **2** not able to be cut or chewed easily [*tough* meat] **3** very difficult or hard [a *tough* job]

town (toun) *n.* **1** a place where there are a large number of houses and other buildings, larger than a village but smaller than a city **2** *another name for* **city 3** the business center of a city or town

trace (trās) *n.* **1** a mark, track, sign, etc. left by someone or something [no human *trace* on the island] **2** a very small amount [a *trace* of garlic in the dressing] ◆*v.* **1** to follow the trail of; track [The hunter *traced* the lions to their den.] **2** to follow or study the course of [We *traced* the history of Rome back to Caesar.] **3** to copy a picture, drawing, etc. by following its lines on a thin piece of paper placed over it —**traced, trac′ing**

trade (trād) *n.* **1** any work done with the hands that needs special skill got by training [the plumber's *trade*] **2** all those in a certain business or kind of work [the book *trade*] **3** the act of giving one thing for another; exchange [an even *trade* of my comic books for your football] ◆*v.* **1** to carry on a business; buy and sell [This company *trades* in tea. Our country *trades* with other countries.] **2** to exchange [I *traded* my stamp collection for a camera.] —**trad′ed, trad′ing**

traf·fic (traf′ik) *n.* the movement or number of automobiles, persons, ships, etc. along a road or route of travel [to direct *traffic* on city streets; the heavy *traffic* on weekends] —**traf′ficked, traf′fick·ing**

trail·er (trā′lər) *n.* a wagon, van, cart, etc. made to be pulled by an automobile, truck, or tractor: some trailers are outfitted as homes

treat (trēt) *v.* **1** to deal with or act toward in a certain way [We were *treated* with respect. Don't *treat* this matter lightly.] **2** to try to cure or heal, as with medicine [The doctor *treated* my cuts.] **3** to act upon, as by adding something [The water is *treated* with chlorine.] —**treat′ed, treat′ing**

tribe (trīb) *n.* a group of people or families living together under a leader or chief [a North American Indian *tribe*; the *tribes* of ancient Israel] —**trib′al** *adj.*

trim (trim) *v.* **1** to make neat or tidy, especially by clipping, smoothing, etc. [She had her hair *trimmed*.] **2** to cut, clip, etc. [He *trimmed* dead branches off the tree.] —**trimmed, trim′ming** ◆*n.* good condition or order [An athlete must keep in *trim*.] —**trim′mer, trim′mest** *adj.* —**trim′ly** *adv.* —**trim′ness** *n.*

trip (trip) *v.* to stumble or make stumble [She *tripped* over the rug. Bill put out his foot and *tripped* me.] —**tripped, trip′ping**

tro·phy (trō′fē) *n.* anything kept as a token of victory or success, as a deer's head from a hunting trip, a silver cup from a sports contest, or a sword from a battle —*pl.* **tro′phies**

trop·i·cal (träp′i kəl) *adj.* of, in, or like the tropics [heavy *tropical* rains; *tropical* heat]

trou·ble (trub′əl) **1** worry, care, annoyance, suffering, etc. [My mind is free of *trouble*.] **2** a difficult or unhappy situation; disturbance [We've had no *trouble* with our neighbors.] —**trou′bled, trou′bling**

trust (trust) *n.* a strong belief that some person or thing is honest or can be depended on; faith [You can put your *trust* in that bank.] ◆*v.* **1** to have or put trust in; rely; depend [I *trust* him to be on time. Don't *trust* that rickety ladder.] **2** to put something in the care of [Her mother *trusted* her with the car.] **3** to believe [I *trust* her story.]

try (trī) *v.* **1** to make an effort; attempt [We must *try* to help them.] **2** to seek to find out about, as by experimenting; test [Please *try* my recipe. *Try* the other window, which may not be locked.] **3** to put to a severe test or strain [Such exercise *tried* my strength.] —**tries, tried, try′ing** ◆*n.* an effort; attempt; trial [He made a successful jump on his third *try*.] —*pl.* **tries**

tiptoe

a	ask, fat
ā	ape, date
ä	car, lot
e	elf, ten
ē	even, meet
i	is, hit
ī	ice, fire
ō	open, go
ô	law, horn
oi	oil, point
o͞o	look, pull
o͞o	ooze, tool
ou	out, crowd
u	up, cut
ʉ	fur, fern
ə	a in ago
	e in agent
	e in father
	i in unity
	o in collect
	u in focus
ch	chin, arch
ŋ	ring, singer
sh	she, dash
th	thin, truth
th	then, father
zh	s in pleasure

tu·ba (too′bə *or* tyoo′bə) *n.* a large brass instrument with a full, deep tone

tun·dra (tun′drə *or* toon′drə) *n.* a large, flat plain without trees in the arctic regions

turn (turn) *v.* **1** to move around a center point or axis; revolve; rotate [The wheels *turn. Turn* the key.] **2** to do by moving in a circle [*Turn* a somersault.] **3** to change in position or direction [*Turn* your chair around. *Turn* to the left. The tide has *turned.*] —**turned, turn′ing**

twelve (twelv) *n., adj.* two more than ten; the number 12

twist·er (twis′tər) *n.* **1** a person or thing that twists ☆**2** a tornado or cyclone

type·writ·er (tīp′rīt ər) *n.* a machine with a keyboard for making printed letters or figures on paper

vessel

Uu

um·pire (um′pīr) *n.* **1** a person who rules on the plays of a game, as in baseball **2** a person chosen to settle an argument ◆*v.* to be an umpire in a game or dispute —**um′pired, um′pir·ing**

un·cle (uŋ′kəl) *n.* **1** the brother of one's father or mother **2** the husband of one's aunt

un·clear (un klir′) *adj.* not clear; hard to see or understand

un·fold (un fōld′) *v.* **1** to open and spread out something that has been folded [to *unfold* a map] **2** to make or become known [to *unfold* one's plans]

u·ni·verse (yoo′ə vurs) *n.* all space and everything in it; earth, the sun, stars, and all things that exist

u·ni·ver·si·ty (yoo′ə vur′sə tē) *n.* a school of higher education, made up of a college or colleges —*pl.* **u′ni·ver′si·ties**

un·known (un nōn′) *adj.* **1** not known, seen, or heard before [a song *unknown* to me] **2** not discovered, identified, etc. [an *unknown* writer] ◆*n.* an unknown person or thing

un·pleas·ant (un plez′ənt) *adj.* not pleasant or agreeable; offensive; disagreeable [an *unpleasant* taste] —**un·pleas′ant·ly** *adv.* —**un·pleas′ant·ness** *n.*

un·pre·pared (un′prē perd′) *adj.* not prepared or ready [We are still *unprepared* for the visitors.]

un·re·al (un rēl′) *adj.* not real; imaginary or made up —**un·re·al·i·ty** (un′rē al′ə tē) *n.*

un·re·lat·ed (un′rē lāt′əd) *adj.* not of the same family or kind

un·til (un til′) *prep.* **1** up to the time of; till [Wait *until* noon.] **2** before [Don't leave *until* tomorrow.] ◆*conj.* **1** up to the time when [He was lonely *until* he met her.] **2** to the point, degree, or place that [She ate *until* she was full.] **3** before [Don't stop *until* he does.]

un·wise (un wīz′) *adj.* not wise; not showing good sense; foolish —**un·wise′ly** *adv.*

ur·gent (ur′jənt) *adj.* **1** needing quick action [an *urgent* situation] **2** demanding in a strong and serious way; insistent [an *urgent* call for help] —**ur′gent·ly** *adv.*

Vv

vague (vāg) *adj.* not clear, definite, or distinct, as in form, meaning, or purpose [*vague* figures in the fog; a *vague* answer] —**va′guer, va′guest** —**vague′ly** *adv.* —**vague′ness** *n.*

val·ley (val′ē) *n.* **1** low land lying between hills or mountains **2** the land that is drained or watered by a large river and its branches [the Mississippi *valley*] —*pl.* **val′leys**

veil (vāl) *n.* a piece of thin cloth, such as net or gauze, worn especially by women over the face or head [a bride's *veil*]

ves·sel (ves′əl) *n.* a ship or large boat

Vi·et·nam (vē′ət näm′) a country in southeastern Asia —**Vi·et·nam·ese** (vē′et nə mēz′ *or* vē′et nə mēs′) *adj., n.*

vi·ta·min (vīt′ə min) *n.* any of certain substances needed by the body to keep healthy: vitamin A is found in fish-liver oil, yellow vegetables, egg yolk, etc.: one kind of vitamin B, called vitamin B_1, is found in cereals, green peas, beans, liver, etc.: vitamin C is found in citrus fruits, tomatoes, etc.: vitamin D is found in fish-liver oil, milk, eggs, etc.: lack of these vitamins or others can cause certain diseases

voice (vois) *n.* **1** sound made through the mouth, especially by human beings in talking, singing, etc. **2** anything thought of as like speech or the human voice [the *voice* of the sea; the *voice* of one's conscience] **3** the right to say what one wants, thinks, or feels [Each voter has a *voice* in the government.] ◆*v.* to put into words, as an idea, feeling, etc.; utter —**voiced, voic′ing** —**voice′less** *adj.*

vote (vōt) *n.* one's decision on some plan or idea, or one's choice between persons running for office, shown on a ballot, by raising one's hand, etc. ◆*v.* **1** to give or cast a vote [For whom did you *vote*?] **2** to decide, elect, or bring about by vote [Congress *voted* for new taxes.] —**vot´ed, vot´ing**

waist (wāst) *n.* **1** the part of the body between the ribs and the hips **2** the part of a garment that covers the body from the shoulders to the waistline

wait·er (wāt´ər) *n.* **1** a man who waits on tables, as in a restaurant **2** one who waits

wait·ress (wā´trəs) *n.* a woman who waits on tables, as in a restaurant

walk·er (wôk´ər) *n.* **1** a person or animal that walks ☆**2** a frame with or without wheels for use by babies in learning to walk or by people who have trouble walking because of injuries or disease

wal·rus (wôl´rəs) *n.* a large sea animal like the seal, found in northern oceans: it has two tusks and a thick layer of blubber

Wash·ing·ton, DC (wôsh´iŋ tən *or* wäsh´iŋ tən) the capital of the United States, in the District of Columbia

watch (wäch *or* wôch) *v.* **1** to keep one's sight on; look at [We *watched* the parade.] **2** to pay attention to; observe [I've *watched* her career with interest.] **3** to take care of; look after; guard [The shepherd *watched* his flock.] —**watch´ing**

wa·ter·fall (wôt´ər fôl *or* wät´ər fôl) *n.* a steep fall of water, as from a high cliff

wax (waks) *n.* **1** a yellow substance that bees make and use for building honeycombs; beeswax **2** any substance like this, as paraffin: wax is used to make candles, polishes, etc. ◆*v.* to put wax or polish on

wea·ry (wir´ē) *adj.* **1** tired; worn out [*weary* after a day's work] **2** having little or no patience or interest left; bored [I grew *weary* of listening to them.] —**wea´ri·er, wea´ri·est** —**wea´ried, wea´ry·ing** —**wea´ri·ly** *adv.* **wea´ri·ness** *n.*

Wednes·day (wenz´dē) *n.* the fourth day of the week

weigh (wā) *v.* **1** to use a scale, balance, etc. to find out how heavy a thing is [to *weigh* oneself] **2** to have a certain weight [The suitcase *weighs* six pounds.]

we're (wir) *contraction* we are

west·ward (west´wərd) *adv., adj.* in the direction of the west

wheat (hwēt *or* wēt) *n.* **1** the cereal grass whose grain is used in making the most common type of flour **2** this grain

where (hwer *or* wer) *adv.* **1** in or at what place? [*Where* is the car?] **2** in what way? how? [*Where* is she at fault?]

where's (hwerz *or* werz) *contraction* **1** where is **2** where has

wheth·er (hwe*th*´ər *or* we*th*´ər) *conj.* **1** if it is true or likely that [I don't know *whether* I can go.] **2** in either case that [It makes no difference *whether* he comes or not.]

which (hwich *or* wich) *pron.* **1** what one or what ones of those being talked about or suggested [*which* will you choose?] **2** the one or the ones that [I know *which* I like best.] **3** that [the story *which* we all know] ◆*adj.* what one or ones [*Which* apples are the best for baking?]

whisk·er (hwis´kər *or* wis´kər) *n.* **1** **whiskers,** *pl.* the hair growing on a man's face, especially the beard on the cheeks **2** a single hair of a man's beard **3** any of the long, stiff hairs on the upper lip of a cat, rat, etc. —**whisk´ered,** *adj.*

whis·tle (hwis´əl *or* wis´əl) *n.* a device for making high, shrill sounds

who's (hoōz) *contraction* **1** who is **2** who has

whose (hoōz) *pron.* the one or the ones belonging to whom [*Whose* are these books?]

wife (wīf) *n.* the woman to whom a man is married —*pl.* **wives**

wild (wīld) *adj.* **1** living or growing in nature; not tamed or cultivated by human beings [*wild* animals; *wild*flowers] **2** not civilized; savage [*wild* tribes] **3** not controlled; unruly, rough, noisy, etc. [*wild* children] —**wild´ly** *adv.* —**wild´ness** *n.*

win·ner (win´ər) *n.* **1** one that wins **2** a person who seems very likely to win or be successful; *used only in everyday talk*

wish (wish) *v.* **1** to have a longing for; want; desire [You may have whatever you *wish*.] **2** to have or express a desire about [I *wish* you were here. We *wished* her good luck.] ◆*n.* something wanted or hoped for [He got his *wish*.] —*pl.* **wish´es** —**wish´ing**

witch (wich) *n.* **1** a person, now especially a woman, who is imagined to have magic power **2** an ugly and mean old woman

with·out (wi*th* out´ *or* with out´) *prep.* free from; not having [a person *without* a worry; a cup *without* a saucer]

wit·ness (wit´nəs) *n.* a person who saw or heard something that happened [A *witness* saw the fire start.] —*pl.* **wit´nes·ses**

wives (wīvz) *n. plural of* **wife**

wom·an (woom´ən) *n.* an adult, female human being —*pl.* **wom´en**

whiskers

a	ask, fat
ā	ape, date
ä	car, lot
e	elf, ten
ē	even, meet
i	is, hit
ī	ice, fire
ō	open, go
ô	law, horn
oi	oil, point
oo	look, pull
oo	ooze, tool
ou	out, crowd
u	up, cut
ʉ	fur, fern
ə	a in ago
	e in agent
	e in father
	i in unity
	o in collect
	u in focus
ch	chin, arch
ŋ	ring, singer
sh	she, dash
th	thin, truth
th	then, father
zh	s in pleasure

wom·en (wim′ən) *n.* *plural of* **woman**

wor·ry (wur′ē) *v.* **1** to be or make troubled in mind; feel or make uneasy or anxious [Don't *worry*. Her absence *worried* us.] **2** to annoy, bother, etc. [Stop *worrying* me with such unimportant matters.] —**wor′ried, wor′ry·ing** ◆*n.* **1** a troubled feeling; anxiety; care [sick with *worry*] **2** a cause of this [He has many *worries*.] —*pl.* **wor′ries**

would·n't (wood′nt) *contraction* would not

wrap (rap) *v.* **1** to wind or fold around something [She *wrapped* a scarf around her head.] **2** to cover in this way [They *wrapped* the baby in a blanket.] **3** to cover with paper, etc. [to *wrap* a present] —**wrapped** or **wrapt** (rapt), **wrap′ping**

wreck (rek) *n.* **1** the loss of a ship, or of a building, car, and so on, through storm, accident, etc. **2** the remains of something that has been destroyed or badly damaged [an old *wreck* stranded on the reef] ◆*v.* **1** to destroy or damage badly; ruin [to *wreck* a car in an accident; to *wreck* one's plans for a picnic] **2** to tear down; raze [to *wreck* an old house] —*pl.* **wrecks**

wrench (rench) *n.* **1** a sudden, sharp twist or pull [With one *wrench*, he loosened the lid.] **2** an injury, as to the back or an arm, caused by a twist **3** a sudden feeling of sadness, as at parting with someone **4** a tool for holding and turning nuts, bolts, pipes, etc.

wrin·kle (riŋ′kəl) *n.* a small or uneven crease or fold [*wrinkles* in a blouse]

wrist (rist) *n.* the joint or part of the arm between the hand and forearm

writ·ing (rīt′iŋ) *n.* **1** the act of one who writes **2** something written, as a letter, article, poem, book, etc. [the *writings* of Thomas Jefferson] **3** written form [to put a request in *writing*] **4** handwriting [Can you read her *writing*?]

yacht

yacht (yät) *n.* a large boat or small ship for racing, taking pleasure cruises, etc. ◆*v.* to sail in a yacht —**yacht′ing** *n.*

yak (yak) *n.* an ox with long hair, found wild or raised in Tibet and central Asia

yawn (yôn *or* yän) *v.* to open the mouth wide and breathe in deeply in a way that is not controlled, as when one is sleepy or tired

your·self (yoor self′) *pron.* **1** your own self: *this form of* **you** *is used when the object is the same as the subject of the verb* [Did you cut *yourself*?] **2** your usual or true self [You are not *yourself* today.] **Yourself** *is also used to give force to the subject* [You *yourself* told me so.] —*pl.* **your·selves** (yoor selvz′)

Spelling Notebook

Spelling Notebook

Modern Curriculum Press
is an imprint of

SAVVAS
LEARNING COMPANY

ISBN-13: 978-0-7652-2483-5
ISBN-10: 0-7652-2483-6

90000>

9 780765 224835